PCs
FOR
DUMMIES®
10TH EDITION

by Dan Gookin

WILEY

Wiley Publishing, Inc.

PCs For Dummies,® 10th Edition

Published by
Wiley Publishing, Inc.
111 River Street
Hoboken, NJ 07030-5774

www.wiley.com

Copyright © 2005 by Wiley Publishing, Inc., Indianapolis, Indiana

Published by Wiley Publishing, Inc., Indianapolis, Indiana

Published simultaneously in Canada

For general information on our other products and services, please contact our Customer Care Department within the U.S. at 800-762-2974, outside the U.S. at 317-572-3993, or fax 317-572-4002.

For technical support, please visit www.wiley.com/techsupport.

Wiley also publishes its books in a variety of electronic formats. Some content that appears in print may not be available in electronic books.

Library of Congress Control Number: 2005927723

ISBN-13: 978-0-7645-8958-4

ISBN-10: 0-7645-8958-X

Manufactured in the United States of America

10 9 8 7 6 5 4 3 2 1

10B/RW/QZ/QV/IN

WILEY

About the Author

Dan Gookin has been writing about technology for 20 years. He has contributed articles to numerous high-tech magazines and written more than 100 books about personal computing technology, many of them accurate.

He combines his love of writing with his interest in technology to create books that are informative and entertaining, but not boring. Having sold more than 14 million titles translated into more than 30 languages, Dan can attest that his method of crafting computer tomes does seem to work.

Perhaps Dan's most famous title is the original *DOS For Dummies,* published in 1991. It became the world's fastest-selling computer book, at one time moving more copies per week than the *New York Times* number-one best seller (although, because it's a reference book, it could not be listed on the *NYT* best seller list). That book spawned the entire line of *For Dummies* books, which remains a publishing phenomenon to this day.

Dan's most recent titles include *Laptops For Dummies*; *Buying a Computer For Dummies,* 2006 Edition; *Troubleshooting Your PC For Dummies,* 2nd Edition; *Power Excel & Word;* and *eBay Photos That Sell.* He also maintains the vast and helpful Web site www.wambooli.com.

Dan holds a degree in communications and visual arts from the University of California, San Diego. He lives in the Pacific Northwest, where he enjoys spending time with his four boys in the gentle woods and on the temperate blue lakes of Idaho.

Publisher's Acknowledgments

We're proud of this book; please send us your comments through our online registration form located at `www.dummies.com/register/`.

Some of the people who helped bring this book to market include the following:

Acquisitions, Editorial, and Media Development

Project Editor: Rebecca Whitney

Acquisitions Editor: Gregory Croy

Technical Editor: James F. Kelly

Editorial Manager: Carol Sheehan

Editorial Assistant: Amanda M. Foxworth

Cartoons: Rich Tennant
(`www.the5thwave.com`)

Composition Services

Project Coordinator: Erin Smith

Layout and Graphics: Carl Byers, Andrea Dahl, Lauren Goddard, Joyce Haughey, Stephanie D. Jumper, Barry Offringa, Lynsey Osborn

Proofreaders: Leeann Harney, Joe Niesen, Dwight Ramsey, TECHBOOKS Production Services

Indexer: TECHBOOKS Production Services

Publishing and Editorial for Technology Dummies

    Richard Swadley, Vice President and Executive Group Publisher

    Andy Cummings, Vice President and Publisher

    Mary Bednarek, Executive Acquisitions Director

    Mary C. Corder, Editorial Director

Publishing for Consumer Dummies

    Diane Graves Steele, Vice President and Publisher

    Joyce Pepple, Acquisitions Director

Composition Services

    Gerry Fahey, Vice President of Production Services

    Debbie Stailey, Director of Composition Services

Contents at a Glance

Table of Contents

Introduction

· ·

*T*hings change quickly in the computer industry, so it's time for *another* revision and update to this classic book, now in its 10th edition. I've done some major work here, shuffled things around, and tidied up all the text so that *PCs For Dummies* can give you the answer to the ever-burning question "How does a computer turn a smart person like you into a dummy?"

You don't have to love a computer. Some folks do, most don't. The reason is simple: Computers are *not* easy to use. True, a computer is easier to use now than it was 10 years ago, but some things remain cryptic. The help files are mystifying. Technical support isn't even in English any more! So, you're left feeling numb and cold and wondering why no one bothers to sit down and explain things to you in plain human terms. Well, wonder no more!

This book explains the basics of your computer, the PC — how it works, what does what, and all that stuff you want to know or maybe didn't realize you wanted to know. Honestly, computers really aren't that difficult to use or understand. It's just that it has taken an author like me and a book like this one a while to get the word out.

Between this book's yellow and black covers you'll find friendly, helpful information about using your PC. This book uses friendly and human — and often irreverent — terms. Nothing is sacred here. Electronics can be praised by others. This book focuses on you and your needs. In this book, you'll discover everything you need to know about your computer without painful jargon or the prerequisite master's degree in engineering. And, you'll have fun.

What's New in This Edition?

I've done my homework! I've sat with beginners and observed how they use their computers. I've made notes about what was obvious to them — stuff I no longer need to write about. I also noted stuff that 'most everyone who uses a computer doesn't know. Even so-called experts have difficulty with some basic computer concepts. So, armed with my new knowledge and understanding of computer users, I sat down at the word processor, cracked my knuckles, winced in pain, waited a few minutes for the pain to subside, and then set about recrafting this book with a newfound emphasis and enthusiasm for the first-time computer user — as well as the old hand who may still find some things befuddling.

This edition of *PCs For Dummies* is specific to any personal computer running the Windows XP operating system, either the Home or Pro edition. If you have an older version of Windows, you have, honestly, an outdated PC, and I strongly urge you to get a new PC with Windows XP and enjoy the benefits of using your new, more powerful computer.

Here are a few of the new topics covered in this edition:

- ✔ Brand-new and highly detailed information on home computer networking, including Internet connections and the ever-popular wireless networking options.

- ✔ Basic information on understanding what a computer is and how it works.

- ✔ Key information on the essence of a file. Truly, by understanding the file, you really get hold of the entire computer software concept.

- ✔ Updated information on broadband (high-speed) modems.

- ✔ Detailed data on the USB port.

- ✔ More information on PC setup and configuration.

- ✔ General up-to-date and current information on all aspects of PC technology, hardware, and software — stuff too numerous to mention here, so why not just start reading the book already?

As in years past, I present all the information in this book in a sane, soothing, and gentle tone that calms even the most panicked computerphobe.

Where to Start

This book is designed so that you can pick it up at any point and start reading — like a reference. It has 31 chapters. Each chapter covers a specific aspect of the computer — turning it on, using a printer, using software, or kicking the computer, for example. Each chapter is divided into self-contained nuggets of information — sections — all relating to the major theme of the chapter. Sample sections you may find include

- ✔ Turning the darn thing off

- ✔ Where's the power cord?

- ✔ Stop, printer! Stop!

✔ Testing the network

✔ Disposing of a CD or CD-R

✔ Downloading a file from the Internet

You don't have to memorize anything in this book. Nothing about a computer is memorable. Each section is designed so that you can read the information quickly, digest what you have read, and then put down the book and get on with using the computer. If anything technical crops up, you're alerted to its presence so that you can cleanly avoid it.

Conventions Used in This Book

This book is a reference. Start with the topic you want more information about; look for it in the table of contents or in the index. Turn to the area of interest and read the information you need. Then, with the information in your head, you can quickly close the book and freely perform whatever task you need — without reading anything else.

Whenever I describe a message or information on the screen, it looks like this:

```
This is a message onscreen.
```

If you have to type something, it looks like this:

Type me

You type the text **Type me** as shown. You're told when and whether to press the Enter key.

Windows menu commands are shown like this:

Choose File⇨Exit.

This line means to choose the File menu and then choose the Exit command. The underlined letters are shortcut keys, which can be pressed instead of using the mouse to choose a menu item: Press the Alt key to activate the menu, and then press the underlined keys — F and then E, in this example.

Key combinations you may have to type are shown like this:

Ctrl+S

This line means to press and hold the Ctrl (control) key, type an *S*, and then release the Ctrl key. It works just like the way pressing Shift+S on the keyboard produces an uppercase *S*. Same deal, different shift key.

What You Don't Need to Read

Lots of technical information is involved in using a computer. To better insulate you from this information, I have enclosed this type of material in sidebars clearly marked as technical information. You don't have to read that stuff. Often, it's just a complex explanation of information already discussed in the chapter. Reading that information only teaches you something substantial about your computer, which is not the goal here.

Foolish Assumptions

I make some admittedly foolish assumptions about you: You have a computer, and you use it somehow to do something. You use a PC (or are planning on it) and will use Windows XP, either the Home or Pro version, as your PC's operating system, or main program. This book doesn't cover any previous versions of Windows.

This book refers to the menu that appears when you click or activate the Start button as the *Start button's menu*. The All Programs menu on the Start panel is referred to as *All Programs,* though it may say *Programs* on your screen.

I prefer to use the Windows Control Panel in Classic view, but I prefer to use the Start button's menu in the newer, Windows XP view. (This topic is covered in Chapter 5.)

Icons Used in This Book

This icon alerts you to needless technical information — drivel I added because I just felt like explaining something totally unnecessary (a hard habit to break). Feel free to skip over anything tagged with this little picture.

This icon usually indicates helpful advice or an insight that makes using the computer interesting. For example, when you're pouring acid over your computer, be sure to wear a protective apron and gloves and goggles.

This icon indicates something to remember, like you kept the refrigerator door open when you left the house this morning or check your zipper before you step before a large audience.

This icon indicates that you need to be careful with the information that's presented; usually, it's a reminder for you not to do something.

Getting in Touch with the Author

My e-mail address is listed here in case you want to write me on the Internet:

```
dgookin@wambooli.com
```

Yes, that is my address, and I respond to every e-mail message. I cannot, however, troubleshoot or fix your PC. Remember that you paid others for your technical support, and you should use them. I am open to answering questions directly related to this book.

You can also visit my Web site, which is chock full of helpful support pages, bonus information, games, and fun, interactive forums:

```
http://www.wambooli.com/
```

The interactive forums are at

```
http://forums.wambooli.com/
```

This book's support page is at this address:

```
http://www.wambooli.com/help/pc/
```

Where to Go from Here

With this book in hand, you're now ready to go out and conquer your PC. Start by looking through the table of contents or the index. Find a topic and turn to the page indicated, and you're ready to go. Also, feel free to write in this book, fill in the blanks, dog-ear the pages, and do anything that would make a librarian blanch. Enjoy.

Part I
Introducing the PC

In this part . . .

*J*ust about anyone can recognize a computer. Computers are common enough now that even someone stomping through a junkyard and searching for the left front end of a 1988 Subaru would be able to recognize one. But, do you know what a PC really is?

There's more to a computer than just a consumer gadget that you can quickly assemble and "be up and running in no time." Despite advances in technology and strides toward making things "user-friendly," the computer remains a highly technical device. If you're going to get the most from your computer, you'll have to be formally introduced. That's what you'll find in this part of the book.

Chapter 1

Computer? PC? What's That?

Guess what? The salespeople lied! They told you that a computer was easy to use. They said that you would be on the Internet in no time. They explained how computer programs are so simple and helpful now that you don't need to take classes or — heaven forbid — buy a book! Yep, them's all lies!

In the great rush to make computers a consumer commodity — right up there with toaster ovens and cell phones — the people who sell computers had to spin these great yarns. Sadly, most people believe the tall tales. And it's possible to squeak by and use a computer with minimal knowledge of what's going on. But you know better.

If you're naturally smart, if you have an IQ that would make Einstein blush, or if you're an alien visitor to Earth and you find all this computer stuff as easy as understanding the Blackmar–Diemer Gambit, phooey on you! Otherwise, my guess is that you've discovered that computers are indeed complex and intimidating and can make you feel like a dummy.

This chapter introduces you to the concept of the computer — basic information that should be necessary to completely understand the beast you may consider buying, have just purchased, or perhaps owned for years. After reading this chapter, you stand a better chance of knowing what it's all about.

Computers at Their Most Dumb

Most gizmos are rather simple: A toaster heats bread; a microwave oven heats water or the water inside of things; a car provides transportation; a telephone allows you to talk with someone else, from across the globe to sitting across the table. The purpose of any device can be boiled down to the simplest description. But what about a computer?

It has been said that computers defy description. At one time, the computer was considered the ultimate solution for which there was no problem. But that's not quite correct. The computer is a simple beast. It does basically one thing: It takes input and then modifies that input to create some form of output (see Figure 1-1). The enormous potential of that simple activity, however, is what makes the computer seem like such a complex device.

Figure 1-1: What a computer does at its simplest level.

To help you grasp the notion of what a computer does, you should understand three basic computer concepts:

- ✔ I/O
- ✔ Processing
- ✔ Storage

This section expands on these ideas, giving you a distillation of what you could have learned in a computer science class, if you had bothered to take one.

I/O

Neither a borrower nor a lender be

—Hamlet, Act I, Scene III

No one would accuse a computer of being a reliable moocher, but it's obsessed over the two letters *I* and *O*. It's *IO* as in "I owe," not as in Io, the third-largest moon of Jupiter.

IO is commonly written as I/O, and it stands for Input and Output, which are the two things a computer does best. In fact, I/O is pretty much the only thing a computer does. You get this whole I/O concept down, and you've tackled the essence of what a computer is and what it can do.

- The devices connected to your computer are divided into input and output camps. There are input devices and output devices.

- *Input* devices are things used to send information to the computer. The keyboard and mouse are two input devices, as are a scanner and a digital camera.

- *Output* devices are things the computer uses to show its output, such as the screen and printer.

- Some devices can do both input and output, such as a hard drive and a modem. The computer can use those devices to supply input as well as send output to those devices.

- Don't let terms like *hard disk* and *modem* bother you! If you're curious, you can look them up in the index. Otherwise, keep reading and nod occasionally like you really get it. If anything, that will impress someone else who's watching.

Processing

If a computer did no processing, it would essentially be like plumbing: Water would come into the system, churn around in a few pipes, and then go out of the system. The water would be the same before, during, and after the journey. But with a computer, you have the added element of *processing*, which means doing something to the input so that you get something else as output.

- Processing is handled by a gizmo inside the computer called (logically enough) a *processor*.

- The processor doesn't really know what to do with all that input. Telling the computer what to do is the job of *software*. The topic of software is covered later in this chapter.

- It's amazing when you think of it: Computer input is all digital. Yet with the proper processing, the output can be anything from a poem to a graphical image to a symphony. That's all thanks to the power of processing.

Storage

The final part of the computer equation is storage, which in a computer is referred to as *memory*. The storage is necessary on the most basic level because the processor needs a place to perform its magic — a scratch pad for mad doodles, if you will.

On a modern computer, storage comes in two forms: temporary and long-term.

RAM is the temporary storage, where the processor does its work, where programs run, and where information is stored while it's being worked on. RAM is the microprocessor's playground, its wood shop, its den.

Disk drives provide long-term storage. The disks also allow information to be saved and recalled for later use — like a closet or storage unit. Disk storage is the place where things go when the microprocessor isn't directly working on them — but from where stuff can be retrieved later, if need be.

- ✔ All computers need storage.

- ✔ RAM is an acronym for Random Access Memory. It's often just called *memory.*

- ✔ RAM is also known as *temporary storage.*

- ✔ Disk drives come in a wide variety of types: removable and nonremovable, and with various names and numbers attached. Because of their variety, disk drives are generally referred to as *long-term storage.*

- ✔ Another term for disk drives is *disk memory,* though I don't prefer that term because it's easy to confuse it with RAM.

- ✔ Don't get all hung up on these terms. Computer jargon, such as *RAM* and *disk drive,* is explained later in this book.

- ✔ The computers on the Apollo moon missions had lots of storage for their day. This was so that the astronauts wouldn't have to manually type in the programs the computer needed to run. Even so, there was a lot more typing and programming going on in the capsule than you would imagine.

The World of Hardware and Software

A computer system is a blend of two different things: *hardware* and *software.* Like other famous pairs — Astaire and Rogers, sweet and sour, pickup and redneck — hardware and software must go well together to create the full computer system.

Hardware is the physical part of a computer — anything you can touch and anything you can see. The computer console, the monitor, the keyboard, the mouse — that physical stuff is hardware.

Software is the brains of the computer. It tells the hardware what to do.

In a way, it helps to think of hardware and software like a symphony orchestra. For hardware, you have the musicians and their instruments. The software is the music. As with a computer, the music (software) tells the musicians and their instruments (hardware) what to do.

Without software, hardware just sits around and looks pretty. It can't do anything because it has no instructions, and nothing telling it what to do next. And, like a symphony orchestra without music, that can be an expensive waste of time (especially at union scale).

No, you must have software to make the computer go and complete the computer system. In fact, it's software that determines your computer's personality.

- If you can throw it out a window, it's hardware.
- If you can throw it out a window and it comes back, it's a cat.
- Computer software is nothing more than instructions that tell the hardware what to do, how to act, or when to lose your data.

- Computer software is more important than computer hardware. Like the master and the slave, it's the software that tells the hardware what to do. This is especially important to note when first buying a computer because most people dwell on the new computer's hardware rather than on the software controlling that hardware.
- Without the proper software, your computer's hardware has nothing to do. That's when the computer magically transforms into a boat anchor.

The computer's operating system

The most important piece of software inside a computer is the *operating system.* It has several duties:

- Control the computer's hardware.
- Manage all the computer software.
- Organize the files and stuff you create on the computer.
- Interface with you, the human.

Doing all these things is a major task. Be thankful that computer designers have seen to it that only one program does all these things! The operating system is no slacker.

On PCs, the most common operating system is Windows. Other operating systems are available, all of which do the things just listed and can handily control the PC's hardware, but Windows dominates the marketplace. This book assumes that Windows is your PC's operating system.

How the operating system does its various jobs is covered elsewhere in this book.

- ✔ The hardware is *not* in charge! Software must rule the computer's roost. And the big bully among all the software programs is the operating system.

- ✔ The computer's most important piece of software is its operating system. It's the computer's number-one program — the head honcho, the big cheese, Mr. In Charge, Fearless Leader, *le roi.*

- ✔ The computer hardware surrenders control of itself to the operating system mere moments after you turn the computer on. See Chapter 4 for information on turning the computer on and off.

- ✔ The operating system typically comes with the computer when you buy it. You never need to add a second operating system, although operating systems do get updated and improved from time to time.

- ✔ When you buy software, you buy it for an operating system, not for your brand of PC. So, rather than buy software for your Dell or IBM, you look in the Windows section of the software store.

Other software

The operating system isn't the only software you use on your computer. If you're a typical computer user, you'll most likely obtain dozens, if not hundreds, of other programs, or computer software, to help customize your computer and get it to do those things you want it to do.

Computer software is known by several different names. In addition to software, you find:

Applications: This category of software is used for productivity or to create things. Applications are the software that does the work.

Programs: Anything that is a "computer program" is also software, but this category includes software that may or may not be used for productivity or to produce output, such as a computer game or CD-playing program.

Utilities or tools: These programs are designed to help you run the computer or work with the hardware. For example, you may use a tool to optimize the performance of your computer's disk drives.

Part IV of this book goes into more detail on computer software.

The stuff you make

You use software to control your computer hardware, and the result is that you produce something. That something — whether it's a document, a piece of music, a video, graphical art, whatever — is stored on the computer in a unit called a *file.*

The operating system is what tells the various applications and programs how and where to save the stuff you create — your files. The operating system helps keep things organized and offers rules for naming and help for finding all those files.

This book covers files and their organization in Chapter 21.

The PC (As in PCs For Dummies)

The kind of computer you have, or will soon have, is a PC, which is why this book is titled *PCs For Dummies.* There are many varieties of computers, from large supercomputers to small handhelds. The largest category by far, however, is the PC.

PC stands for *personal* computer. The design of the PC is based on its earliest ancestor, the IBM PC. Back then, PCs were referred to as *microcomputers.* And though many, many microcomputers were available, the IBM PC proved the most popular and successful.

Specifically, a PC today is any computer that can run the Windows operating system. There are subtle differences between the PC's hardware from one manufacturer to the next, but, universally, if the computer runs Windows, it's a PC. (Note that this doesn't include cars, sewing machines, or heart–lung machines that also may run Windows.)

✔ In the big picture, what a PC specifically is *not* is a Macintosh. If you have a Macintosh — any shape or variety — you should get the book *Macs For Dummies,* a well-written tome by my friend David Pogue.

✔ If you have a laptop PC, I highly recommend getting the book *Laptops For Dummies*, a well-written tome by my friend Dan Gookin.

The Most Important Question: Will Your PC Explode?

I can happily inform you that, no, your computer will not explode. Not under normal circumstances anyway. But if you're culturally literate, it's entirely possible that you could believe the PC capable of spontaneous combustion, despite its never happening in real life.

Anyone who's ever seen an old episode of TV's *Star Trek* or any Irwin Allen television show from the 1960s knows that computers are capable of exploding, and doing so in a quite dramatic fashion. When given the most subtle yet illogical directions, the typical TV computer fidgets and heats up, and eventually explodes in a shower of sparks and chunky debris.

In real life, computers die a much more silent death. The typical dead PC simply refuses to turn on when the switch is thrown. Oh, sure, sometimes the power supply may go "poof!" But that is so nondramatic compared to something like the exploding war computers of Eminiar VII in *Star Trek* Episode 23.

Now, although your computer will not explode — or even blow up — I do admit that they can be much more friendly. I would love to say that the computer is really rather easy to understand, but it's not. Even folks who readily take to computers discover new and useful things every day. Of course, you already have taken a giant stride into making the computer more of a friend than a potential powder keg: You have this book, which starts off with this friendly chapter, a pleasant introduction to the PC.

- ✔ If you don't already own a PC, I can recommend a great book: *Buying a Computer For Dummies,* written by yours truly and available from Wiley Publishing, Inc. It covers the basics of the PC, how to select one just right for you, and how to set it up for the first time.

- ✔ Computers aren't evil. They harbor no sinister intelligence. In fact, when you get to know them, they're rather dumb.

Chapter 2

The Nerd's-Eye View

*Y*ou would think that 25 years after the dawn of the computer revolution, most folks would know what a computer looks like. They don't. Most commonly, people think that the monitor is *the computer*. It's not! Silly. So, how can you tell what's the computer and what's just a lowly peripheral? Why, you read this here chapter, of course!

Of the two parts of a computer system, hardware and software, it's the hardware that gets the most attention — despite the software being more important. This chapter provides you with the bird's-eye — or, rather, *nerd's-eye* — overview of what is a PC and where you can find interesting and useful things on that device.

Variations on the Typical PC

There is no such thing as a typical PC, just as there is no such thing as the typical car. Though PCs and cars all have common parts, the arrangement and design are different from manufacturer to manufacturer. Here's a quick overview of the various types of PCs available and what they're officially called:

Mini-tower: The most popular PC configuration, where the computer sits upright on a desktop or tucked away out of sight below the desk.

Desktop: Once the most popular PC configuration, with a slab-like console lying flat on the desktop with the monitor squatting on top.

Desktop (small footprint): A smaller version of the desktop, typically used in low-priced home systems. The *footprint* is the amount of desk space the computer uses.

Tower system: Essentially a full-size desktop standing on its side, which makes this PC tall, like a tower. Towers have lotsa room inside for expansion, which makes them the darlings of power-mad users. Towers typically sit on the floor, often propping up one end of the table.

Notebook/laptop: A specialty type of computer that folds into a handy, lightweight package, ideal for slowing down the security checkpoints in airports. Laptop PCs work just like their desktop brethren; any exceptions are noted throughout this book.

Choosing the proper PC system depends on your needs. Power users love the expandability of the tower, or maybe mini-tower. Folks on the go love laptops. Small-footprint desktops can fit on any desk. (Just remember that the amount of clutter you have always expands to fill the available desk space.)

Your Basic PC Hardware

Figure 2-1 shows a typical computer system. The big, important pieces have been labeled for your enjoyment. It's important that you know which piece is which and what the proper terms are.

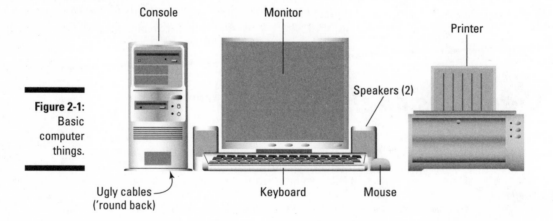

Console   Monitor   Printer

Figure 2-1: Basic computer things.

Speakers (2)

Ugly cables ('round back)   Keyboard   Mouse

Console: The main computer box is the console, though it may also be called the *system unit* (geeky) or the *CPU* (incorrect). It's a box that contains your computer's *soul:* electronic guts plus various buttons, lights, and holes into which you plug the rest of the computer system.

Monitor: The monitor is the device where the computer displays information, its output.

Keyboard: It's the thing you type on; it's the primary way you communicate with the computer, with input.

Mouse: No rodent or pest, the computer mouse is a helpful device that lets you work with graphical objects that the computer displays on the monitor.

Speakers: PCs bleep and squawk through a set of stereo speakers, either external jobbies you set up, as shown in Figure 2-1, or speakers built into the console or the monitor. Pay more money and you can even get a subwoofer to sit under your desk. Now, *that* will rattle your neighborhood's windows.

Printer: It's where you get the computer's printed output, also called *hard copy.*

You may find, in addition to these basic items, other things clustered around your computer, such as a scanner, a digital camera, a game pad (or joystick), an external disk drive, a high-speed modem, and many, many other toys — er, vital computer components.

One thing definitely not shown in Figure 2-1 — and something you will never see in a computer manual and especially not in advertisements — is the ganglia of cables that lives behind each and every computer. What a mess! These cables are required in order to plug things into the wall and into each other. No shampoo or conditioner on Earth can clean up those tangles.

 ✔ Ensure that you know where the console, keyboard, mouse, speakers, monitor, and printer are in your own system. If the printer isn't present, it's probably a network printer sitting in some other room.

 ✔ Silly but true: Most beginners (and anyone who doesn't know better) believe the monitor to be "the computer."

 ✔ Chapters in Part II of this book go into more detail on the individual computer components just introduced and illustrated in Figure 2-1.

 ✔ CPU stands for *central processing unit.* It's another term for the computer's *microprocessor* (see Chapter 6). Even so, some folks foolishly refer to the console as the CPU. Boy, are they wrong!

Looking About the Console

That console, that main box that really is your computer system, doesn't stand alone. Into the console you plug every other gizmo that you use as part of the computer system. To accommodate them, the console has many, many holes into which those things plug. Not only that, the console has doors and slots so that you can access important things inside the console directly. Topping everything off like nuts on a sundae, the console has interesting buttons to press and switches to throw. This section mulls it all over.

✔ Try to find on your own PC the things mentioned in this section. Get to know their locations as well as their official computer names.

✔ Not every console is the same. Use this section as a general guide.

Major points of interest on the console, front

The front of the console is for you, dear computer user. That's where you interact with the computer system directly, by adding or removing disks, observing lights, punching buttons, and perhaps even plugging one or two special items into the PC's tummy.

Use Figure 2-2 as your reference as you go hunting for the following items:

CD-ROM or DVD drive: Like a music or video player, your computer digests CDs and DVDs through a slot or tray on the front of the console. Some computers may have a dual CD/DVD drive, and others may have one of each. Read more about this in Chapter 8.

Future expansion: Some spots on the console's nose may look like they're CD-ROM or disk drives, but they're not! They're simply blanks that cover holes — holes you can use for adding things to your computer someday.

Floppy drive: This slot eats floppy disks. Some software comes on floppy disks, and you can use these disks to move files from one PC to another. Not every PC sold today comes with a floppy drive.

Air vents: Okay, this one isn't impressive, but most consoles sport some type of air vent on the front. Don't block the air vents with books or sticky notes! The thing's gotta breathe.

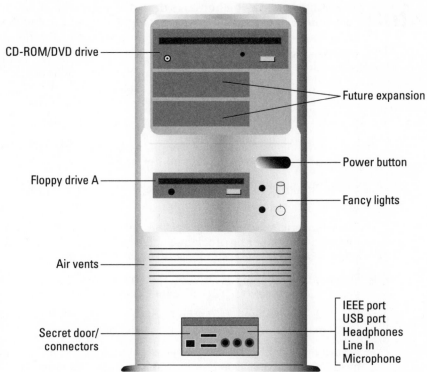

CD-ROM/DVD drive

Future expansion

Power button

Floppy drive A

Fancy lights

Air vents

Figure 2-2:
Things to
note on the
front of the
console.

Secret door/
connectors

IEEE port
USB port
Headphones
Line In
Microphone

The secret panel: Some PCs, especially home models, have a secret panel or door that pops open. Behind it, you can find connectors for joysticks, microphones, headphones, or other handy items you may need to plug and unplug from time to time. Having the secret panel is handier than having to reach around behind the computer and fumble for plugs and holes.

Buttons and lights: Most of a computer's buttons are on the keyboard. A few of the more important ones are on the console, and these buttons on fancier PCs are accompanied by many impressive tiny lights. These buttons and lights include the following:

✔ **Power button:** It's no longer a plain on–off button — it's the *power button,* and it can do more than just turn the computer off or on. See Chapter 4 for the details.

✔ **Reset button:** Rare, but still found on some computers is a button that forces the computer into a restart during times of woe. Consider it a plus if your PC has such a button.

✔ **Sleep button:** This rare button is designed specifically to put the computer into a coma and suspend all activity without turning the computer off. On some PCs, this button and the power button are the same.

✔ **Disk drive lights:** These lights flash when the hard drive, floppy drive, or CD-ROM drive is working. On a hard drive, the light is your reassurance that it's alive and happy and doing its job. On all other types of drives (with removable disks), the light indicates that the computer is using the drive.

Other fun and unusual things may live on the front of your console, most of which are particular to a certain computer brand.

✔ The front of the console may also boast a brand label or manufacturer's tattoo.

✔ Some newer computers have stickers that show the secret Windows installation number or proclaim such nonsense as "I was built to run Windows 3D" or "A Pentium Wazoo lurks inside this box."

✔ For more specific information on the connectors lurking behind a secret panel, see the section "The I/O panel," later in this chapter.

✔ Don't block the air vents on the front of the console. If you do, the computer may literally suffocate. (It gets too hot.)

✔ A hard drive light can be red or green or yellow, and it flickers when the hard drive is in use. Don't let it freak you out! It's not an alarm; the hard drive is just doing its job.

Things of note on the console's rump

The console's backside is its busy side. That's where you find various connectors for the many other devices in your computer system: a place to plug in the monitor, keyboard, mouse, speakers, and just about anything else that came in the box with the PC.

Use Figure 2-3 as a guide for finding the following important things on the back of your PC's console. Note that some things may look different, some may be missing, and some newfangled things may not be listed here.

Power connector: This thing is where the PC plugs into a cord that plugs into the wall.

Fan: Air gets sucked in here, blows around inside the console to keep things cool, and then puffs out the vents.

Voltage switch: Use this item to switch power frequencies to match the specifications for your country or region.

Expansion slots: These slots are available for adding new components on *expansion cards* to the console and expanding your PC's hardware. Any connectors on the expansion cards appear in this area, such as the audio and video connectors on a DVD expansion card.

Vents: The breathing thing again.

I/O panel: Aside from the power cord, and anything attached to an expansion card, the rest of your PC's expansion options and plug-in type things are located in a central area I call the I/O panel. Details of what you can find there are covered in the next subsection.

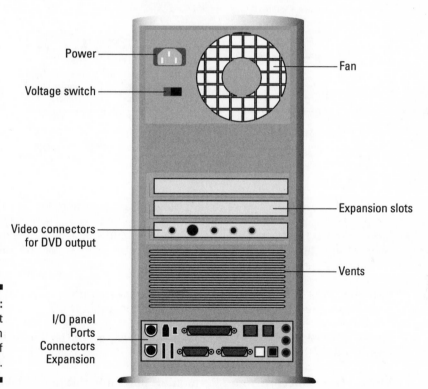

Figure 2-3:
Important
doodads on
the back of
the console.

The I/O panel

To either help keep all the connectors in one spot or just create the most intensely cable-crammed location on the console, your PC most likely has an I/O panel, normally found on the console's rear. This is where you add various expansion options to the PC as well as plug in the standard devices shown way over in Figure 2-1.

Use Figure 2-4 as your guide for what's what. The items you find on your PC's I/O panel may be labeled with text, or they may include the symbols listed in Table 2-1.

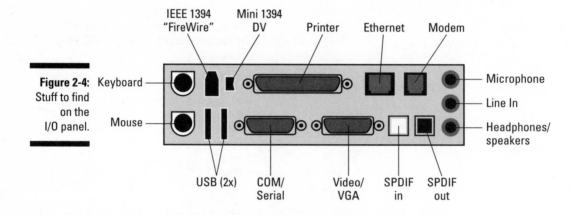

Figure 2-4: Stuff to find on the I/O panel.

Keyboard connector: The keyboard plugs into this little hole.

Mouse connector: It's generally the same size and shape as the keyboard connector, although this hole has a mouse icon nearby to let you know that the mouse plugs in there.

USB port: Plug snazzy devices into these Certs-size Universal Serial Bus (USB) slots. See Chapter 7 for more information about USB.

Serial, or COM, ports: PCs have at least one of these ports, named COM1. A second one is called COM2.

Video/VGA connector: Your PC's monitor plugs into this hole, which looks like the serial port, but it has 15 holes rather than 9. A second, digital monitor connector may be available for plugging in LCD monitors. Also, these connectors may be located on an expansion card rather than the I/O panel.

SPDIF In/Out: These connectors are used to attach the fiber optic cable, used for digital audio. Audio coming into the computer plugs into the In hole; the sound the computer generates goes out the Out hole.

Microphone jack: The computer's microphone plugs into this hole.

Line-in jack: This jack is where you plug in your stereo or VCR to the PC for capturing sound.

Speaker/sound-out jack: It's where you plug in your PC's external speakers or headphones, or where you hook up the PC to a sound system. (Also check the "secret panel" on the front of the console for a headphone connector.)

Dial-up modem: This is where you connect your PC's modem to the phone jack in the wall. If two phone or modem holes are on the I/O panel, the second one is for a telephone extension. Note that this is *not* where you connect a broadband (DSL or cable) modem.

Ethernet (network) connector: This is where you plug in a local area network (LAN) connector, or where you attach a broadband modem to the PC. Not every computer has one of these connectors.

Printer port: The PC's printer plugs into this connector.

IEEE ports: These ports are used for many things, similar to the USB ports. They may be labeled IEEE, 1394, or FireWire. A smaller version of the port may be labeled DV, for Digital Video.

Not pictured in Figure 2-4 but available on many PCs are the following connectors:

S-Video Out: If your PC sports a DVD drive, the S-Video connector allows you to connect an S-Video-happy TV to your PC.

Joystick port: A port used for older-style joysticks, though most all PC joysticks now sold plug into the USB port.

The good news? You connect all this stuff only once. Then your PC's butt faces the wall for the rest of its life and you never have to look at it again (well, unless you add something in the future).

✔ The keyboard and mouse connectors *are* different! Be certain that you plug the proper device into the proper hole, or else the keyboard and mouse don't work!

✔ See Chapter 7 for more information on these holes and what plugs into them.

✔ See Chapter 13 for more on modems.

Helpful hieroglyphics and hues

Even though most PC connectors are different, manufacturers have a set of common colors and symbols used to label the various holes, connectors, and ports on the console's butt. They're listed in Table 2-1 to help you find things, in case the need arises.

Table 2-1	Shapes, Connections, Symbols, and Colors		
Name	*Connector*	*Symbol*	*Color*
COM/Serial			Cyan
Digital video			White
Ethernet/RJ-45			None
IEEE 1394			None
IEEE 1394 mini			None
Infrared			None
Joystick			Mustard
Keyboard			Purple

Name	Connector	Symbol	Color
Line In (audio)			Grey
Microphone			Pink
Modem			None
Monitor			Blue
Mouse			Green
Power			Yellow
Printer			Violet
SPDIF In		IN	Pink/white
SPDIF Out		OUT	Black
Speakers/Headphones			Lime
S-Video			Yellow
USB			None

Chapter 3

Insert Tab A into Slot B

*T*here's nothing difficult about setting up a computer. A child could do it. Well, a child with an IQ of about 240. Or maybe just a child who's lucky. They say if you get a big enough hammer . . . and hammering away will eventually get you something, but something more akin to modern art than a truly functional computer.

This chapter is about setting up your computer — specifically, what goes where and also how various things plug into each other. It can really be as easy as inserting the proverbial Tab A into the primordial Slot B — especially when you know exactly where Tab A is and how it fits into Slot B.

✔ This chapter covers basic computer setup. Turning the computer on is covered in Chapter 4.

✔ See Chapter 7 for additional information on what do to next, specifically after adding USB, IEEE, or other expansion options to your computer.

Setting Up Your PC

Your computer runs faster when you take it out of the box.

Unpack the boxes

Computers can come in one, two, or multiple sets of boxes. If you're lucky, one of the boxes says "Open me first." Open that one first. Otherwise, attempt to locate the box containing the console. Open that one first.

Be sure to look through everything. Sometimes, manufacturers stick important items inside boxes inside boxes, or tucked away between pieces of packing material. Look over everything.

Open other boxes as well to be certain that you have all the pieces necessary for your computer system. (Refer to Chapter 2 for a review of the pieces.) If you're missing anything, call someone!

- ✔ Keep the packing slip, warranty, sales receipt, and other important pieces of paper together.

- ✔ Don't fill out the warranty card until after the computer is set up and running fine. (If you have to return the computer, the store likes it best if you have *not* filled in the warranty card.)

- ✔ Keep the boxes and all the packing material. You need them if you have to return the computer. Also, the boxes are the best way to ship the computer if you ever have to move. Some movers don't insure a computer unless it's packed in its original box.

- ✔ Your computer may have come with a roadmap or flow chart type of diagram that tells you how to set everything up. If so, follow those instructions first and use the instructions here as suggestions.

Set up the console first

The console is the main computer box, the locus of all the PC's activities, so it's best if you set it up first. Put it on the desktop or location where you imagine you'll soon become the computing maven you've always dreamed that you would be.

Don't back the console up against the wall just yet. You need to start plugging things into the console's back. Not until everything is connected to the console do you want to push it back up against the wall. (Even then, leave some room so that you don't crimp the cables.)

- ✔ The console needs to breathe. Don't set up the computer in a confined space or inside a cabinet where there's no air circulation.

- ✔ Avoid setting the console by a window where the sun will heat it up. Computers don't like to operate in extreme heat — or cold for that matter.

- ✔ A computer by a window also makes a tempting target for a smash-and-grab thief.

It's a PC, not an oven or a refrigerator

Your PC wants to operate in just about the same temperatures as you, the human, enjoys. Most computers list their happiest operating temperatures on the case somewhere. Generally speaking, temperatures between 40 and 80 Fahrenheit (4 to 27 Celsius) are best for a computer. When it gets too hot, the computer starts to act funny and may spontaneously restart itself. When temperatures get too cold, the computer may not even start!

Also avoid humidity, which can really gum up a computer. I've heard from readers in tropical climes who've reported mold growing inside PCs — the humidity was that bad! If you're going to compute where it's humid, do so in an air-conditioned room!

A General Guide to Plugging Things into the Console

All major parts of your computer system plug directly into the console, which means that once you have the console set up, the next step in assembling your computer is to unpack other pieces parts and hook them into the console.

Don't plug anything into the wall just yet! Even so, as you begin to set up your computer system and attach various gizmos, ensure that those devices with an on–off switch have the switch in the Off position.

This section covers the basics of connecting many popular things to the console. Use this information when you first set up the computer, as well as later when you expand or add to your computer system.

Unless you read otherwise, it's okay to plug in most computer gizmos while the computer is on. There are some exceptions to this rule, so carefully read this section!

Audio

The PC uses the tiny *mini-DIN* connector for standard audio. Most computer audio gadgets — speakers and microphones, for example — use this connector. If not, you can buy an adapter at any audio store or Radio Shack.

- ✔ PC speakers connect to the Line Out, speaker, or headphone jack on the console.
- ✔ Microphones connect to the microphone connector.

✔ The Line In connector is used to connect any non-amplified sound source, such as your stereo, VCR, phonograph, Victrola, or other sound-generating device.

✔ Yes, the difference between the Line In and microphone jack is that Line In devices aren't amplified.

✔ Be sure to check the front of the console for another spot to plug in the headphones. It's much more handy than using the connector on the back.

✔ If your PC has DVD audio, be sure to plug the speakers into the DVD card's output, not the standard audio output on the I/O panel.

IEEE, 1394, FireWire

On a PC, the IEEE port is used primarily for connecting audio or video devices to the computer, most notably a digital videocamera. Even so, external disk drives and scanners are available, which you can also use with the IEEE port.

Generally speaking, most PCs don't come with an IEEE port, so the USB port is used instead. Even so, you can add an IEEE port to your PC by installing a simple expansion card.

Know your computer cables

Unless your computer system is a wireless gizmo, the devices in it connect to the console by using a cable. The cable is known by which hole, or *port*, it plugs into, as well as the cable's length. For example, USB cables plug into USB ports and come in varying lengths.

The ends of a computer cable are configured so that you cannot plug the cable in backward. Generally, the connector for the console is one shape, and the connector for the gizmo is another shape. There are exceptions, in which case it doesn't matter which end of the cable plugs in where.

Some cables are permanently attached to their devices: The mouse and keyboard have such cables, for example. Other cables are separate. That just means that you must remember to plug in both ends.

Extra cables, if you need them, can be purchased at any computer or office supply store or over the Internet. As a suggestion, measure the distance for which you need a cable and then double it to get a cable of the proper length. For example, if it's 2 feet between your console and where you want a microphone, get a 4-foot cable.

You can plug any IEEE device into the computer at any time. The computer or the device can be on or off when you plug things in or remove them. Be sure to check with the device's documentation for any exceptions to this rule.

✔ There are two types of IEEE connectors: small and large. The small one is used specifically with digital video and is often labeled DV. Be sure to look for one of these in the secret panel on the front of the console (if the console has such a panel).

✔ IEEE devices require an IEEE cable, which may or may not come with the device.

✔ See Chapter 7 for more information on all things IEEE.

Keyboard and mouse

The PC keyboard plugs into the keyboard port on the back of the console. The mouse plugs into the mouse port. Note that the two ports look identical, but they are different. Don't plug the keyboard or mouse into the wrong port or else neither device works.

✔ If you're using a USB keyboard or mouse, plug the keyboard or mouse into any USB port.

✔ Some USB keyboards and mice come with a tiny adapter, designed to convert the USB port into a keyboard or mouse port connector.

✔ Don't plug the keyboard or mouse into the keyboard or mouse port while the computer is on. It may damage the keyboard, mouse, or computer. This warning doesn't apply when plugging a keyboard or mouse into a USB port.

Modem

A dial-up modem connects to the phone company's wall jack by using a standard telephone cord. (The cord probably came with the PC.) It works just like plugging in a telephone, and you leave the cord connected all the time. (The modem "hangs up" after a connection, just like a telephone.)

You can use the modem's second phone jack, if available, to connect a real telephone to the computer so that you can use the phone when the computer isn't on the line. The second phone jack is labeled Phone and may have a telephone symbol by it. (The first jack is labeled Line.)

There are also external dial-up modems, which connect to either the USB port or the serial port. You still need a telephone cord to connect the external modem to the phone company's wall jack. Note that external modems have on–off switches.

- ✔ Broadband modems — either cable, DSL, or satellite — plug into the computer's networking jack. See "Network," later in this chapter.
- ✔ Be careful not to confuse the modem's jack with the networking jack. They look similar, but the networking jack is slightly wider.

Monitor

The monitor plugs into the VGA, or graphics adapter, jack on the back of the console. The plug goes in only one way. If you have a digital monitor, find and use the digital jack. Some digital monitors come with a digital-to-VGA adapter if your console lacks a digital jack.

If the console has two VGA connectors, you want to use the one on an expansion card rather than the one on the console's I/O panel.

Network

Plug the network, or Cat-5, cable into the network jack on the back of the console. This is how you connect your PC to a network, or how you connect to a broadband modem.

Another name for the network jack is RJ-45. It's similar in size to the modem's jack, so try not to confuse them.

Part III of this book covers computer networking.

Printer

Plug your computer's printer into the printer port. The standard PC printer cable has two distinct ends, only one of which can be plugged into the console. The other plugs into the computer.

If you're using a USB printer, use any USB port to connect the printer to the console.

✔ For printers with both printer and USB options, use the USB option.

✔ If you use a standard printer cable, be sure to get a bidirectional cable. It's often necessary for the printer software to work properly.

✔ Printers can also be accessed via the computer network. See Part III of this book for more information on networking.

Optical audio

Newer PCs sport SPDIF connectors that allow you to use digital audio devices with the computer. The digital audio devices must also have SPDIF connectors, and you must use special (and not cheap) fiber optic cable to connect these high-end toys.

✔ Plug optical audio input into the computer's SPDIF In connection. To use the computer's optical audio output, plug the cable into the SPDIF Out connector.

✔ Be careful not to bang, touch, or taunt the clear glass ends of the optical cable. Better cables come with little protective caps that you can keep on the ends when the cable isn't connected.

✔ Optical audio is optional.

✔ SPDIF stands for Sony/Philips Digital Interconnect Format. It's also written S/PDIF or S/P-DIF.

S-Video

The S-Video connector is designed to send video output from the computer to a monitor or television screen, or to any video gizmo that has S-Video input. You can, for example, connect the console to a large-format TV to play a computer game. You can do this rather than hook up a standard monitor to your PC.

✔ S-Video is for video output only; it doesn't transmit any audio.

✔ See Chapter 10 for more information on computer monitors.

Serial

The serial, or COM, port isn't as popular as it once was, though you may still find external modems or mice that connect to this port. Otherwise, you can leave it alone.

✔ COM is short for *communications*.

   ✔ When you have two serial ports, the first is COM1 and the second is COM2.

   ✔ Another term for the serial port is RS-232.

USB

USB devices plug into the USB port — any USB port, though some devices specifically want to be connected to the console or to a powered USB hub.

USB cables have two different ends, dubbed A and B. The A end is flat and exists on the console or the back of any USB hub. The B end is trapezoidal in shape and plugs into the USB device. Most USB cables are of the A-B variety. A-A extension cables also exist, so try not to confuse them.

   ✔ You'll probably add your digital camera or scanner to the console by using a USB cable.

   ✔ Many USB devices act as hubs and provide even more USB connectors for even more gizmos.

   ✔ USB cables come in a variety of lengths, but the cables are never longer than 3 or 4 meters. Any longer and the signal may be compromised.

   ✔ Newer USB devices are generally faster and better than the original USB standard. These newer devices are referred to as high-speed or USB 2.0 devices, and they require a USB 2.0 port. Most PCs come with this port, though an older PC can add the port by adding an internal expansion card.

   ✔ USB devices can be connected or disconnected whether the power is on or off. If the power is on, the computer instantly recognizes the device and makes it available.

   ✔ Some USB devices should not be unplugged until the computer is done using them. See Chapter 7 for more information on that, as well as other details on using USB.

Wireless gizmos

Just because the gizmo says that it's wireless, don't think that it means wire-free. For example, a wireless keyboard or mouse may not connect to the console by using a wire, but a wireless transmitter *is* wired to the console, to either the USB, IEEE, or keyboard/mouse ports. Beyond that point, however, it has no more wires.

Wireless networking is more or less truly wireless. The networking adapter on the console has a tiny antenna — no wires. But the rest of the network will, at some point, require a wire or two. See Chapter 19 for wireless networking nonsense.

Plugging Stuff into the Wall

The last thing you need to do, after plugging your computer components into the console and setting them all up, is to plug all those gizmos into the wall. The things need power!

The mighty power strip

You may have noticed that you have far many more devices that need to be plugged in than you have available sockets in the wall. No problem! That's why power strips were invented! The idea is to plug everything into a power strip and then plug that single power strip into the wall, as illustrated in Figure 3-1.

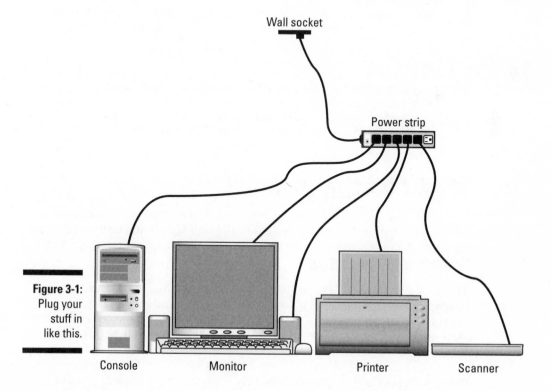

Figure 3-1:
Plug your stuff in like this.

Wall socket

Power strip

Console   Monitor   Printer   Scanner

Follow these steps:

1. Ensure that all your gizmos with on–off switches are in the Off position.

2. Ensure that the power strip is in the Off position.

3. Plug everything into the power strip.

4. Turn your gizmos to the On position.

Now you're ready to turn on the computer system, which is done by turning the power strip on. But not yet! The official on–off information is in Chapter 4. See that chapter for more information, though I highly recommend finishing this entire chapter before you plow ahead.

- ✔ Most power strips have six sockets, which is plenty for a typical computer system. If not, buy a second power strip, plug it into its own wall socket, and use it for the rest of your computer devices.

- ✔ Try to get a power strip with line noise filtering. Even better, pay more to get a power strip that has line conditioning! That's super nice for your electronic goodies.

- ✔ I recommend the Kensington SmartSockets power strip. Unlike cheaper power strips, the SmartSockets lines up its sockets in a perpendicular arrangement, which makes it easier to plug in bulky transformers.

- ✔ Don't plug one power strip into another power strip; it's electrically unsafe!

- ✔ Don't plug a laser printer into a power strip. The laser printer draws too much juice for that to be effective — or safe. Instead, you must plug the laser printer directly into the wall socket. (It says so in your laser printer's manual — if you ever get around to reading it.)

The UPS power solution

UPS stands for *u*ninterruptible *p*ower *s*upply, and it's the best thing to have for hooking up your computer system to the wall socket. Basically, a UPS is a power strip combined with a battery to keep your computer running when the power goes out.

The notion behind a UPS is not to keep computing while the power is out. Instead, the UPS is designed to keep your basic computer components — the console and monitor — up and running just long enough for you to save your work and properly shut down the computer. That way, you never lose anything because of a power outage.

Surges, spikes, and lightning strikes

The power that comes from the wall socket into your computer isn't as pure as the wind-driven snow. Occasionally, it may be corrupted by some of the various electrical nasties that, every now and then, come uninvited into your home or office. Here's the lowdown:

Line noise: Electrical interference on the power line, most commonly seen as static on the TV when someone uses the blender.

Surge: A gradual increase in power.

Serge: Some guy from Europe.

Spike: A sudden increase in the power, such as what happens when lightning strikes nearby.

Dip: The opposite of a surge; a decrease in power. Some electrical motors don't work, and room lights are dimmer than normal. This is also known as a *brownout.*

Power outage: An absence of power coming through the line. People in the 1960s called this a *blackout.*

If possible, try to get a power strip with surge protection for your computer. You have a price to pay, but it's worth it. For an even better power strip, find one with both surge protection and noise filtering or line conditioning.

The most expensive form of protection is spike protection. That causes the power strip to lay down its life by taking the full brunt of the spike and saving your computer equipment.

Note that spikes come through not only the power lines, but also the phone lines. So, if lightning strikes are a common occurrence in your area, get a power strip with phone line protection, as well as network protection if you're using a broadband modem.

For more information about nasty things that can walk into your house through your wall sockets, contact your electrical company. It may offer its own solutions to help you keep your valuable electronics safe, such as power protection right at the breaker box.

Figure 3-2 illustrates the proper way to set up your computer system with a UPS and power strip. Note that some UPS systems also have non-battery-backed-up plugs so that you can plug everything into the UPS directly. Just be sure to plug the monitor and console into the battery-backed-up sockets.

✔ Ignore what it says on the box: A UPS gives you *maybe* five minutes of computer power. Be like Stan and save your stuff to disk, and then shut down Windows and turn off the computer. You can print, scan, modem, or do whatever when the power comes back on.

✔ Leave the UPS on all the time. You need to turn it off only when the power is out and the computer has been properly shut down.

✔ In addition to emergency power, a UPS provides higher levels of electrical protection for your equipment. Many models offer surge, spike, and dip protection, which keep your PC running smoothly despite any nasties the power company may throw your way.

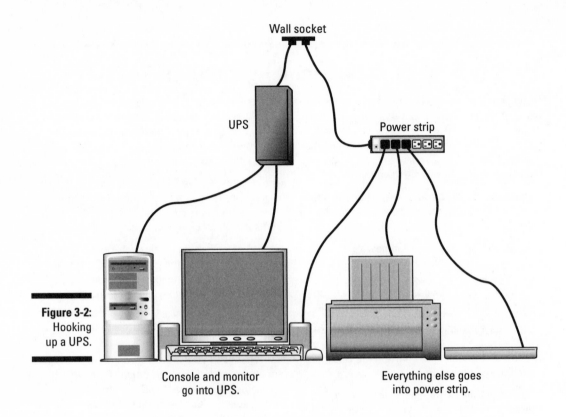

Wall socket

UPS

Power strip

Figure 3-2:
Hooking
up a UPS.

Console and monitor
go into UPS.

Everything else goes
into power strip.

Using the UPS (a short play)

A large boom is heard. The lights flicker and then go out. ROGER *is left sitting in the dark, but his computer is still on. The UPS beeps* once every few seconds. FELICIA *rushes in.*

FELICIA: The power is out! The brioche I put in the toaster oven is ruined! Did you lose that urgent doodle you were creating in Paint?

ROGER: No, darling, I'm still working on it. See? Our UPS has kept the computer console and monitor on during this brief outage.

FELICIA: Oh! That explains the beeping.

ROGER: Yes, the UPS beeps when the power has gone out. It does that just in case I don't notice the pitch darkness we happen to be in.

FELICIA: Well, hurry up and print your doodle!

ROGER: Nay! I shan't print. Printing can wait, which is why I did not connect the printer to the UPS. It's as powerless as the toaster oven.

FELICIA: What can you do? Hurry! The UPS battery won't last forever!

ROGER: Relax, gentle spouse. I shall save to disk, thus. [Ctrl+S] Now I may shut down the computer, assured with the knowledge that my doodle file is safely stored on the internal hard drive. There. *(He turns off the computer and monitor. He shuts off the UPS and the* beeping *stops.)* Now we can weather the storm with peace of mind.

Two hours later, after the power is back on, FELICIA and ROGER are sipping wine:

FELICIA: Honey, you sure are smart, the way you used that UPS.

ROGER: Well, I'm just thankful I read Dan Gookin's book *PCs For Dummies,* published by Wiley. I think I shall buy more of his books.

FELICIA: Who knew that we could find such happiness, thanks to a computer book?

They canoodle.

Chapter 4

Computer On, Computer Off

Some would find a computer frightening enough without knowing that the evil device has no true on–off switch. Some of the most evil computers in all of fiction seem to figure this one out right away. Just as Our Hero realizes, "Hey! It's a computer — I'll just unplug it," the wicked computer is one step ahead. "You cannot unplug me!" the computer says in its tinny, mechanical voice, "I've hooked myself directly into the power system. Bwa-ha-ha!"

Although your computer may not have a big red on–off switch, it does have a *power button*. You use that button to turn the PC on and off. You can also use that button for other purposes as well because the computer actually lets you define what it is the power button does. That's supposed to be friendly, not scary! Even so, I've devoted this entire chapter to the sole topic of turning the computer on and then turning it off again.

How to Turn On Your PC

When everything is plugged in and ready to go (refer to Chapter 3), you turn on the computer this way:

1. **Turn on everything but the console.**

2. **Turn on the console last.**

Or, if everything is plugged into a power strip, just turn on the power strip.

If the console and monitor are plugged into a UPS (which should be kept on all the time) and everything else is plugged into a power strip, do this:

1. **Turn on the power strip, which turns on all the computer's external devices, or** *peripherals.*

2. **Press the monitor's power button to turn it on.**

3. **Press the console's power button to turn it on.**

Success is indicated by your computer system coming to life; you can hear the fan and disk drives whir and warble into action, and various lights on the console, keyboard, and other devices may flash at you or glow softly. The scanner and printer may creak their weary bones into action. Get ready to start computing!

✔ By turning the console on last, you allow time for the other devices in the computer system to initialize and get ready for work. That way, the console recognizes them and lets you use those devices in your computer system.

✔ Not all computer devices have their own on–off switches. For example, some USB scanners and USB disk drives use the USB port's power. To turn these devices off, you must unplug the USB cable (though that's not necessary unless the device is behaving improperly).

✔ You don't have to turn everything on when the computer starts. For example, if you don't plan on printing, there's no need to turn the printer on. In fact, you don't need to turn on most printers until you're ready to print, anyway.

✔ Some devices can be left on all the time. For example, your printer may have a special low-power mode that allows you to keep it on all the time, yet it uses very, very little energy. It's often better to keep such devices on all the time than to turn them on or off several times a day.

✔ It's generally a good idea to keep the DSL or cable modem on all the time.

✔ Also see the later section "Should You Leave the Computer On All the Time?" for information on keeping your computer on all the time.

✔ The largest button on the front of the monitor turns it on. Some older models may have the on–off switch in back. Indeed, many computer devices have their switches in the back, usually next to where the power cord attaches.

✔ When something doesn't turn on, check to see whether it's plugged in. Confirm that all the cables are properly connected.

Ignore these other terms for "starting a computer"

Any of the following terms is roughly equivalent to "starting the computer." Use them at your own risk, usually in the presence of a licensed, high-tech professional.

Cold start Cycle power Hard start

Power on Power up Soft boot Warm boot

Boot Reboot Reset Restart

The PC Setup program

At some point during the startup process, you see a message on the monitor about pressing a certain key, or keyboard combination, to enter the PC's Setup program. *Pay attention to those keys!*

You don't always need to run or access the PC Setup program, but it's good to know how to get there when you do — for example, when you're adding more memory to the PC, updating some types of hardware, or disabling chipset features — technical stuff, and rare, but often necessary.

- ✔ Write down on this book's Cheat Sheet the keys used to access the PC Setup program.

- ✔ Common keys to press for getting into the PC Setup program include Del or Delete, F1, F2, F10, F11, and the spacebar.

- ✔ The PC Setup program is part of your computer's hardware. It's not part of Windows.

- ✔ One feature of the PC Setup program is that you can apply a system password for your computer. Although I strongly recommend using passwords on the Internet and for your computer accounts, I recommend against setting a system password in the PC Setup program. Unlike with those other passwords, if you forget the system password, there's nothing you can do and your computer is pretty much useless.

Trouble in Startup Land!

Hopefully, Windows starts right up and you get on with your work. You may experience a few unwelcome detours along the way.

The most common warning happens when you leave a floppy disk in the PC's floppy drive. You see a message displayed regarding a "non-system" disk — something scary like that. Anyway, remove the floppy disk from drive A and press the Enter key on the keyboard, and the computer starts along its merry way.

For other startup problems, such as starting in the oddly named Safe mode, please refer to my book *Troubleshooting Your PC For Dummies* (Wiley Publishing, Inc.).

Here Comes Windows!

Starting a computer is a hardware thing. But the hardware is dumb, remember? It needs software to keep things hopping, and the most important piece of software is your computer's operating system. For most PCs, that operating system is *Windows.* So, after starting your computer's hardware, the next thing you have to deal with is Windows.

Log in, mystery guest

The first time you run Windows on your PC, you do some extra setup and configuration. After that, you may also find that you have to *log in* and identify yourself. This is done first of all as a security measure (especially if you've applied a password to your account), but also to keep your stuff separate from anyone else who may use the same computer.

Choose your account from the list and, optionally, type a password if you're prompted to do so. Figure 4-1 shows a typical friendly Windows login screen. Here's how it works:

1. **Click on your account name or the cute picture by your account.**

   If you don't have an account name, you can use the Guest account, if it's present. (Refer to a book more specific to Windows for information on setting up accounts.)

2. **Enter your password into the box, if one appears.**

   Carefully type your password into the box.

3. **Click the green arrow or press the Enter key to have Windows check your password.**

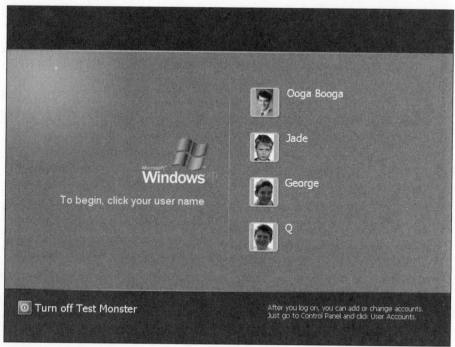

Figure 4-1:
Let us in, the
users beg.

If everything goes well, you next see Windows main location, its home plate, its lobby, which is called the *desktop*. Keep reading in this section. If you goof up your password, try again. You can use the Password Hint link to remind you of your password — but you must type a password to get into the system!

✔ The login screen shown in Figure 4-1 is the Welcome screen. There's also a more terse version of the same thing, a screen that simply lists blank spots for a user name and password. You must type your password into a Password box and then click the OK button to log in.

✔ The word *login* comes from the word *log,* as in a list of activities or experiences. The *login* is just like entering your name in a log.

✔ It's possible to avoid the login screen. If the computer has only one account and that account lacks a password, the Welcome screen doesn't appear. I don't recommend this technique, however, because passwords are important. Future versions of Windows will demand that all users — even only users — log in. You may as well get used to it now.

Welcome to the desktop

Windows pretty face is something called the *desktop,* or the main starting place for doing anything in Windows. A typical desktop is shown in Figure 4-2. Believe it or not, that's your instinctive, intuitive, friendly, ready-to-use computer staring at you in the face. You've made it.

What you do next depends on the reason you bought your computer. This book has some ideas in it, but remember that this book is a *reference,* not a tutorial. As such, the reference for turning on your computer is all done.

Turning the Computer Off (Shutdown)

In the past 100 or so years that society has been electrified, there's really been no easier operation than turning something off. That is, unless the thing you're turning off is a computer. Leave it to the computer industry to make something like turning off a PC as illogical as possible.

Figure 4-2: Why it's called a desktop, the world may never know.

It's not just a question of turning the computer off, but in which way to turn the computer off: All the way? Temporarily? Or just a weensy bit? Mix in some jargon and the fact that the computer doesn't have an on–off switch (no, it's a *power button*), and you have the reason that more pages in this chapter are devoted to turning a PC off than to turning the darn thing on.

Your options for turning off the PC

Here are your choices for turning off the computer, from not turning it off at all to an angry tug on the power cord. See the subsections that follow for the details:

Keep the computer on all the time: A viable option, given the glut of other choices. See the section "Should You Leave the Computer On All the Time?" toward the end of this chapter.

Log Off: A way to tell Windows that you're done without having to turn the computer off and then on again.

Stand By: The computer slips into a special, power-saving Sleep mode, like going into a low-power coma.

Hibernate: The computer does turn itself off, but when you turn it back on it again, it comes back to life much faster. Think "suspended animation."

Restart: You turn the computer off and on again in one step, mainly when installing or upgrading software or sometimes to fix minor quirks — like slapping Windows upside its head.

Shut Down: The one real option that turns the darn thing off.

Yank the power cord out of the wall: This method is satisfying, but not recommended.

Log yourself off

I'll be honest: No one does this. Or, if they do, it's infrequently. Although multiple people can use the same computer, rare is the time that you really need to log off. In fact, if you're the only one using your computer, you can merrily skip this entire section; don't bother ever logging off.

By logging off, you allow users on the same PC to get in and use their accounts to, well, do whatever. But by logging off, you ensure that your computer session has properly ended, and you save time over restarting the computer.

Here's how to log off and let someone else use the computer:

1. **Click the Start button.**

2. **Click the Log Off button at the bottom of the Start panel.**

   That just may be it, or you may see the Log Off Windows dialog box, as shown in Figure 4-3. If so, do Step 3:

3. **Click the Log Off button.**

Figure 4-3:
Get outta
here, you
bum!

As the computer logs you out, you're prompted to save any unsaved files, and any open programs or windows are closed. You're done for the day. Time for someone else to use the PC.

If you see the Switch User button (refer to Figure 4-3), you can use it to quickly log out and let someone else log in. This option is faster than logging out in that it doesn't require you to save your stuff or close your programs. When you return (log in again), all your stuff is waiting for you just as you left it.

Another quick way to log out and *lock* the computer is to press the Win+L key combination. The Win key is the Windows key on your keyboard; L stands for Lock. To unlock the system and get back in, just log in to Windows as you normally would. Many users use this Win+L trick when they step away from the computer to ensure that no one nearby snoops at stuff while they're gone.

Please stand by (Sleep mode)

Stand By mode, also known as Sleep or Suspend mode, was designed as an energy-saving measure. What it does is to place your PC into a special low-power mode — almost like the computer is asleep (hence the name). The monitor goes blank, the hard drive spins down, and the computer sits there not doing anything other than saving electricity.

To put your PC into Stand By mode, comply with these steps:

1. **Save your work!**

   This step is important: You must save your documents or files to disk before putting the PC into Stand By mode. If you want to be extra safe, close your programs. You may lose data if a power outage occurs while the computer is quiescent.

2. **Click the Start button.**

3. **Click the Shut Down button at the bottom of the Start panel.**

   The Turn Off Computer dialog box appears, as shown in Figure 4-4.

Figure 4-4: Options for turning off your PC.

 4. **Click the Stand By button.**

   The computer then appears to have turned itself off, but it's really just resting. Don't be fooled!

You wake the computer up by pressing a key on the keyboard or jiggling the mouse. The PC comes back to life, all refreshed and rested and resuming operations where you left off.

Sleep mode is controlled through the Power Options icon, in the Windows Control Panel. That's where you can set options to automatically put the PC into Sleep mode or to control which parts of the PC sleep and which don't.

Cybernation hibernation

Rather than turn off your computer, you should consider using Hibernation instead. It's really better than turning the computer off, especially if you're always in a hurry. Here's how:

1. **Click the Start button.**

2. **Click the Shut Down button at the bottom of the Start panel.**

   You see the famous Turn off computer dialog box (refer to Figure 4-4). But — what? No Hibernate button!

3. **Press and hold the Shift key.**

   Either Shift key activates the Hibernate button, which is inexplicably in the same place as the Stand By button. Fine. Keep holding that Shift key!

4. **Click the Hibernate button.**

   The computer's hard drive churns for a few seconds, and then it shuts off.

Yes, the computer is really off.

Wiggling the mouse or slapping the keyboard doesn't wake up the PC. To unhibernate, punch the console's power button. Unlike in a normal startup, the computer quickly jumps to life and returns to its former state — and restores things the same as they were the last time you used the PC.

- Not every PC can hibernate.

- If you don't see the Hibernate option in Step 3, your PC may not have it. Check with the Windows Control Panel to be sure; open the Power Options icons and check that dialog box for a Hibernate tab.

- Hibernation saves electricity, in that the computer is really turned off, and time, in that it takes less time to turn the computer on again.

- If you have a PC with multiple operating systems — a *multiboot* system — you have to select Windows XP from that menu first. After that, Windows unhibernates and restores things to the way they were.

Restarting Windows

You need to reset or restart Windows in two instances. Windows tells you to restart after you install something new or make some change, or whenever *Something Strange* happens. For some reason, a restart clears the computer's head, and things return to normal.

Here's how to restart Windows:

1. **Click the Start button.**

2. **Click the Shut Down button at the bottom of the Start panel.**

   The Turn Off Computer dialog box appears (refer to Figure 4-4).

3. **Click the Restart button.**

Windows shuts itself down — almost as though it were turning the computer off. But, just at the moment the system would have turned off, it starts back up again — a restart.

✔ If any files are unsaved, you're asked to save them before shutting down.

✔ As the computer shuts down, you may encounter various End Now dialog boxes. These are stubborn programs that refuse to quit. If you see any, click the End Now button to expedite the restart process.

✔ Windows may initiate a restart on its own; or, when upgrading, you may have to click a button in a window to restart the computer.

✔ Remember to remove any floppy disks from drive A before restarting. If you leave a disk in there, the computer tries to start itself from that disk, which is dumb, but no one ever said that computers are smart.

Turning the darn thing off

Yes, these steps really work:

1. **Click the Start button.**

2. **Click the Sh̲u̲t Down button at the bottom of the Start panel.**

   You see the Turn Off Computer dialog box, as shown earlier in this chapter, in Figure 4-4.

3. **Click the Turn Off button.**

   After a spell and a fashion, the computer turns itself off.

If you had any unsaved documents or files, Windows asks you to save them before it fully shuts down.

After turning off the console, go ahead and turn off the other components in your computer system: monitor, scanner, and other external devices. Or, if you have a power strip, simply flip its switch to turn everything off.

If you have a UPS, however, *do not* turn it off; you want to leave it on so that its battery remains charged.

✔ Some stubborn programs may require you to deliberately shut them down. That's fine. Do so properly; avoid using artillery, if possible.

✔ If the computer shuts down and then immediately restarts, you have a problem. Refer to your dealer or computer manufacturer for assistance, or check out my other PC book, *Troubleshooting Your PC For Dummies,* published by Wiley.

Power Button, What Is Your Function?

Yes, it's true that the PC no longer has an on–off switch — it has a *power button*. So what's the big deal? The big deal is that the power button is *programmable*. You can tell the computer what to do when you press the power button, from "do nothing" to "turn off the computer." The choice is up to you.

Normally, pressing the power button is the same as shutting down Windows; when you press the power button, the computer automatically carries out the steps shown in the preceding section. But that's just one of five potential things the power button can do. To see them all, comply with these steps:

1. **Open the Windows Control Panel.**

   See Chapter 5 for information on opening the Control Panel.

2. **Double-click the mouse on the Power Options icon to open it.**

   The Power Options Properties dialog box appears.

3. **Click the Advanced tab.**

   Look for this text in the dialog box: "When I press the power button on my computer." A drop-down list below that text has options that tell the computer what to do when you press the power button. You see up to five choices:

   - **Do nothing.** This option effectively disables the power button; press it and nothing happens.

   - **Ask me what to do.** Pressing the power button displays the Turn Off Computer dialog box, as shown earlier in this chapter, in Figure 4-4.

   - **Stand by.** The computer goes into Stand By mode.

   - **Hibernate.** The computer hibernates.

   - **Shut down.** The computer shuts down.

   For example, if you want the computer to just shut down when you press the power button, choose the option that reads Shut Down.

4. **Select a function for the power button.**

5. **Click OK.**

Not all computers have programmable power buttons, and often the selection of power button functions is limited by the computer's design. Don't be disappointed if your PC lacks some of the abilities of others, or even lacks the ability to assign a function to the power button.

Regardless of which settings you make from the preceding list, when you press and hold the power button for about two or three seconds, it instantly turns the computer off. Remember this trick, but use it only in times of desperation. Otherwise, shut down the PC properly, as described in this chapter.

Some PC cases do have a true on–off button in addition to a power button. This button is on the back of the console and is labeled | and O, for on and off, respectively. Use this button rather than the power button only in times of dire emergency.

Should You Leave the Computer On All the Time?

I've been writing about computers for over 20 years now, and this debate has yet to be settled. Should you leave your computer on all the time? Does it waste electricity? Is it better for the PC to be on all the time — like the refrigerator or Darth Vader night light? Will we ever know *the truth?* Of course not! But people have opinions.

"I want to leave my computer off all the time"

Hey, I'm with you.

"I want to leave my computer on all the time"

I say Yes. If you use your computer often, such as for a home business, or you find yourself turning it on and off several times during the day, just leave it on all the time.

The only time I ever turn my computers off is when I'll be away for longer than a weekend. Even then, I just hibernate the computers (well, those computers that have the hibernation feature) rather than turn them off.

Does this waste electricity? Perhaps, but most computers have Stand By mode and save energy when they're not being used. Modern PCs don't use that much electricity, and having one on all the time doesn't raise your electrical bill significantly, not like a Jacuzzi or a time machine.

Also, computers enjoy being on all the time. Having that fan going keeps the console's innards at a constant temperature, which avoids some of the problems that turning the system off (cooling) and on again (heating) cause.

What should you do? Do whatever you feel like doing! I keep my computers on all the time mostly because I use them all the time and it's easier for me to have immediate access to them than to wait for the dumb things to start up all the time.

- ✔ If you use your PC only once a day (during the evening for e-mail, chat, and the Internet, for example), turning it off for the rest of the day is fine.

- ✔ Most businesses leave their computers on all the time.

- ✔ Whatever you do with your PC, it's always a good idea to turn the monitor off when you're away. Some monitors can *sleep* just like PCs, but if they don't, turning them off can save some electricity.

- ✔ If you do leave your computer on all the time, don't put it under a dust cover. The dust cover gives the computer its very own greenhouse effect and brings the temperatures inside the system way past the sweltering point, like in a sweaty Southern courtroom drama.

- ✔ Another good idea: Turn off the computer during an electrical storm. Even if you have spike protection or a UPS, *don't* let that nasty spike of voltage into your computer during a lightning storm. Unplug the computer. And remember to unplug the phone line. You can't be too careful.

Chapter 5

Places to Go, Things to See in Windows

*S*oftware rules the PC's roost, and the O Supreme One of all software in your computer is the *operating system,* the main program that controls all the other programs. It would be impressive if the operating system were evil or twisted in some dramatic manner. But, it's not. No, the operating system is merely in charge because some program has to be. Besides, the operating system is too busy minding the computer's hardware and obeying your every whim to turn to the dark side.

This is a hardware book, yet a lot of the hardware things this book discusses relate directly to Windows. Because software is in charge of the hardware, and Windows is in charge of all the software, this chapter covers some of the more important places in Windows you need to visit to manage or adjust your computer's hardware.

For more information on the various parts of Windows, including the desktop, taskbar, and system tray — and their individual pieces parts — please refer to this book's companion *PCs For Dummies Quick Reference* (Wiley Publishing, Inc.).

The Desktop

Windows main screen is the *desktop*. That's where the actual windows appear, those that frame the programs you run or show you a list of files or icons. The desktop can also have its own icons, such as shortcut icons to programs, files, or folders you often use. It can also be splashed with a fancy picture or background.

Figure 5-1 shows a typical Windows XP desktop. You can see various icons on either side of the screen, a pretty background, plus the Start button and taskbar on the bottom of the screen. (The Start button and taskbar are covered later in this chapter.)

Desktop background   Icons

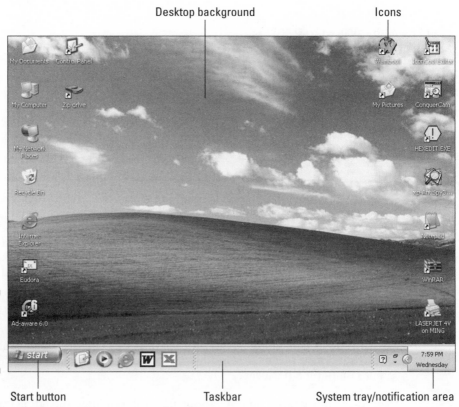

Figure 5-1:
The
Windows
desktop.

Start button   Taskbar   System tray/notification area

✔ The *desktop* is merely the background on which Windows shows you its stuff — like an old sheet you hang from the wall to bore your neighbors with by showing your Cayman Islands vacation slide show.

✔ Icons are tiny pictures representing files or programs on your computer. See Chapter 20 for more information on icons.

✔ You can change the desktop wallpaper to any image. See Chapter 10.

✔ Also see Chapter 10 for information on changing the size of the desktop, or its *resolution*.

✔ The desktop is called a desktop for traditional reasons. Several generations of computers ago, it really did look like a desktop, complete with paper pad, clock, glue, scissors, and other desktop-y things.

Taming the Taskbar

The desktop is more like a corkboard where you pin icons than a place where you can grab hold of Windows and strangle it, if the desire is there. If you really want to wrap your paws around Windows, you must notice the taskbar.

The taskbar is typically located on the bottom of the desktop, as shown in Figure 5-2. Four important areas are noted in the picture, though the Quick Launch bar may not be visible on your PC's taskbar.

Start button   Quick Launch bar   Window button   System tray

Figure 5-2: The taskbar.

You use the taskbar to control the windows on the screen; it allows you to quickly switch between those windows, or *tasks,* by clicking a window's button. The taskbar is also home to the Start button, which is where you *really* control Windows, as well as other doodads covered throughout the remainder of this chapter.

The System Tray, or Notification Area

The tiny tub on the opposite end of the taskbar from the Start button (refer to Figure 5-2) displays the current time and day, and also wee little icons that represent special programs running in Windows. The location is called the *system tray,* or *notification area.*

✔ You can see more information about the special programs by either double-clicking or right-clicking their wee icons.

✔ Some icons display pop-up bubbles with messages in them as various things happen in windows.

✔ There's no way to completely disable the system tray. You can hide icons, but you cannot turn the entire thing off without buying a special utility to do so. (I don't recommend doing so.)

The Start Button

The Start button is where you start a number of activities in Windows. It truly is the place to go when you want to start a program, start some activity, adjust the way Windows works, or even shut down the computer.

 The Start button lives on one end of the taskbar, usually in the lower-left corner of the desktop. Clicking the Start button with the mouse displays the Start button menu. That's where the fun — or anguish — starts!

✔ You can also pop up the Start button menu by pressing the Win key on your computer's keyboard. If your computer doesn't have a Win key, press Ctrl+Esc to pop up the Start button menu.

✔ You make the Start button menu go away by pressing the Esc key on the keyboard.

The Start button menu

You use the Start button menu to start programs as well as get at key locations elsewhere in Windows. Figure 5-3 shows an example of what the menu may look like.

Important things to find on the Start button menu are listed in the figure. Note that the Start button menu can be customized, so what you see on your screen may look different from what's shown in the figure.

✔ To customize the Start button menu, right-click the Start button and choose Properties from the pop-up menu. Click the Customize button in the dialog box that appears, and you can find many options for adjusting how the Start button menu looks and behaves.

✔ Figure 5-3 shows the Windows XP Start button menu. A Classic Start menu is available, which looks different. This book assumes that you have the Windows XP Start button menu, as shown in Figure 5-3.

Recently used programs

Pin-on area

Programs

Account information

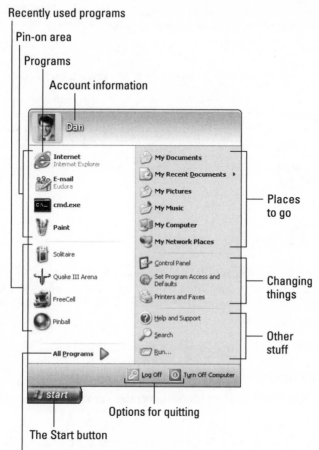

Places to go

Changing things

Other stuff

Figure 5-3:
The Start
button
menu.

Options for quitting

The Start button

Access all programs on the computer

The All Programs menu

All the programs — software and applications — installed on your computer are on the Start button menu's All Programs menu. Clicking that item displays a pop-up menu full of choices — in fact, the menu is so full that it may fill more than one column of options on the screen.

The All Programs menu is organized into programs and submenus. To run a program, click its icon or name on the menu. Or, you can see more programs

organized into the many submenus by clicking a submenu name. Note that
there are submenus on submenus for extra added craziness.

- ✔ Chapter 23 has more information on the All Programs menu.

- ✔ The All Programs menu may be called More Programs in some versions
  of Windows XP.

- ✔ The Programs submenus are rather slippery. They pop up and disappear
  as your mouse roves over them. Be careful! Accessing them can be aggra-
  vating if you're a sloppy mouse mover or your mouse is too sensitive.

- ✔ Refrain from beating your mouse into the table when it behaves
  erratically.

The Control Panel

One important place to know in Windows, especially in regard to your PC
hardware, is the Control Panel. The *Control Panel* is a special window that
lists icons relating to many aspects of your computer's hardware, software,
and general configuration.

To display the magical Control Panel window, do this:

1. **Click the Start button.**

2. **Click the Control Panel menu item on the right side of the Start button
   menu.**

If you don't see the Control Panel item on the Start button menu, open the My
Computer icon on the desktop. Click to choose Control Panel from the list of
Other Places on the left side of the window. Or, you can click the downward-
pointing arrow on the Address bar and select Control Panel from the drop-
down list.

Figure 5-4 shows a typical Control Panel window, chock full of icons. Later
chapters in this book cover what many of those icons do.

Note that Figure 5-4 shows the Control Panel in Classic view, which is what I
prefer and how this book references things. It's faster than using Category
view. To switch to Classic view, click the mouse on the text "Switch to Classic
View" on the left side of the window.

Figure 5-4:
The Control
Panel.

Networking Control

If you plan to put your PC on a network or use a broadband (cable or DSL) Internet connection, you need to know where Networking Central is in Windows. It's a sneaky Window named Network Connections.

To display the Network Connections window, click the Start button and choose Network Connections from the Start button menu. Sadly, this option may not appear on the Start button menu, in which case you do this:

1. **Open the Control Panel.**

   Refer to the preceding section.

2. **Open the Network Connections icon.**

   There's your window, which is covered in more detail in Part III of this book.

Another networking place to know is the My Network Places window, which can be accessed by opening the My Network Places icon on the desktop or choosing My Network Places from the Start button menu. The window displays various network connections available to your computer, on either the local area network or the Internet. Again, more information on this window is in Part III.

Places for Your Stuff

Windows has places where you can store your stuff — the files you create. The big name here is the *file system*. That includes all the disk drives on your computer, as well as the stuff you store on those disk drives. The whole subject is tossed around in Part IV of this book. For now, consider knowing these three important places:

 My Computer: This main icon details all the disk storage in your computer, as well as any network drives you're using or a scanner or digital camera. You display the My Computer window by opening the My Computer icon on the desktop or accessing it from the Start button menu.

 My Documents: This is your home place for the stuff you save on the computer — the things you store or create. The window is accessed by opening the My Documents icon on the desktop or via the Start button menu.

 Recycle Bin: This icon is on the desktop. It represents File Hell — or that location where files are sent when you delete them. It's more like File Limbo in that it's possible to recover files from the Recycle Bin when you change your almighty mind.

Getting Windows to Help You

Windows is huge! To document the entire operating system would require not only a single book — a fat book — but, rather, multiple fat volumes of that book. Not even Microsoft sells such a book. Instead, what it did was put all its documentation and helpful information on the computer itself. It's called the Windows Help system.

To access the Windows Help system, you press the F1 key on the keyboard. I know: F1? What's up with that? Felp? "F any 1 can help me?" I just don't get it, but that's the key to use.

Pressing F1 in the midst of doing anything in Windows displays helpful information about what you're doing.

To get general help, choose the Help and Support command from the Start button menu, and you see the Help and Support Center. There, you can type a question or pick a topic to search for help, as shown in Figure 5-5.

Note that Windows may dial in to the Internet to complete your help request. This is normal (and you notice it only if you have a dial-up Internet connection).

The help engine is its own program. When you're done using help, remember to quit: Click the X Close button in the upper-left corner of the window.

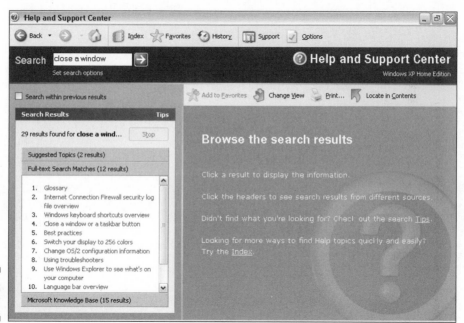

Figure 5-5:
Help?

Part II
Computer Guts

The 5th Wave   By Rich Tennant

"Well, here's your problem. You only have half the ram you need."

In this part . . .

There's more to your computer hardware than just its keyboard and monitor. You may touch the keyboard and mouse, you may look at the monitor, and occasionally you may slap the printer, but a computer system is more than those physical things. If you plan on getting as much as possible from your computer, you'll need to know the details — the *guts*. That's the stuff that lurks inside the console, and the real names for all those doodads, gadgets, gizmos, and other hardware that make up your computer system. In this part of the book, you'll find out how to name, use, adjust, and abuse all that stuff.

Chapter 6

Inside the Box

*B*eneath the console's sleek, 21st century exterior lies a tangled chaos of electronic enigma. It's a tropical jungle of twisty, vine-like cables connecting various circuit boards to power supplies and disk drives, tossed in with a high-tech salad of circuits, transistors, capacitors, resistors, and other components, many of which are sharp and pointy. Scary? Not really, but it isn't exactly inviting.

Despite the forbidden and complex nature of the console's innards, it's not a forbidden place. Most computer consoles open easily, and that's for a reason: Sometimes, you need to get in there to add new stuff to your PC. It's rare, but it happens. When it does, you have this chapter as a reference to tell you what's what and, most importantly, how not to electrocute yourself.

A Look Around, Inside the Console

You don't have to open up the computer console — nope, not ever. You have plenty of options for expanding your computer system without opening the case. Even so, I highly recommend that you become familiar with the internal configuration of your computer, or at least have a passing knowledge of what's what and what's where, and its proper name.

Your PC's innards

Figure 6-1 highlights the important things to note inside your PC's console. The figure shows a sideways view, as though you took off the right side of the console and looked inside. (The left side of the image shows the front of the console.)

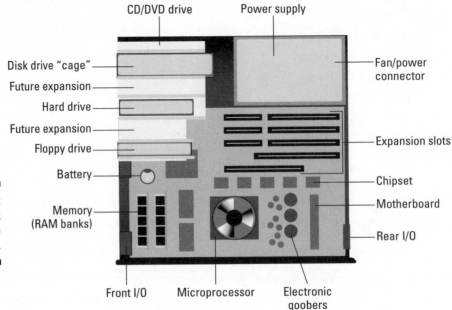

Figure 6-1:
A peek
inside the
console.

CD/DVD drive · Power supply · Disk drive "cage" · Fan/power connector · Future expansion · Hard drive · Future expansion · Expansion slots · Floppy drive · Battery · Chipset · Memory (RAM banks) · Motherboard · Rear I/O · Front I/O · Microprocessor · Electronic goobers

Missing from Figure 6-1 are the myriad cables that festoon the console's abdomen. Also, the detail on the motherboard is a bit sparse, and the typical PC's console is a lot less roomy. And, if you've owned the computer for a while, some dust is in there too — maybe even cat hair!

The three main parts of the console's tummy are

✔ The disk drive cage

✔ The power supply

✔ The motherboard

The *disk drive cage* is a contraption used to hold internal disk drives, a CD-ROM, a DVD, a hard drive, plus maybe a floppy drive. The cage also has room for even more disk drives (the so-called "future expansion"), usually right behind some knock-out panels on the console's front.

The *power supply* feeds the console that all-important stuff called electricity. You can read more about the power supply in the section "The Source of PC Power," at the end of this chapter.

Finally, the *motherboard* is the computer's main circuitry board. It's important, so it's talked about later in this chapter, starting with the section "The Mother of All Boards."

Everything inside the PC's case is a *modular* component. That term means that individual pieces can be replaced without having to toss out the entire console. (Modularity is one of the keys to the PC's success over the years.)

Opening the case (if you dare)

You don't have to go inside the console if you don't want to. Instead, return the console to your computer dealer or fix-it person whenever work needs to be done. But, if you have even the slight inclination toward fixing things, or you just have a lot of life insurance, it's okay to open up the console to add or replace things inside.

Here are the general steps I recommend for opening the console:

1. **Turn off the computer.**

   Refer to Chapter 4.

2. **Unplug the console; remove the power cord.**

   Turning the console off isn't enough. You really need to unplug the power cord. Unplugging other cables isn't necessary unless you need to do so to move the console around.

3. **Move the console away from the wall or locate it in a place where you have room to work.**

4. **Open the console's case.**

   The steps for opening the case depend on the case. Some cases require a screwdriver and the removal of several screws. Other cases may just pop off or swing open.

Now you're ready to work inside the console. Refer to Figure 6-1 and try to find things — but look at all 'dem cables! What a nightmare!

✔ Never plug the console in when the case is open. If you need to test something, close the case!

✔ Typically, you open the case to do one of three things: Add more memory; add an expansion card; or replace the PC's battery.

✔ While you work in the console, try to keep one hand touching the case or, preferably, something metal, like the disk drive cage. That way, your electric potential is the same as the console's, and you reduce the chances of generating static electricity — which can damage your computer.

Closing the case

When you're done doing whatever motivated you to open the console, close it up! Check to ensure that all the wires have been reconnected and that your internal operations are all wrapped up and no tools or screws are left loose inside the case.

Reattach the lid or cover, and then plug the console back into the power cord. Turn the computer on and pray that it still works.

   ✔ It may be a good idea not to screw on the case until you're certain that the upgrade was successful.

   ✔ See Chapter 15 for specific information on updating your PC's hardware.

The Mother of All Boards

The computer's largest circuitry board is the *motherboard*. It's where the computer's most important electronics exist. The motherboard is home to the following essential PC components, many of which are illustrated earlier in this chapter, in Figure 6-1:

   ✔ Microprocessor

   ✔ Chipset

   ✔ Memory

   ✔ Battery

   ✔ Expansion slots

   ✔ I/O connectors

   ✔ Electronic goobers

The microprocessor, chipset, battery, and expansion card items all have their own sections in this chapter. Refer to them for more information. Computer memory is a big deal, so it's covered exclusively in Chapter 9.

The *I/O connectors* are simply places on the motherboard where the console's I/O panels are plugged in. There's also a connector where the disk drives plug in, as well as a power connector for electricity from the power supply. The electronic goobers are those miscellaneous pieces of technology that engineers put on the motherboard to look impressive.

> ✔ The motherboard is the main piece of circuitry inside your PC.

> ✔ Though many computer chips can be on the motherboard, the main chip is the *microprocessor*. The motherboard exists to support that one chip.

The Microprocessor

At the heart of every computer beats the *microprocessor*. That's the computer's main chip — the computer's muscle.

Note that the microprocessor is *not* the computer's brain. Software is the brain. The microprocessor is just hardware, and it does only what the software tells it to do.

The microprocessor's job is really rather simple: It can do basic math, it can fetch and put information to memory, and it does all the input/output (I/O) stuff, which you didn't read about in Chapter 1. The key to the microprocessor's success is that, unlike your typical brooding teenager, the microprocessor does things very fast.

> ✔ When your jaw is tired, you can refer to the microprocessor as the *processor*.

> ✔ Another term for a microprocessor is CPU. *CPU* stands for *central processing unit*.

> ✔ Modern PC microprocessors run very hot and therefore require special cooling. You notice inside the PC that the microprocessor wears a tiny fan as a hat. That helps keep the thing cool.

Naming a microprocessor

A long time ago, in an economy far, far away, computer microprocessors were named after famous numbers, like 386 and 8088. The trend now is toward microprocessor names, but not human names, like John or Mary. No, now microprocessors are named after potential science fiction heroes or pharmaceuticals. Here's a smattering:

Pentium: The premium microprocessor, developed by industry leader Intel.

Celeron: A less-expensive version of the Pentium and often used in low-end, or *home,* PCs.

Athlon: An imitation Pentium from Intel rival AMD. The Athlon is just as good as the Pentium, though less expensive.

Duron: The Celeron imitation, from AMD.

Other names or numbers may be used along with the main names just listed. Those suffixes aren't worth noting because the computer industry changes them too often for anyone to care. The only important yardstick used to judge a microprocessor (aside from price) is its speed, which is covered in the next subsection.

- The two most popular types of Pentium chips that are now sold are the Pentium 3 and Pentium 4. The Pentium 4 is the newer, better one of the two.

- The Pentium also has some higher-end siblings: the Itanium and Xeon microprocessors, used exclusively in high-end server computers.

- Intel is the world's leading manufacturer of computer microprocessors. The company developed the 8088, which dwelt in the bosom of the first IBM PC.

- Another way to describe a microprocessor is by which type of socket on the motherboard it plugs into. This information is important only to those folks who choose to build their own PCs.

- Little difference exists between a true Intel and a non-Intel microprocessor. As far as your PC's software is concerned, the microprocessor is the same no matter who made it. I must note, however, that computer gamers prefer AMD microprocessors.

The measure of a microprocessor

Microprocessors are gauged by two factors: their muscle power and how fast they go.

Microprocessor muscle is measured in bits — specifically, how many bits at a time the chip can toss around. For a typical PC microprocessor, that's either 32 bits or 64 bits, and 32 bits is the most common.

It helps to think of bits in a microprocessor like cylinders in a car: The more you have, the more powerful the engine. Or, a better example is lanes on a freeway: The more you have, the quicker that larger chunks of data (traffic) can move around.

Current microprocessor speed is measured in gigahertz (GHz), or billions of cycles per second. The higher the value, the faster the microprocessor, with average speeds between 2.0 GHz (slower) and 4.0 GHz (faster).

Sadly, speed isn't really a realistic gauge of how fast a microprocessor does its microprocessing. Speed is a relative thing when it comes to computers, but even so, a Pentium running at 2.4 GHz is slower than a Pentium running at 3.0 GHz — not that you would notice.

"Okay, wise guy, so which microprocessor lives in my PC?"

It's not easy, after you get home, to confirm that your PC has the microprocessor you bought. Even if you crack open the case, you can't really see the microprocessor because it's wearing that little fan hat — and even if you peeled off the hat, the numbers and names printed on the chip may not be of any use to you.

One way to discover which type of microprocessor dwells in your PC's bosom is to use Windows. The System Properties dialog box shows a brief microprocessor and RAM summary, similar to the one shown in Figure 6-2.

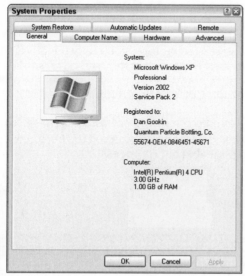

Figure 6-2:
The System
Properties
dialog box.

To summon the System Properties dialog box, press Win+Break on your keyboard (that's the Windows key plus the key labeled Break or Pause Break). You can also open this dialog box by opening the System icon in the Control Panel.

In Figure 6-2, you can see that the PC sports a Pentium 4 microprocessor running at 3.00 GHz. The computer sports 1GB of RAM. That jibes with what I paid for, but not every computer's System Properties dialog box is quite as explicit.

- Not every System Properties dialog box displays information as complete as that shown in Figure 6-2. When Windows doesn't really know, it may say something vague, as in "x86 Family."

- One of my favorite microprocessor snooper programs is CPU-Z. Here's the Web site:

  ```
  http://www.cpuid.org/cpuz.php
  ```

- See Chapter 9 for more information on RAM.

"Can I upgrade my PC's microprocessor?"

Some computers are sold with the idea that you can upgrade later to a faster microprocessor. That is true: In many PCs, you can buy a new CPU, remove the old one, and plug in the new one. Boom! You get instant speed. But I don't recommend doing this.

To truly take advantage of newer technology, you really need more than a new microprocessor. What you need is a new motherboard, some new memory, and, while you're at it, new disk drives. Otherwise, the power of the new CPU gets lost in the old CPU's antique circuitry.

Another issue is cost. Individually, microprocessors are expensive, especially the newest, best ones. It's just easier to buy yourself a whole new computer than to worry about an upgradeable microprocessor.

Expansion Slots

Your computer's abilities can be expanded in a number of ways. One of the most direct ways to add extra circuitry or options to the computer is to plug an *expansion card* directly into the motherboard via one of the *expansion slots*. The idea is that you can expand your system by adding options not included with the basic PC.

The number and type of slots available in your computer depend on the size of the console's case as well as on the motherboard's design. Some home systems and most laptops have no expansion slots. That keeps the price down on the home systems, and, well, laptops are too petite to worry about hulking expansion cards. Mini-desktop PCs typically have from three to five expansion slots, and those hulking tower PCs can have up to eight expansion slots.

Expansion slots come in three delicious flavors:

ISA: The most ancient type of expansion slot is the ISA, which stands for (get this) Industry Standard Architecture. That's because it never really had a name until another, better type of expansion slot came along. ISA slots hang around to be compatible with older expansion cards. Most PCs have one or two ISA expansion slots for compatibility reasons.

PCI: The PCI slot is the most common form of internal expansion for a PC (for a Macintosh too, but that's not the subject here). Chances are good that if you buy an expansion card, it's a PCI card.

AGP: The final expansion slot is the AGP, or Accelerated Graphics Port. This special type of slot takes only video expansion cards, usually the nice spendy ones that do all sorts of amazing graphics. Not every PC has this type of slot, and if your PC does, it has only one of them.

The backsides of most ISA and PCI cards stick out the rear of the console; the card's back replaces the metallic slot cover to reveal special connectors or attachments for the expansion card.

Having expansion slots in your PC is a good thing, but not entirely necessary. Most of the goodies available via expansion cards can also be added to the computer by using external USB or IEEE devices.

- If given the choice, choose a PCI expansion card over an ISA model.
- Small-footprint PCs have the fewest expansion slots. Tower computer models have the most.
- For more information on video expansion cards, see Chapter 10.
- Expansion cards are sometimes called *daughterboards*. Get it? Motherboard, daughterboard? I'm looking forward to *auntboard* or perhaps *secondcousinboard*.
- Most expansion cards come squirming with cables. This mess of cables makes the seemingly sleek motherboard look more like an electronic pasta dish. Some cables are threaded inside the PC; others are left hanging limply out the back. The cables are what make the internal upgrading and installation process so difficult.

Tick-Tock Goes the Clock

One piece of hardware that's native to all PCs but not exactly visible on the motherboard is the internal clock. The clock is battery operated, which enables it to keep track of the time, day or night, whether the PC is plugged in or not.

The computer displays the current time — as it believes it to be — on the system tray on the taskbar. If you point the mouse at the time and hold the mouse still, the current day and date pop up. But there's more to the clock than that nifty trick.

The computer uses the internal clock to not only track the time and to schedule things, but also to time-stamp files. That way, you can determine which files are created when, sort your stuff, and do other time-related things.

- ✔ Windows displays a date-and-time icon on the system tray on the taskbar. (Refer to Chapter 5.)
- ✔ The date-and-time format is based on your country or region. You can change that display by going to the Control Panel and opening the Regional and Language Options icon.

"My clock is all screwy!"

Computers make lousy clocks. A typical PC loses about a minute or two of time every day. Why? Who knows!

Generally speaking, the clock runs slow or fast because of all the various things going on inside the computer. The more that goes on, the more the clock is wrong. Especially if you put your computer to sleep, or "hibernate" it, the clock can get really nuts. (Refer to Chapter 4 for more hibernation information.)

On the positive side, the computer's clock is well aware of daylight savings time: Windows automatically jumps the clock forward or backward, and does so without having to know the little ditty "Spring forward, fall back." Or is it the other way around? Whatever — the computer knows and obeys.

What do you do if the clock is wrong? Why, set it, of course. Keep reading!

Setting the clock

To set the date and time on your PC, double-click the time on the taskbar: Click-click. The Date and Time Properties dialog box magically appears, as shown in Figure 6-3.

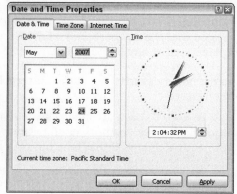

Manipulate the controls in the Date and Time Properties dialog box to change or set the date or time.

For example, type **10:00 AM** if it's 9:58 AM or so. Then, when the telephone time lady (or whoever) says that it's 10 o'clock, click the Apply button in the Date and Time Properties dialog box. That action sets the time instantly. Click OK when you're done.

Internet time to the rescue!

One way to tame the wild computer clock is to have the computer itself automatically synchronize the time with one of the many worldwide time servers. A *time server* is a computer designed to cough up accurate time information for any computer that checks in on the Internet.

To configure your PC to use a time server and synchronize itself with time on the Internet, open the Date and Time Properties dialog box, as described in the preceding subsection. Then click the Internet Time tab (refer to Figure 6-3).

Put a check mark by the option Automatically Synchronize with an Internet Time Server. Optionally, choose a time server from the drop-down list.

Windows automatically adjusts the PC's clock whenever you're connected to the Internet. There's nothing else you need to do — ever!

Boring Details about Your PC's Battery

All computers have an internal battery, which is part of the motherboard. Its primary purpose is to help the PC's clock keep time even when the computer is off or unplugged.

A typical PC battery lasts for about six years, possibly more. When it dies, you know because the computer's date and time are way off, or perhaps the PC even has a message telling you that the motherboard's battery needs replacing. You can get the replacement at any Radio Shack.

- ✔ Yes, you have to open the console's case to get at the battery. Don't expect it to be easy to find, either!

- ✔ The PC's battery may also be used to back up special system information, such as the number of disk drives, memory configuration, and other trivia the computer needs to know all the time, but may not remember otherwise.

- ✔ The motherboard's battery is in addition to any other batteries in the computer, such as the main battery used to power a laptop.

The Chipset

Rather than refer to the various and sundry computer chips on the motherboard as The Various And Sundry Computer Chips On The Motherboard, computer scientists have devised a single descriptive term. All those chips are called the *chipset*.

The chipset is what makes up your computer's personality. It contains instructions for operating the basic computer hardware: keyboard, mouse, networking interface, sound, and video, for example.

Different chipsets are available depending on what types of features the computer offers. For example, some motherboards may come with advanced graphics in the chipset or maybe wireless networking. Sadly, there's no easy way to tell based on the chipset's weirdo names or numbers; you must refer to the chipset's documentation to see what you're really getting. (Even then, the info is really only interesting to diehard computer nerds.)

- ✔ Different PCs use different chipsets, depending on which company manufactured the motherboard.

- ✔ An older term for the chipset, particularly the main ROM chip in a PC, is BIOS. *BIOS* stands for Basic Input/Output System. There's a BIOS for the keyboard and mouse, one for the video system, one for the network, and so on. Altogether, they comprise the *chipset*. (See Chapter 9 for more info on ROM.)

The Source of PC Power

Lurking inside your PC's console is something that does no thinking and isn't used for data storage. That's the *power supply.* It does several wonderful things for Mr. Computer:

✔ Brings in electricity from the wall socket and converts it from wild AC current into mild DC current

✔ Provides electricity to the motherboard and everything living on the motherboard

✔ Provides juice to the internal disk drives

✔ Contains fans that help keep the inside of the console cool

✔ Contains or is directly connected to the PC's power button

The power supply is also designed to take the brunt of the damage if your computer ever suffers from electrical peril, such as a lightning strike or power surge. In those instances, the power supply is designed to die, and to sacrifice itself for the good of your PC. *Don't panic!* You can easily replace the power supply and discover that the rest of your PC is still working fine.

✔ Thanks to the fans, the power supply is the noisiest part of any PC.

✔ Power supplies are rated in *watts.* The more internal hardware stuff your PC has — the more disk drives, memory, and expansion cards, for example — the greater the number of watts the power supply should provide. The typical PC has a power supply rated at 150 or 200 watts. More powerful systems may require a power supply upward of 300 watts.

✔ One way to keep your power supply — and your computer — from potentially going Poof! (even in a lightning strike) is to invest in a surge protector, or UPS. Refer to Chapter 3 for details.

Chapter 7

The Basic Ports

One key to the PC's success over the past 25 years is its expandability. You can not only expand a computer on the inside of the console (via the expansion slots), but you can also add a nearly infinite number of gadgets to your computer system on the outside of the console. That's done by plugging the gizmo into one of the computer's basic *ports,* as discussed in this chapter.

What Is a Port?

Perhaps you've been on the port side of a ship, looking out a porthole at a seaport and seeing people with portable computers? If so, you've used the word *port* about as much as you could, except for the peculiar way the word *port* is used when it comes to computers.

In the computer world, a hardware *port* is a place on the computer where information can be sent or received or both. Often, it's called an *I/O port* because it's used for both input and output. Information flows out of the computer through the port, and into the computer from whatever gizmo is attached to the port.

For technological as well as historical reasons, the typical PC has a variety of ports. There are specific ports, such as the printer port, mouse port, and keyboard port. Then there are general ports, such as the serial, USB, and

IEEE 1394 and FireWire ports. The rest of this chapter covers what is what and how each port is best used.

- ✔ Also refer to Chapter 3 for information on plugging things into the various PC ports.

- ✔ On the software side, *port* means something else! It refers to rewriting a program to be compatible with another computer, operating system, or computing platform.

Legacy Ports

When the PC was first designed, external thingamajigs were attached to the console by using specific and aptly named ports. If you wanted to attach a keyboard, mouse, or printer, for example, you would use a specific keyboard, mouse, or printer port.

Since that time, those older, or *legacy,* ports have been gradually phased out on a PC, and replaced by the versatile USB port. For example, you can now have a PC where the mouse, keyboard, and printer plug into the USB port. But on most PCs, those older ports still exist and are still used just as they were on the first IBM PC.

Mouse and keyboard

The mouse and keyboard ports are designed specifically for what they do: The mouse plugs into the mouse port, and the keyboard into the keyboard port. And, despite the fact that both ports look alike, they are unique, and strange things happen when you connect things improperly.

Some wireless keyboards and mice still use the traditional keyboard and mouse ports. You plug the wireless base station into the keyboard or mouse port (or both), and then you can use the wireless keyboard and mouse.

The printer port

It should be no surprise that the computer's printer can plug into the printer port. But you probably didn't know that the port was originally called the LPT port. LPT was an IBM acronym-thing for Line Printer. It may also be called a PRN port, which is how the word *printer* looks when your computer's keyboard is broken.

The magical KVM switch

KVM is an acronym for *k*eyboard, *v*ideo, and *m*ouse. The *KVM switch* is a box you can use to attach a single keyboard, monitor, and mouse to two (or more) computers. That way, you can use two computers without having to buy each one its own keyboard, monitor, or mouse. Often, people use the KVM switch so that they can use their current computer as well as access an older computer or second computer system.

Alas, there's no inverse-KVM switch, or a device that lets a single computer have two keyboards, monitors, and mice attached so that two people can use a single computer at the same time. That is possible with the Linux and Unix operating systems, but not with Windows.

I highly recommend using the USB connector (covered later in this chapter), rather than the traditional printer port and printer cable, to connect your PC's console to a printer. It's just better.

In the old days, you could use the printer port to add an external device to the computer, scanner, or disk drive. The device was daisy-chained on the printer port, as illustrated in Figure 7-1. This technique is no longer necessary; it's easier and better to use the USB port to add an external device to the console.

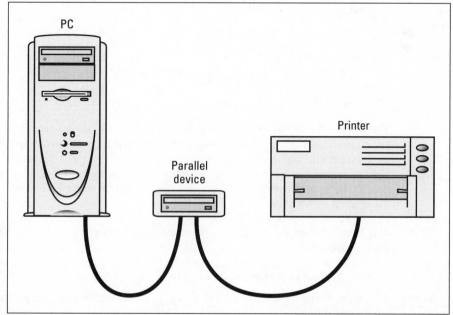

Figure 7-1: The old printer port daisy-chain.

Folks with two computers often use something called an A-B switch to share a single printer between those two computers. A-B switches are still available today, though the better solution is to *network* the computers and the printer, which also works better in sharing a high-speed Internet connection. See Part III of this book for the details.

The serial port

The original PC's serial port was at one time the *versatile* port. Unlike with the other legacy ports, you could plug in a variety of devices to the serial port: printer, mouse, modem, and scanner, for example. That function has been taken over by the faster and easier-to-use USB port, which is covered starting in the next section.

✔ The serial port is also known as the COM or COM1 port. Some old-timers may call it the RS-232C port.

✔ Modern serial ports use a 9-pin connector, though some serial devices may use the older 25-pin connector. If so, you need to buy a 9-to-25 converter, either a tiny box-like gizmo or a 9-to-25 pin cable.

✔ Serial ports are used with *dial-up* modems. High-speed modems — cable, DSL, and satellite — plug into the PC's network adapter. See Part III of this book.

King USB

The most versatile port on your PC is the USB, where the U stands for *universal* and means that this port can be used to plug in an entire universe of peripherals, often replacing the function of many other individual ports on the computer.

The variety of USB devices is legion. Here's just a sampling of what you can plug into a USB port: monitors, speakers, joysticks, scanners, digital cameras, videocameras, Webcams, floppy drives, CD and DVD drives, hard drives, flash drives, media card readers, networking gizmos, tiny fans, lamps, time machines — and the list goes on and on. More and more USB devices are appearing every day.

The best news about USB? It's *easy.* Just plug the gizmo in. Often, that's all you need to do!

✔ USB stands for Universal Serial Bus. Say "you S bee."

 ✔ USB ports, as well as USB devices, sport the USB symbol, as shown in the margin.

✔ Refer to Chapter 2 for information on finding the USB port on your PC's console.

✔ If your PC lacks a USB port, you can buy a USB expansion card. It costs about $20. Be sure to get a USB 2.0 expansion card. (The reasons are explained in the nearby sidebar, "USB version number nonsense.")

Connecting a USB device

One reason the USB port took over the world is that it's smart. Dumb things never take over the world. Witness the Tablet PC. But I digress.

Adding a USB device to your computer is easy. Often, all you need to do is plug it in — and you don't need to turn off the computer first. When you plug a USB device into the console, Windows instantly recognizes it and configures the device for you.

Note that in some cases you must install software first before you initially plug in some USB devices. After that, you can attach and detach the devices almost at will. There's one exception, and that goes for USB storage devices, which is covered in the later section "Removing a USB device."

Where's the power cord?

Another advantage of USB is that many types of USB devices don't require a separate power cord. Instead, they use the power supplied by the USB ports themselves. These are known as *USB-powered* devices.

USB version number nonsense

Two versions of USB are available: the current, fastest version of USB 2.0, which includes the High Speed USB standard and the older version, USB 1.1. Most newer PCs have the USB 2.0 standard, which means that they can handle all USB devices, whether they're the older 1.1 type or the newer High Speed USB type.

Older PCs may have only the USB 1.1 type, which means that some USB disk drives may not work on those systems. You know instantly when this happens because Windows pops up an error message stating that it's unable to read the USB 2.0, or High Speed USB, gizmo. The solution? Go out and buy your PC a USB 2.0 expansion card.

Some folks find it uncomfortable that USB-powered devices lack an on-off switch. That's okay; it's fine to leave the device on, as long as you keep the computer on. But, if you really, *really* want to turn the gizmo off, simply unplug the USB cable.

  ✔ USB devices that require lots of power, such as printers and certain external disk drives, also have their own power cords.

  ✔ USB gadgets that require power may insist on being plugged into a USB-powered hub. That means the USB connection must be made either directly to the computer itself or to a USB hub that supplies power. See the section "Expanding the USB universe," later in this chapter, for information on powered versus unpowered hubs.

Removing a USB device

This is cinchy: To remove a USB device, just unplug it. That's it! Well, unless that device is a disk drive of sorts. In that case, you must officially *unmount* the drive before you unplug it.

Why bother? Because some program may be using the drive. If you yank out the drive while the computer is busy writing information to it, you lose not only the file being updated or created, but also possibly other information on the drive. Therefore, you should always be sure that you properly unmount the drive. Here's how:

1. **Open the My Computer icon on the desktop.**

   Or, somehow display the contents of the My Computer window.

2. **Locate the category heading Devices with Removable Storage.**

   Choose View⇨Arrange Icons by⇨Show in Groups if you cannot find the Devices with Removable Storage area.

3. **Click to select the removable disk.**

    In many cases, the disk has a generic icon associated with it, though some USB gizmos may sport a unique icon.

4. **Choose File⇨Eject from the menu.**

5. **Unplug or detach the USB disk drive.**

Note that the icon may not disappear from the My Computer window until the device is detached.

If you see an error message, the disk drive is either busy or being used. You have to wait and try again. If the error is persistent, you should turn off the computer. Detach the device. Then restart the computer.

A shortcut method of unmounting a USB disk drive is to find the Safely Remove Hardware icon on the system tray. When you click that icon, a pop-up list of removable disk drives appears. Choose your drive from the list, and Windows attempts to unmount that drive. A pop-up bubble appears and tells you that the drive can be safely removed upon success.

- ✔ Always properly remove your USB disk drives!

- ✔ USB disk drives include those flash memory drives, such as jump drives or keychain USB disk drives. Digital camera media cards are also included in the lot.

- ✔ I recommend plugging any external disk drives on your PC into the UPS. That way, Windows doesn't complain when the power goes out and the external disk drive suddenly becomes unavailable.

Expanding the USB universe

There never seems to be enough USB ports when you need them. Fortunately, when you need more USB ports, you can quickly add them by plugging a USB *hub* into your computer system.

A USB hub allows you to greatly expand your PC's USB universe. A typical expansion hub, as shown in Figure 7-2, connects to your PC's USB port. But then it turns around and instantly provides even more USB ports for those devices that need them.

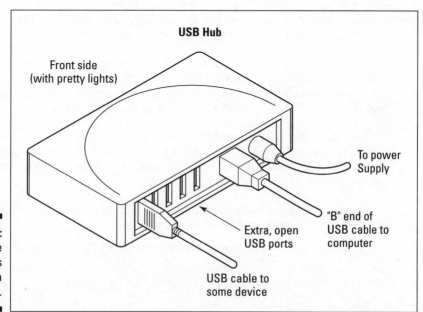

Figure 7-2: Add more USB ports with a USB hub.

✔ If one hub isn't enough, buy another! You can connect hubs to hubs, if you like. As long as the cables fan out from the PC and nothing loops back on itself, it all works.

✔ Using hubs, you can expand your PC's USB universe to the maximum 127 USB devices. You'll probably run out of desk space before that.

✔ Note that some USB devices prefer to be plugged directly into the console. These types of devices say so on their boxes and in the manuals.

✔ A hub that also plugs into the wall socket is known as a *powered* USB hub. (The console is also a powered USB hub.) This type of hub is necessary for some USB devices to operate.

✔ An example of an unpowered hub is a keyboard that has USB ports on it. Those ports are designed to connect non-USB powered devices, such as mice.

✔ The first hub (your PC) is the *root* hub.

IEEE, or the Port of Many Names

A second type of versatile port is called IEEE 1394, but it's more commonly known by the frightening moniker *FireWire*. It may even have other names, or even new names by the time this book goes to print. One thing is for certain: You say "Eye triple E" not "Ieeeee!" as in "My pants are on fire!"

IEEE and USB 2.0 are very similar. Both are high-speed ports. Both allow you to expand your computer. Both can be used to add disk drives or high-speed scanners. Both can be plugged in and unplugged without having to turn the PC on or off. Both have hubs you can use to expand the system.

On the PC, the IEEE is best used for digital video. If you have a videocamera with a mini-DV connection, often labeled DV on the camera, IEEE is the best way to get that video information into your PC. Beyond that situation, anything IEEE can do, you're better off doing with USB on a PC.

The only sad news is that most PCs don't come with an IEEE port standard. Even so, you can easily add IEEE ports to your computer by installing an inexpensive expansion card. Even then, why bother? For now, USB is just a better option.

✔ Even if you don't have IEEE, most digital videocameras have a secondary USB connection that works just fine.

✔ IEEE uses its own, unique cables, which aren't the same as USB cables.

✔ If an external disk drive has two IEEE connectors, you can use either one. The second connector allows you to daisy-chain on a second IEEE device.

✔ Both ends of the standard IEEE cable are the same. But for digital video, you need an IEEE cable with one standard end and one DV end.

 ✔ Some IEEE ports are marked by the FireWire symbol, as shown in the margin.

✔ Unlike USB cables, IEEE cables are quite expensive. Maybe that's when you pronounce it "Ieeeee"?

 ✔ Another term for IEEE is *I-Link*. Officially, the standard is known as the *High Performance Serial Bus*.

Chapter 8

Disk Drives Me Crazy

. . . .

. . . .

Do disk drives spin because they're happy? Computer scientists tell us that happiness could be a reason, though it's probably more logical to assume that the tiny motor inside the disk drive is responsible for all the spinning. I'm still up in the air about it. What I do know is that disk drives are an important component of your computer system. No PC is sold without at least one type of disk drive, and most often two or three types. What those types are and other hardware aspects of your PC's disk drives are covered in this chapter.

The Big Spinning Deal with Disk Drives

Disk drives are necessary in a computer system, to provide for long-term storage. Information saved on a disk drive stays there, even when the computer's power is off.

> ✔ The *drive* is the device that reads the disk. The term disk drive is often used to describe only the drive.

> ✔ The *disk* is the thing that contains the data — the media inside the drive.

> ✔ Refer to Chapter 1 for more information on how disk drives are necessary to a computer system.

No, you don't have to read this disk drive history

Sometimes, it makes no sense why the PC needs to have three (or more) different types of disk drives. Wouldn't just one do? Perhaps. But things may make sense to you after reviewing this wee bit of personal computer history.

Once, there were these two caveman, Og and Gronk. Now fast-forward to the late 1970s, during the dawn of the personal computer age. Back then, permanent storage for a personal computer was provided by cassette tape.

I'm serious: cassette tape. You can stop laughing now.

Cassette tape was slow, awkward, and unreliable, but cassette recorders were far cheaper than those early monster floppy disk drives. And those floppy drives were way, way cheaper than the hulking primitive hard drives of the era.

Eventually, the price of floppy disk drives dropped from about $800 a unit to $100. Hard drives dropped in price as well, while increasing in capacity. Things weren't cheap, but ample storage was available for most PC users.

At the time of the first IBM PC, floppy drives were standard in personal computers. Hard drives were rare. In fact, it was the second-generation IBM PC, the IBM PC/XT computer, that came with a hard drive in addition to a floppy drive. The hard drive held a whopping 10MB of data.

In the early 1990s, another type of disk drive joined the floppy and hard drives on personal computers. The CD-ROM drive was used to read data CDs, just as a musical CD player tooted out musical CDs. The CD, or compact disc, provided computer users with reliable, removable, high-capacity data storage — but the storage was "read only," which means that it wasn't possible to create your own CD.

Eventually, the high-capacity DVD drive joined the CD drive. About that time, around the year 2000, computer CD and DVD drives could *create* those disks as well as read their data.

The most recent development isn't a disk drive at all. *Flash memory* drives are all solid state — no moving parts. They're found primarily in digital cameras, though they can be used on PCs for backup storage or to help move large files between PCs.

Over the years, there were other disk standards as well. Some of these provided stopgap measures, until more practical or inexpensive solutions came around. Of all the types of disk drives, the ones that survived and are still in use now are the floppy drive, hard drive, CD or DVD drive, and flash memory drive.

Typical disk drives found in a PC

Of the entire dang doodle history of long-term, permanent storage, the following rabble are most likely to be the common disk drives found in a standard PC:

✔ **Floppy drives:** A floppy drive eats floppy disks, which, sadly, store only a puny 1.44MB of information. That was enough space 10 years ago. Now, it's useless, which is why floppy drives are being phased out of the PC's design.

✔ **Hard drives:** The PC's primary long-term storage device is the hard drive. This drive stores many gigabytes of information, more than enough for Windows, your software, and all the data you can create and take from the Internet. Unlike other types of drives, the hard drive cannot be removed from the computer.

✔ **CD/DVD, or "shiny media," drives:** These drives can eat computer data discs and music CDs or videos. Some drives can only read the discs. Other drives can read and write to the discs. Sometimes the CD and DVD drives are separate, and sometimes they're included as the same unit.

If your PC is typical, it should have one of each: floppy drive, hard drive, and CD or DVD drive. Sometimes, you may find a single CD drive, sometimes you may see both a CD and a separate DVD drive, or you may have a CD/DVD combo.

Though flash memory drives are popular, they aren't readily sold with PCs today. A few models sport them, but mostly you need to buy a special adapter or reader, which is covered later in this chapter.

 No matter what, all disk drives of all types that are connected to your computer show their smiling icon faces in the My Computer window, as shown in Figure 8-1. To see that window, open the My Computer icon on the desktop. (Refer to Chapter 5.)

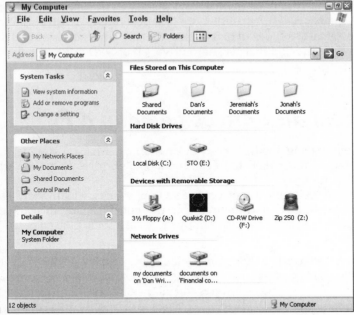

Figure 8-1:
Your PC's
assortment
of disk drive
flavors.

Ask Mr. Science: How Does a Disk Drive Work?

Glad you asked, Billy!

Disk drives have two parts: the disk, where information is recorded, and the drive, which spins the disk. The drive also contains hardware that controls how information is read from and written to the disk.

In a hard drive, the actual disk is a chunk of metal coated with magnetic oxide — the same stuff used to record on cassette tape or videotape. The magnetic oxide stores electronic impulses by orienting its magnetic particles in one direction or another.

Most hard drives contain multiple disks, or *platters,* as shown in Figure 8-2. They're all hermetically sealed — in an airtight environment. That way, the hard drive can be extra precise without having to worry about contaminants or nasty particles in the air.

Rather than magnetic oxide, CD and DVD drives use a thin, metal foil sandwiched between two plastic disks. The metal has tiny pits in it, which are detected by a laser beam.

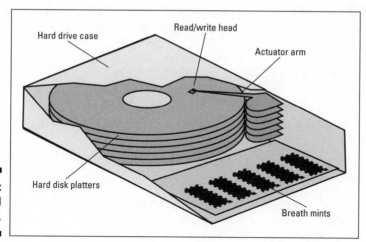

Figure 8-2:
A hard
drive's guts.

It's the drive's job to spin the disk, which allows the information on the disk to be read, or information to be written, to the disk. On a hard drive, reading and writing are done by a doohickey called the *read-write head.* CD and DVD drives use a laser beam to read information. To create a CD or DVD, a secondary and more powerful laser is used to burn tiny pits into the recordable disc's surface.

The final part of the disk drive is the *interface,* or wires through which information is sent to and from the computer's motherboard and the microprocessor. On a PC, the ATAPI interface is used inside the console. External disk drives use another interface — typically, USB. (Refer to Chapter 7.)

- ✔ ATAPI stands for AT Attachment Packet Interface, as though that clears up anything. You lose no points if you fail to remember that term.

- ✔ Floppy disks use Mylar for their disk material, also coated with magnetic oxide.

- ✔ Flash memory drives have no disks. They use a special RAM, or memory, chip instead. See the section "This Just In: Flash Memory Drives," at the end of this chapter.

Disk Drive ABCs

Each disk in your PC's system is assigned a letter of the alphabet. This is how Windows recognizes the disk. It doesn't say "The CD drive." No, Windows knows a drive by a letter of the alphabet, such as D or E or something else.

Windows uses the letters *A* through *Z* to identify disks in your computer system. This system is remarkably similar to the letters in our own, English alphabet.

On just about every PC, the first three letters are consistently assigned:

- Drive A is always the computer's floppy drive.

- Drive B isn't used. It was historically the PC's second floppy drive, but letter B is just skipped over.

- Drive C is always the computer's primary hard drive, the one from which Windows was started.

After drive C, the drive letters can be wildly inconsistent from PC to PC. Typically, drive D is the CD or DVD drive, but that's not always the case. Here's the twisted logic Windows uses to assign drive letters after C:

- If any additional hard drives are in the console, they're given drive letters D, E, and onward, one letter for each extra hard drive beyond drive C.

- Any internal CD or DVD drive is given the next drive letter after the last hard drive has been given a letter. So, if the only hard drive is C, the CD drive gets drive D. If the last hard drive is drive F, the CD drive gets G. And, if there's a separate DVD drive, it gets the next letter.

- The order in which drive letters are given to the CD or DVD drives depends on the order in which the computer finds the drives when the computer starts up.

- Yes, sometimes Windows gets confused and may assign a letter to your CD drive before assigning a letter to an internal hard drive. Don't ask me why.

- Any external disk drives are given letters as the system finds them when the computer starts up. Each disk drive is given the next letter in the alphabet.

- After the computer starts adding any disk drive, such as plugging in a USB flash memory drive, it results in that drive being given the next letter in the alphabet.

Disk drives on the network can be added to your computer system. When you add the drive, however, you get to choose which drive letter it uses, from any of the available (unused) drive letters.

✔ Because each PC assigns disk drive letters differently, never assume that you know which letters belong to which drive when you use a new computer. For example, the CD drive isn't always drive letter D. That's why installation manuals are often vague about which disk drive to insert the CD into.

✔ Make a note of your PC's disk drive assignments on this book's Cheat Sheet.

The Little You Need to Know about Floppy Disks

There's no reason for you to use floppy disks with a PC any more. They're too pathetic to hold data and, generally, are way too unreliable for me to recommend them for backups or anything else.

✔ If you're using a floppy disk with your computer, consider buying a flash disk drive and memory card reader instead. See the sections on flash disk drives later in this chapter.

✔ If your computer has a floppy disk, then it's always drive A.

✔ The floppy drive uses a specific icon in Windows, as shown in the margin.

✔ The only time I've seen floppy disks used is to create a restore disk for antivirus or backup software. In instances like that, follow the instructions on the screen or in the manual, and they tell you what to do. Remember that creating the floppy disk is optional. Hopefully, those program writers will think of some other way to do their stuff and not use floppy disks any more.

✔ This book's companion, *PCs For Dummies Quick Reference* (from the Wiley Publishing empire), contains more information on floppy disks, if you *really* need to know.

Driving a Hard Disk

The *hard disk* is the primary place for storing stuff on your computer. It's your main source of permanent storage. On nearly every PC, the hard drive is given letter C and referred to as "drive C" or "the C drive."

Which disk is the *boot* disk?

The *boot disk* is the disk drive that contains the computer's operating system, or the software that controls the hardware. Normally, when a PC starts, it looks for the operating system first on the floppy drive and then on the hard drive.

The PC looks on the floppy drive for historical reasons: The original IBM PC didn't have a hard drive, and the thing was started by using a floppy disk. The computer still does that and, in fact, if you neglect to remove a floppy disk from drive A, the computer displays an error message as it fails to find software on that startup disk. (Remove the floppy disk and press Enter to fix that problem.)

The PC can also boot, or start itself, from the CD-ROM. That's normally done to run disaster recovery software. Some PCs may prompt you to "boot from the CD-ROM" if you leave a startup CD (or *bootable* CD) in the CD-ROM drive when the computer starts. If so, answer the prompt or just ignore it so that the computer continues to load software from the hard drive.

You can control which disk drives are used to start, or boot, the PC by using the PC Setup program. When the computer first starts, read the screen and press the keys that are indicated to enter the PC Setup program. On one of that program's menus, you can tell the computer which disk (or disks) to use to start the PC.

Hard drives are measured by how much information they can store. This value is specified in *gigabytes,* or billions of bytes, and abbreviated GB. (See Chapter 9 for more information on what a *byte* is.)

The typical PC hard drive stores anywhere from 20GB to 100GB of information, which is plenty of storage for Windows and many other programs, and lots of room for you to lose your stuff.

Hard drives use the hard drive icon (as shown in the margin) inside Windows.

✔ The hard drive is where Windows lives, where you install software, and where you keep the stuff you create or save on your computer. That's what the hard drive is designed for.

✔ Most PCs have one physical hard drive installed inside the console.

✔ Extra hard drives can be added to your PC, to give you even more storage. You can generally add a second internal hard drive to the console, plus nearly unlimited external hard drives via the USB port.

✔ A single physical hard drive can be divided into multiple logical hard drives. This division is done by *partitioning* the drive. For example, to Windows, a single 100GB hard drive could be two 50GB logical disk drives, C and D. Partitioning is *not* a beginner's duty, and it's generally done only when installing a new hard drive or setting up a secondary hard drive.

CD and DVD Kissin' Disk Drive Cousins

Your PC has at least a CD drive. It may also have a separate DVD drive. Or, as is most common recently, the computer has a combination drive that eats both CD and DVDs. Both drives are similar in many ways.

The typical CD or DVD drive is *read-only*. That term means that information can only be read from the disc; you cannot use the read-only drive to create a CD or DVD. You may find the drives labeled by using the acronym ROM, where the RO stands for Read-Only. (The M is for *m*emory, but it should really be S, for *s*torage.)

CDs are used in the PC world for installing new programs on your computer. CDs may also simply contain lots of data, such as the Encarta Encyclopedia. DVDs are similar, though they store many times the amount of information as CDs. Even so, most new software comes on CDs rather than on DVDs.

The computer's CD and DVD drive can also be used to play musical CDs or watch movies on your computer — though I'm certain that this is not the real reason that you bought a PC in the first place.

✔ The CD-ROM drive reads both computer and musical CDs.

✔ The DVD drive reads both computer and video DVDs.

✔ You can also call it a DVD-ROM drive, though no one important uses that term.

✔ A single DVD drive can read both DVDs and CDs. So, if all you have on your computer is a DVD drive, it's really a DVD/CD drive.

✔ CD stands for *c*ompact *d*isc. The British spelling is used for historical reasons, mainly that Shakespeare is rumored to have burned his first folio to a CD.

✔ DVD is an acronym for *d*igital *v*ersatile *d*isc. Or, it may be *d*igital *v*ideo *d*isc.

 ✔ Both CD and DVD drives use similar icons in Windows. The icon may change appearance, depending on which type of disk is in the drive.

> ✔ A typical CD holds up to 640MB of information. A typical music CD can store up to 80 minutes of music.

> ✔ DVD technology is now capable of storing 4GB of information on a disc. Some future versions of DVDs are rumored to be able to hold more than 17GB of information.

CD and DVD drives that create CDs and DVDs

Some CD and DVD drives are designed to not only read from the discs but also create them. The type of CD drive that can create CDs is called CD-R or, often, CD-R/RW. The letters *R* and *RW* represent the two recordable CD formats.

On the DVD side, the drive names get weird because there are many recordable DVD formats. The two most popular, however, are DVD-R and DVD+R. Others are listed in the nearby sidebar, "Types of recordable CD and DVDs."

You need to buy the proper discs to create your own CDs or DVDs. For CDs, I recommend any CD-R. Avoid CD-RWs because they tend to be expensive and, often, multiple CD-Rs are better than a single CD-RW. (More on that in Chapter 24.)

For the DVD, ensure that you buy the proper disc for your drive. If the drive eats only DVD-Rs, don't buy DVD+R disks, or vice versa.

> ✔ The drive must say CD-R/RW or DVD-R or +R for it to be a recordable drive. Plain old CD and DVD drives cannot be used to create CDs or DVDs.

> ✔ You can get a combination CD/DVD drive that can record to both disk formats. It's often called the SuperDrive, though it's really just a combination CD-R/RW and DVD-R (or +R) drive. If your PC lacks one of these, you can easily add an external USB version of the drive.

> ✔ Sony makes a versatile DVD drive that can record to multiple DVD formats. It can also record to CDs.

About the speed rating (the X number)

CDs have speed ratings measured in X. The number before the X indicates how much faster the drive is than the original PC CD-ROM drive (which plays as fast as a musical CD player). So, a 32X value means that it's 32 times faster than the original PC CD-ROM drive.

Types of recordable CDs and DVDs

Don't expect to find any sanity behind the various recordable CD and DVD disk formats. Here's a more or less complete list, with my comments:

CD-R: The disk can be written to once. Information can be written one little bit at a time or all at once. For a musical CD, the music can only be copied over all at once. Note that there are different types of CD-R discs, one for music and one for data. Buy the right one!

CD-RW: This disk works just like a CD-R, though it can be completely erased and used again. These discs cost more than CD-Rs, and the CD drive must be capable of working with CD-RW disks.

DVD-R: The most popular DVD recordable format, compatible with both computers and home-movie DVD players.

DVD-RW: An erasable version of the DVD-R format. As with a CD-RW, these recordable DVDs can be completely erased and recorded to again.

DVD+R: The second most popular DVD recordable format, much faster than DVD-R but not as compatible.

DVD+RW: The fully erasable version of the DVD+R format.

You need to buy the proper discs for your drive; some drives are very specific about which discs they can write to, though other drives may be compatible with multiple formats. It should say so on the box or spool. Also be on the lookout for DVDs that allow recording on both sides of the disc. It should say so on the package.

A recordable CD-R/RW drive has three Xs in its rating:

- The first is the drive's write speed, or how fast a CD-R can be written to.
- The second X is how fast the drive can rewrite to a CD-RW.
- The final X indicates how fast the drive can be read from.

High write and read speeds on a CD drive are especially important if you plan on importing lots of music discs. The higher the speed, the less time it takes the computer to read all the music from the drive. (See Chapter 24 for more information.)

Which drive is which?

Upon inspection, it's not exactly clear which disk drive could be the CD and which is the DVD. You have to look *closely*.

CD drives have the CD logo on them. If it's a recordable drive, it also has the word *Recordable* and maybe even *RW*.

DVD drives have the "DVD" logo on them. If you don't see the DVD logo, your PC has a mere CD-ROM drive.

Inserting a CD or DVD

Generally speaking, the disc is always inserted label side up. Aside from that, how you stick the disc into the drive depends on how the drive eats discs:

Tray type: The most popular type of CD-ROM or DVD drive uses a slide-out tray to hold the disc. Start by pressing the drive's eject button, which pops out the tray (often called a *drink holder* in many computer jokes). Drop the disc into the tray, label side up. Gently nudge the tray back into the computer. The tray slides back in the rest of the way on its own.

Slide-in type: Another type of disk drive works like the CD player in most automobiles; the drive is merely a slot into which you slide the disc: Pushing the disc (label side up) into the slot causes some gremlin inside the drive to eventually grab the disc and suck it in all the way. Amazing.

When the disc is in the drive, you use it just like any other disk in your computer.

✔ When you insert the disk upside down (label side down), the drive can't read it and most likely simply ejects the disk automatically.

✔ An exception to the label-side-up rule is a DVD with data recorded on both sides. For example, some DVD movies have the TV version on one side and the wide-screen, or letterbox, version on another. If so, make sure to put the proper side up in the drive.

✔ Some CDs are clipped. That is, they aren't round discs, but, rather, are business card size or some other special shape. These discs work fine in the tray type of CD-ROM/DVD drive, but don't insert them into the slide-in type of drive.

Ejecting a CD or DVD

Follow these steps to eject a disc from the CD-ROM or DVD drive:

1. **Open the My Computer window.**

2. **Click to select the CD-ROM or DVD drive icon.**

3. **Choose File⇨Eject from the menu.**

   The disc spits from the CD-ROM drive.

You may be tempted to eject the disk by punching the eject button on the front of the drive. Don't! If Windows is using the drive, you see an ugly error message on the screen when you try to eject a disc this way.

In times of urgency, such as when the computer is locked up (or turned off), you can eject a CD or DVD by pushing a bent paper clip into the tiny hole (the "beauty mark") on the front of the CD/DVD drive. That action manually ejects the disc when the computer is too stupid to do it by itself.

This Just In: Flash Memory Drives

Thanks to the versatility of the USB port, flash memory drives have become popular for the PC. They're called by many names: jump drive, Flash Drive, memory stick, SmartMedia, and on and on. They all use the same type of memory chip, and they all universally plug into a USB port for instant recognition by Windows.

Flash memory drives come in a variety of formats, shapes, and sizes. The capacity of a flash memory drive depends on how much you pay for it. Storage ranges from a handful of megabytes (MB) on up to several gigabytes (GB) of storage — which is great for such a tiny, portable drive.

To use the flash memory drive, just plug it into one of the PC's USB ports. Some drives, such as those used in digital cameras, may require a media card reader, which plugs into the USB port. You then stick the memory card into the media reader.

The memory card "mounts" itself in the My Computer window, which gives the drive a drive letter, and instantly you have access to the flash memory card, just as you do any other disk drive in your computer system.

To eject the drive, refer to Chapter 7, the section "Removing a USB device."

✔ Most flash memory drives require USB 2.0. Older PCs may not have this type of USB port, but you can easily add USB 2.0 via an expansion card.

✔ Do not remove a flash memory drive while the computer is using it!

✔ Flash memory works by using a special flash memory chip. The chip doesn't require power to maintain its contents, so you can remove a flash memory drive from the PC and its data stays intact because the flash memory drive isn't damaged.

Chapter 9

Memories . . . Like a PC Full of RAM

Of all hardware computable

One thing is indisputable

To make things go

And fast, not slow

Your PC needs some RAM

With memories undeniable

And DRAM chips quite reliable

Your programs fly

The disks won't die

On a PC full of RAM

Memory is one of the computer's basic resources. The more you have, the happier the computer seems to be. Not having enough memory is like trying to put too many people into a bus: It's cramped, hot, and smelly; nothing gets done quickly; and you can really tell who had tacos for lunch. But, when you have enough memory, it's like swimming in the ocean — with no jellyfish or sharks. And free tacos. But, I digress. More memory is better. This chapter tells you why.

What Is Memory?

If your computer were a sport, memory is the field on which competition would take place. Memory is where the action is.

Software is in charge. It tells the microprocessor what to do. But, the microprocessor is only a minicalculator. It's fast, but, like the absent-minded professor, the microprocessor doesn't remember much. It has some storage, but not a lot.

To provide those Elysian Fields upon which the microprocessor can dance and play, your computer comes with memory. The microprocessor uses the memory for storage, but it can also manipulate the contents of memory. That's basically how your programs work with data: The data is stored in memory, and the microprocessor manipulates the contents of memory.

- ✔ All computers need memory.
- ✔ Memory is to computers as legal pads are to human beings: It's where information is jotted down and saved for later.
- ✔ The more memory in your PC, the better. With more computer memory, you can work on larger documents and spreadsheets, enjoy applications that use graphics and sound, and boast about all that memory to your friends.
- ✔ The term RAM is used interchangeably with the word *memory*. They're the same thing. (In fact, RAM stands for Random Access Memory, in case you have been working any crossword puzzles lately.)

How computer memory works

Memory in your computer is used for storage — fast and changeable storage because all memory is accessible by the microprocessor. The software you run tells the microprocessor how to interact with memory, what to store in memory, and what to do with the stuff stored in memory.

Whenever you create a document with your word processor, each character you type is placed in a specific location in memory. After the character is stored, the microprocessor doesn't need to access it again, unless you're editing, searching or replacing, or doing something active to the text.

After you create something in the PC's memory, you save it to disk. When you need to access the information again, it's opened up and loaded back into memory from disk. After the information is there, the microprocessor can again work over it.

✔ Turning off the power makes the *contents* of memory go bye-bye. The memory chips themselves aren't destroyed, but the chips require electricity in order to maintain their contents.

✔ Computer memory is *fast.* The microprocessor can scan millions of bytes of memory — the equivalent of Shakespeare's entire folio — in fractions of a second, which is far less time than it took you to even trudge through *Hamlet* in the 11th grade.

✔ Your disk drives provide long-term storage for information. This type of storage is necessary because computer memory is lost when the power is turned off or when you restart Windows.

✔ When you open a file on disk, the computer copies that information from disk into the computer's memory. Only in memory can that information be examined or changed. When you save information back to disk, the computer copies it from memory to the disk.

✔ Always save your stuff to disk. Make it your mantra: "Save! Save! Save!"

Chips off the old block

Memory dwells on the PC's motherboard, and sits very close to the microprocessor for fast access and ready dispatch. Memory comes in the form of tiny chips, called *DRAM* chips. They're permanently attached to teensy-weensy memory expansion cards, called *DIMMs.*

Figure 9-1 shows what a DIMM looks like, though in real life a DIMM is slightly smaller than what's shown in the figure. A DIMM also has chips on both sides, which is why it's a DIMM, or *Dual* Inline Modular Memory thing, and not a SIMM, or Single Inline Modular Memory thing.

Figure 9-1: DIMM's about this big.

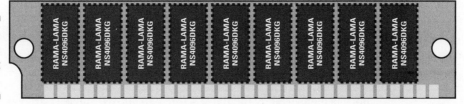

Each DIMM card contains a given chunk of RAM, measured in one of the magical computer memory values of 4, 8, 16, 32, 64, 128, 256, or 512 megabytes — or, perhaps even values of 1, 2, or 4 gigabytes.

Boring details on RAM, ROM, and flash memory

RAM stands for *Random Access Memory*. It refers to memory that the microprocessor can read from and write to. When you create something in memory, it's done in RAM. RAM is memory and vice versa.

ROM stands for *Read-Only Memory*. The microprocessor can read from ROM, but it cannot write to it or modify it. ROM is permanent. Often, ROM chips contain special instructions for the computer — important stuff that never changes. For example, the chipset on the motherboard is in

ROM (refer to Chapter 6). Because that information is stored on a ROM chip, the microprocessor can access it. The instructions are always there because they're not erasable.

Flash memory is a special type of memory that works like both RAM and ROM. Information can be written to flash memory, like RAM, but it isn't erased when the power is off, like RAM. Sadly, flash memory isn't as fast as RAM, so don't expect it to replace standard computer memory any time soon.

Each of those memory slots that the DIMM cards are plugged into is a *bank* of memory. So, a PC with 512MB of RAM may have four banks of 128MB DIMMs installed or two banks of 256MB DIMMs.

- ✔ DRAM stands for Dynamic Random Access Memory. It's pronounced "dee-ram," and it's the most common type of memory chip installed in a PC.

- ✔ Other types of memory chips exist, each with a name similar to DRAM, such as EDORAM or NIFTYRAM or DODGERAM. Most of these are merely marketing terms, designed to make one type of memory sound spiffier than another.

Here a Byte, There a Byte, Everywhere a Byte-Byte

Memory is measured by the byte. A *byte* can store a single character. For example, the word *frog* is 4 bytes long and requires 4 bytes of computer memory storage. The word *prince* is 6 characters long and requires 6 bytes of memory to store. I would put a joke in here about a toad being 2 bytes away from a prince, but I'm just not being that clever this afternoon.

Bytes, however useful, are puny. Although the experimental hobby computers of the 1970s may have had 256 or 1,000 bytes, PCs now have many times that amount. So, rather than waste time talking about millions or billions of bytes, handy abbreviations and swanky computer jargon are used to refer to a specific quantity of memory, as shown in Table 9-1.

Table 9-1		**Memory Quantities**	
Term	*Abbreviation*	*About*	*Actual*
Byte		1 byte	1 byte
Kilobyte	K or KB	1,000 bytes	1,024 bytes
Megabyte	M or MB	1,000,000 bytes	1,048,576 bytes
Gigabyte	G or GB	1,000,000,000 bytes	1,073,741,824 bytes
Terabyte	T or TB	1,000,000,000,000 bytes	1,099,511,627,776 bytes

Although it's handy to say "kilobyte" rather than mouth out "1,024 bytes," it's hard to visualize how much data that really is. For comparison, think of a kilobyte (KB) as about a page of text from a novel. One *megabyte* (MB) of information is required in order to store one minute of music on a CD or as much text information as in a complete encyclopedia.

The *gigabyte* (GB) is a huge amount of storage — 1 billion bytes. The *terabyte* (TB) is 1 trillion bytes, or enough RAM to dim the lights when you start the PC.

A *trilobite* is an extinct arthropod that flourished in the oceans during the Paleozoic era. It has nothing to do with computer memory.

Other trivia:

- ✔ The term *giga* is Greek, and it means *giant*.
- ✔ The term *tera* is also Greek. It means *monster!*
- ✔ A specific location in memory is an *address*.
- ✔ Hard disk storage is also measured in bytes.
- ✔ A PC running Windows XP requires at least 256MB of memory in order to work well.
- ✔ A typical hard drive now stores between 40 and 100 *gigabytes* of data. At the high end, some hard drives hold 500GB, or nearly half a terabyte of information. Gadzooks!

- ✔ Bytes are composed of 8 bits. The word *bit* is a contraction of *bi*nary digi*t*. Binary is base 2, or a counting system that uses only ones and zeroes. Computers count in binary, and their bits are grouped into clusters of eight, for convenient consumption as bytes.

Why the magical numbers?

Computer memory comes in given sizes. You see the same numbers over and over:

1, 2, 4, 8, 16, 32, 64, 128, 256, 512, 1024, 2048, 4096, and so on.

Each of these values represents a *power of two* — a scary mathematical concept that you probably slept through in high school. To quickly review: $2^0 = 1$, $2^1 = 2$, $2^2 = 4$, $2^3 = 8$ and on up to $2^{10} = 1024$, and so on, until you get a nosebleed.

These specific values happen because computers count by twos — ones and zeros — the old binary counting base of song and legend. So, computer memory, which is a very binary-like thing, is measured in those same powers of two. RAM chips come in quantities of 64MB or 256MB, for example, or maybe 2GB.

Notice that, starting with 1024, the values take on a predictable pattern: 1024 bytes is really 1K; 1024K is really 1M, and 1024M is 1G. So, really, only the first 10 values, 1 through 512, are the magical ones.

Some Memory Q&A

I can be anywhere — shopping at the grocery store, volunteering at some civic function, or leaving the local strip bar — and it doesn't matter where I am, yet people stop and ask me questions about computer memory. Over the years, I've collected the questions and have distilled the lot into the several subsections that follow. This section should cover up any loose ends or random access thoughts you may have about computer memory.

"How much memory is in my PC right now?"

This information may be a mystery to you, but it isn't a secret to your computer. The System Properties dialog box shows you how much memory lives inside the beast: Right-click the My Computer icon on the desktop and choose Properties from the shortcut menu that appears. The System Properties dialog box appears (refer to Figure 6-2, over in Chapter 6).

The amount of memory (shown as RAM) appears right beneath the type of microprocessor that lives in your PC. In Figure 6-2, it says that the computer has 1.00GB of RAM — plenty. Click the OK button to close the dialog box.

"Do I have enough memory?"

Not if you forgot that you asked that same question in the preceding edition of this book.

"Does my PC have enough memory?"

Knowing how much memory is in your PC is one thing, but knowing whether that amount is enough is entirely different!

The amount of memory your PC needs depends on two things. The first, and most important, is the memory requirement of your software. Some programs, such as photo-editing programs, require lots of memory. It says right on the box how much memory is needed. For example, the Photoshop photo-editing program demands 192MB of RAM.

To test your PC's memory, you need to make the computer *very* busy. You do this by loading and running several programs simultaneously. I'm talking about *big* programs, like Photoshop or Word or Excel. While all those programs are running, switch between them by pressing the Alt+Esc key combination.

If you can easily switch between several running programs by using Alt+Esc, your PC most likely has plenty of memory. But, if you press Alt+Esc and the system slows down, you hear the disk drives rumbling, and it takes a bit of time for the next program's window to appear, your PC could use more memory.

Close any programs you have opened.

- ✔ Generally speaking, all PCs should have at least 256MB of RAM, which is what you need, at minimum, to run Windows XP.
- ✔ One sure sign that your PC needs more memory: It slows to a crawl, especially during memory-intensive operations, such as working with graphics.
- ✔ Not enough memory? You can upgrade! See the section "Adding More Memory to Your PC," at the end of this chapter.

"Will the computer ever run out of memory?"

Nope. Unlike the hard drive, which can fill up just like a closet full of shoes and hats, your PC's memory can never really get full. At one time, back in the dark ages of computing, the "Memory full" error was common. That doesn't happen now, thanks to something called *virtual memory*.

"What is virtual memory?"

Windows uses a clever technique to prevent your computer's memory from ever becoming full: It creates *virtual memory*.

Virtual memory is a fake-out. It lets the computer pretend that it has much more memory than it has physical RAM. It does that by swapping out vast chunks of memory to the hard drive. Because Windows manages both memory and hard drive storage, it can keep track of things quite well, by swapping chunks of data back and forth. *Et, voilà!* You never see an "Out of memory" error.

Alas, there's trouble in paradise. One problem with virtual memory is that the swapping action slows things down. Although it can happen quickly and often without your noticing, when memory gets tight, virtual memory takes over and things start moving more slowly.

- ✔ The solution to avoiding the use of virtual memory is to pack your PC with as much RAM as it can hold.

- ✔ Windows never says that it's "out of memory." No, you just notice that the hard drive is churning frequently as the memory is swapped into and out of the disk drive. Oh, and things tend to slow down dramatically.

- ✔ You have no reason to mess with the virtual memory settings in your computer. Windows XP does an excellent job of managing things for you.

"What is video memory?"

Memory used by your PC's video system is known as *video memory*. Specifically, memory chips live on the video adapter card. Those memory chips are used specifically for the computer's video output and help you see higher resolutions, more colors, 3-D graphics, bigger and uglier aliens, and girlie pictures that your husband downloads from the Internet late at night but says that he doesn't.

As with regular computer memory, you can upgrade video memory if your PC's video card has room. See Chapter 10 for more information on video adapters.

Shared video memory is used on some low-end computers to save money. What happens is that the computer lacks true video memory, but instead borrows some main memory for use in displaying graphics. This is fine for simple home computers, but not nearly good enough to play cutting-edge games or to use photo-editing software.

Adding More Memory to Your PC

The best thing you can do for your PC is to add more memory. It's like adding Geritol to your computer's tired blood. *Bam!* More memory provides an instant boost to the system.

Adding memory to your computer is LEGO-block simple. The only difference is that the typical LEGO block set, such as the Medieval Castle or Rescue Helicopter set, costs less than $100. Your computer, on the other hand, may cost 5 to 20 times that much. Adding memory isn't something to be taken lightly.

Upgrading memory involves five intricate and tedious steps:

1. **Figure out how much total memory you need.**

   Your PC should have at least 256MB, which is enough to run Windows XP. After that, you can upgrade the RAM to 512MB, 1,024MB, 1GB, 2GB of RAM — or more!

2. **Figure out how much memory you can install.**

   This step is technical. It involves knowing how memory is added to your computer and in what increments. If you have an empty bank of memory, this step is quite simple. But, if your PC doesn't have any empty memory banks, it can be complex — and expensive. Better leave this task to your dealer or computer guru.

3. **Buy the memory.**

   Don't get cheap on me! You may think that you're prudent for saving money, but cheap memory is bad memory.

4. **Pay someone else to plug in the chips and do the upgrade.**

   Oh, you can do it yourself, but I would pay someone else to do it.

5. **Gloat.**

After you have the memory, brag to your friends about it. Heck, it used to be impressive to say that you had 640K of RAM. Then came the "I have 4 megabytes of memory in my 386" or "I'm swimming in 8 megabytes of memory in my 486." Now? Anything less than 256MB and your kids roll their eyes at you.

Now, for a shocker: You may think that upgrading from 512MB to 1GB RAM requires the addition of only 512MB of more memory. Wrong! It all depends on how the memory is now configured on the motherboard, as shown in Figure 9-2.

1GB = 1GB

Slot 4
Slot 3
Slot 2
Slot 1

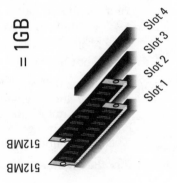

512MB 512MB = 1GB

Slot 4
Slot 3
Slot 2
Slot 1

Figure 9-2: Possible ways to upgrade memory.

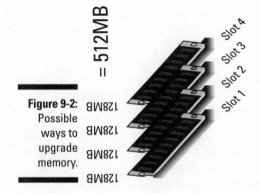

128MB 128MB 128MB 128MB = 512MB

Slot 4
Slot 3
Slot 2
Slot 1

256MB 256MB 256MB 256MB = 1GB

Slot 4
Slot 3
Slot 2
Slot 1

Suppose that your PC has four memory slots and each has only a 128MB DIMM in it. Therefore, to upgrade, you have to ditch all those DIMMs and buy either four 256MB DIMMS (the cheapest option) or two 512MB DIMMS (the next cheapest) or one single 1GB DIMM (the most expensive option, but the most logical for future expansion).

✔ Before you buy memory, check to see how the memory is configured on the motherboard. Open memory banks are a *good thing*.

✔ My favorite place to get memory chips online is Crucial, at www.crucial. com. The Web site asks a series of questions and then provides memory solutions to solve your problems exactly.

✔ If you want to try upgrading memory yourself, go ahead. I know that Crucial, as an example, provides a well-written booklet for doing the upgrade as part of the memory it sells. When in doubt, however, I strongly recommend having someone else do it.

Chapter 10

Minding Your Monitors

● ●

In This Chapter

▶ Understanding PC graphics

▶ Finding the monitor

▶ Discovering the graphics adapter

▶ Changing the display resolution

▶ Using a screen saver

▶ Applying a theme

▶ Saving monitor power

▶ Taking a screen dump

● ●

*I*t may look like a TV, but it's really called the *monitor,* and it's the main gizmo through which the computer communicates with you, the human. In a way, the monitor is really the computer's face. Its gentle and quizzical expressions tell you how the computer is doing, and it presents you with the information you requested or shows you the stuff you're working on. When you get angry, the monitor also makes a great target.

This chapter helps you to understand what the computer monitor is, how it works, how to adjust things, and how to speak about the monitor in intelligent terms — or, really, anything other than "That TV Thing."

Some Terms to Know

Computer jargon is infamous and confusing enough, but monitors seem to be a special case. That's because *three* terms are used to describe similar things: monitor, screen, and display. Fortunately, they aren't complex technical terms, though it's still easy to confuse them:

✔ The *monitor* is the box.

✔ The *screen* is the part of the monitor on which information is displayed.

✔ The *display* is the information that appears on the screen.

Sadly, most people use these terms interchangeably, as in "My screen says that the computer doesn't like me" or "My monitor says that the computer doesn't like me" or even "The display is showing how much the computer doesn't like me." They all describe the same thing: that the computer loathes your presence.

Your PC's Graphics System

The monitor may get all the attention, but it's really only the visible half of what I call your Computer's Graphics System. It has two components:

- ✔ The monitor
- ✔ The graphics adapter

The monitor is the dumb part. All it does is display information. The monitor lives outside the console, so it gets more attention than the true brains of the operation, the graphics adapter.

It's the graphics adapter that tells the monitor what to display and where, plus how many colors to use and the overall resolution of the image. It's the graphics adapter that determines your PC's graphics potential.

Figure 10-1 illustrates the monitor/adapter relationship. The graphics adapter can be a separate expansion card, as shown in the figure, or its circuitry can be part of the chipset on the motherboard. A cable then connects the monitor to the console. The monitor, of course, plugs into the wall for power.

Aren't there supposed to be USB monitors?

One feature of the Universal Serial Bus (USB) is that it can be used to attach a monitor to your computer, effectively replacing the graphics adapter. Although it's something that the USB port is capable of doing, the reality is that the USB standard is too slow and performance suffers.

Although USB monitors seem to be in the same league with Bigfoot and true tax reform, a USB gizmo lets you attach an external monitor to your laptop. The gizmo plugs into the USB port and then allows you to plug a PC monitor into the gizmo's standard monitor connector. Sadly, this is not a USB monitor solution — it's just a trick for using two monitors (or a video projector) on a laptop.

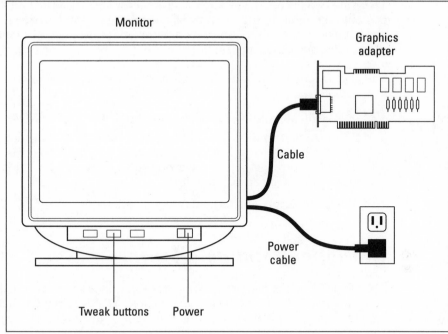

Figure 10-1:
The monitor and graphics adapter.

- Monitor
- Graphics adapter
- Cable
- Power cable
- Tweak buttons
- Power

✔ Your PC needs both a monitor and a graphics adapter.

✔ The graphics adapter is also known as a *video card*.

✔ If your PC has more than one monitor (and it can, you know), it must have one graphics adapter for each monitor or a special graphics adapter that supports multiple monitors. (The dual-monitor thing is possible only with Windows XP Pro.)

Two types of monitors: LCD and CRT

PC monitors come in two different flavors, each of which is known by a popular TLA (*three-letter acronym*): LCD and CRT.

✔ The *CRT* monitor is the traditional, glass-screen, television-set-like monitor.

✔ The *LCD* monitor is the newer, flatter type of computer screen.

Between the two, the LCD monitor is better, though it's more expensive. Traditional CRT monitors are quite cheap, but they are heavier and bulkier and use more electricity, and they're harder on the eyes than LCD monitors. If you have a choice, get an LCD monitor.

There are two exceptions where a CRT monitor is better. The first comes with computer graphics. A CRT monitor is better able to emulate true colors than an LCD. The second exception is computer games, where CRT monitors display the images faster than an LCD.

- ✔ CRT stands for *cathode ray tube*. Note that it's *cathode* ray tube, not *catholic* ray tube.

- ✔ LCD stands for *liquid crystal display*. It isn't a hallucinogenic.

- ✔ Be aware that some CRT monitors are advertised as "flat screen." This term isn't misleading: The glass on the front of the monitor is indeed flat, and it provides a better viewing surface than the traditional convex glass. But it's *not* an LCD monitor.

- ✔ All LCD monitors are flat.

Glorious graphics adapters

The most important half of the computer's graphics system is the graphics hardware itself, known as the *graphics adapter*. It's the circuitry that runs the monitor and controls the image that the monitor displays.

Graphics adapters come in various price ranges and have features for artists, game players, computer designers, and regular Joes like you and me and guys named Joe. You should look for three key things in a graphics adapter:

- ✔ The amount of memory
- ✔ Whether it has a GPU
- ✔ The type of adapter

PC graphics require special memory that's separate from the computer's main memory. This memory is known as *video RAM*, or, often, *VRAM*. The more memory, the more colors and high resolutions and fancier tricks the graphics adapter is capable of.

Graphics adapters can have from 0M (no memory) up to 512MB and beyond. In the case of graphics adapters, more isn't necessarily better. Only if your applications demand more memory, or can take advantage of the extra video memory, is the price worth it. Otherwise, a typical PC has between 16MB and 128MB of video RAM.

Those 0MB graphics adapters "share" video memory with main memory. Obviously, for anyone interested in playing games or creating computer graphics, it's a bad deal.

Another measure of a graphics adapter's muscle is whether it has its own microprocessor, or *graphics processing unit* (GPU). That microprocessor is specially geared toward graphical operations, and, by having it, the graphics adapter takes a load of work away from the PC's main microprocessor and things really fly on the screen.

Finally, there's the way the graphics adapter plugs into the motherboard. The best models use the AGP port, which gives them direct access to the microprocessor and system memory. Low-end graphics adapters are often included with a PC's chipset. Even so, it's possible to install a better graphics adapter and use the PC Setup program to disable the cheesy adapter that's built into the motherboard.

✔ The more memory the graphics adapter has, the higher the resolutions it can support and the more colors it can display at those higher resolutions.

✔ Two popular models of GPUs are available: the Radeon and the GeForce. Both are approximately equal in power and popularity.

✔ Refer to Chapter 6 for more information on the AGP expansion slot.

✔ Many graphics adapters are advertised as supporting 3-D graphics. That's okay, but they work only if your software supports the particular 3-D graphics offered by that graphics adapter. (If so, the side of the software box should say so.)

✔ If your PC has a DVD drive, you need a graphics adapter capable of producing the DVD image on the monitor. A graphics adapter typically has an S-Video Out port on it, which lets you connect a TV to the computer for watching things on a larger screen.

✔ Graphics adapters were once known by various acronyms in the PC world. The most popular acronym was VGA, which stands for Video Gate Array (not Video Graphics Adapter, as is commonly believed). Other acronyms exist, with some incorporating VGA into their alphabet soup. The names are primarily for marketing reasons and have no significance for PCs in general.

Getting to Know and Love Your Monitor

A PC's monitor is really a *peripheral*. It's separate from the console. In fact, you don't need to have the same brand of computer and monitor. You can mix and match. You can even keep your old PC's monitor with a new console you may buy — as long as the monitor is in good shape, why not?

Despite all the features and technical mumbo-jumbo, all monitors serve the same function: They display information that the computer coughs up.

The physical description

Each monitor has two tails (refer to Figure 10-1). One is a power cord that plugs into the wall. The second tail is a video cable that connects to the graphics adapter port on the back of the console. The graphics adapter port is also known as the *VGA port*.

You usually find the monitor's on–off button on the front of the monitor, most likely near the lower-right corner or maybe on the monitor's right side. (It's a total bias against left-handed people, and part of the larger adroit conspiracy.)

Additional buttons adorn the front of the monitor, which you use to control the monitor's display. These buttons may be visible, like a row of ugly teeth, or they may be hidden behind a panel. The section "Adjusting the monitor's display," later in this chapter, discusses what they do.

Some monitors display a message when the monitor is turned on and the PC is not (or the monitor isn't receiving a signal from the PC). The message may read No Signal or something like that, or it may urge you to check the connection. That's okay. The monitor pops to life properly when you turn on the console and it receives a video signal.

All the technical information you need to know

Lots of technical nonsense is used to describe a monitor's abilities. Of that pile of jargon, only the following terms are really necessary:

- ✔ **Size:** Monitors are judged by their picture size, measured on a diagonal, just like TVs. Common sizes for PC monitors are 15, 17, 19, and 21 inches. The most common size is 17 inches, though I love the 19-inch monitors and absolutely swoon over the 21-inch monsters! Oooooooo! (That's me swooning.)

- ✔ **Dot pitch:** This term refers to the distance between each dot, or *pixel,* on the screen (as measured from the center of each pixel). The closer the dots, and the tinier the dot pitch value, the finer the image.

- ✔ **Interlace/non-interlacing:** You want a monitor that's *non-interlacing,* which means that the image appears on the monitor in one swipe rather than two. An interlacing monitor flickers, which makes your eyeballs go nuts.

Other aspects of the display — such as resolution, colors, and video memory — are all part of the graphics adapter hardware, not the monitor. These terms are covered elsewhere in this chapter.

Oh, and other terms, ugly and verbose, are used to describe a monitor. Most of them are marketing terms, which don't do you any good after you own the monitor.

Adjusting the monitor's display

In the early days, you were lucky if your PC's monitor had contrast and brightness knobs. The adjustments you can make to your monitor now are endless. Sometimes, you make adjustments using a row of buttons that adorn the front of your monitor and look almost like a second keyboard. At other times, you use a combination of generic buttons, similar to the annoying way digital clocks are set.

Generally, the buttons on your monitor are of two types. The first type has a menu button and then two or four control buttons adorned with arrows or plus and minus symbols. Pressing the menu button pops up an onscreen display, such as the one shown in Figure 10-2. You use the buttons on the monitor (up, down, plus, and minus) to manipulate the menu and adjust the monitor.

Figure 10-2:
A typical onscreen display.

The second type, often hidden behind a flap or door, has specific buttons with icons that adjust specific things, as shown in Figure 10-3. The idea is to use these buttons to adjust what the icons represent. Sometimes, you have to press more than one button to make a specific adjustment.

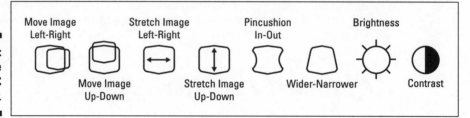

Figure 10-3:
Icons on the
typical PC
monitor.

✔ This is one area of the PC that I really wish they would standardize.

✔ The onscreen information appears over any other image displayed on the monitor. Don't let it freak you out.

✔ Use the buttons to adjust the image size to make full use of the monitor's display area.

✔ Monitors may also display frequency information (31 kHz/60 Hz, for example) when they change screen modes, such as when you play a game and the screen changes to another resolution.

✔ Most monitors also have a Save or Store button, which remembers the settings you have entered and makes them permanent. Use it.

Adjusting the Display in Windows

The graphics adapter controls the monitor, and software rules over the graphics adapter. Which software? Specifically, a thingie called a *video driver* controls the graphics adapter. But lording it over the video driver is the operating system. Windows gives you plenty of options for adjusting the display and what you see on the screen. This section mulls over several interesting and useful examples.

Summoning the Display Properties dialog box

You tweak the display in Windows through the Display Properties dialog box. Here's how you muster it:

1. **Right-click the desktop.**

2. **Choose Properties from the pop-up menu.**

   The Display Properties dialog box appears, ready for action, as shown in Figure 10-4.

Figure 10-4:
The Display
Properties
dialog box.

 You can also summon the Display Properties dialog box by opening the Display icon in the Control Panel, but in nearly a dozen years of using Windows, I have rarely done that.

Some Display Properties dialog boxes may have custom tabs for your display adapter. For example, some versions of the ATI adapter may add tabs for doing special things with that graphics adapter. I don't cover those things here, mostly because ATI doesn't send me any free stuff.

 To preview any changes made in the Display Properties dialog box, click the Apply button. Your monitor may blink or flicker, and Windows asks whether everything is okay. Click the OK button if it is.

Adjusting the display size (resolution) and colors

The monitor's physical dimensions cannot change, but you can set the amount of stuff you see on the screen by adjusting the monitor's *resolution*. That's the number of dots, or *pixels,* the monitor displays. Each pixel can be a different color, and, altogether, thousands of them on the monitor's screen create the image you see. The resolution is the number of pixels measuring horizontally by vertically.

To set the screen's resolution, you use the Settings tab in the Display Properties dialog box, as shown in Figure 10-5.

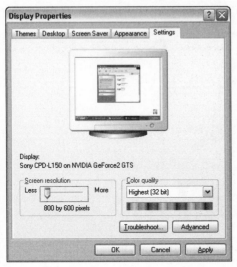

Figure 10-5:
Change
your
monitor's
resolution
and colors
here.

The Screen Resolution slider sets the display resolution, measured in pixels horizontally and vertically. The larger the numbers, the more information is displayed. Smaller values yield less information, but make everything appear bigger.

Use the preview window in the upper center of the dialog box to get an idea of how the new resolution affects the display.

The Color Quality area determines how many colors are available at a specific resolution. The colors range from 16 (which is pretty dern ugly) to the highest rating, also known as 32 bits.

✔ The resolution and color settings are related. Higher resolutions have fewer colors, so you may want to set the color setting first and then see which resolutions are available for that setting.

✔ You need only the highest color settings if you plan to use graphics applications, such as photo editing.

✔ Higher resolutions work best on larger monitors.

✔ Some LCD monitors allow only selected resolutions, such as 800 x 600 or 1024 x 768.

✔ The maximum number of resolution and color settings depends on the graphics adapter and not on the monitor size. The more video RAM the graphics adapter has, the more options are available.

✔ Some computer games automatically change the monitor's resolution to allow the games to be played. This change is okay because the resolution should return to normal after playing the game.

Making things easier to see

If you have trouble seeing small things, adjust your display so that they appear as big as possible: Choose a low resolution, such as 800 x 600 or even 640 x 480. Take advantage of the various View➪Zoom commands available in applications, which greatly enlarge the text or subject matter.

You can also direct Windows to use larger icons on the display. In the Display Properties dialog box, click the Appearance tab and then click the Effects button. In the Effects dialog box, put a check mark next to the Use Large Icons option. Click OK.

Changing the background (wallpaper)

The background, or *wallpaper,* is what you see when you look at the desktop. It can be a solid color, or it can display any graphics image stored on your hard drive or found on the Internet. This process is all handled on the Desktop tab in the Display Properties dialog box, as shown in Figure 10-6.

Figure 10-6: Select desktop wallpaper here.

To use a solid color, choose (None) from the top of the scrolling Background list and then select a color using the Color button. Yes, you can choose from only 20 colors; I hope you can find something to match your drapes.

Images are more fun than solid colors, and Windows gives you a host of image files to choose from on the Background scrolling list. You can click to select an image and then see how it looks in the preview window, at the top of the dialog box. If you can't find the image you're looking for, use the Browse button to go fetch one from a specific location on the disk.

If the image doesn't quite fill the screen, you can use the Position button to adjust it. Choose Tile to have the image pattern replicate to fill the screen; the Stretch option forces an image to resize itself and cover the whole desktop.

 ✔ The Browse dialog box works just like the Open dialog box. See Chapter 21.

 ✔ To set an image from the Web as your wallpaper, right-click the image and choose the Set As Background command from the pop-up menu.

 ✔ Creating your own wallpaper is easy. You can do so in the Windows Paint program, or you can use a scanned image or a shot from a digital camera.

Adding a screen saver

The *screen saver* is an image or animation that appears on the monitor after a given period of inactivity. After your computer sits there, lonely and feeling ignored, for 30 minutes, for example, an image of a fish tank appears on the monitor to amuse any ghosts in the room.

To set a screen saver, you use the Screen Saver tab in the Display Properties dialog box, as shown in Figure 10-7. Choose a screen saver from the drop-down Screen Saver list. Use the Settings button (if it's available) to adjust the screen saver's action. The preview window shows you what the screen saver looks like teensy; use the Preview button to see what the screen saver looks like full-screen.

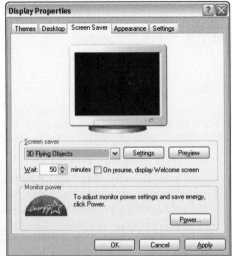

Figure 10-7:
Select a
screen
saver here.

One key setting is the Wait box, which tells Windows how many idle minutes pass before the screen saver kicks in.

Make your settings and then click the OK button. If you don't touch the mouse or keyboard after the given amount of Wait time, the screen saver appears on your monitor.

- ✔ A safe key to press for switching off the screen saver is Ctrl. Unlike other keys on your keyboard, this key doesn't mess with any application that appears after the screen saver vanishes.

- ✔ A cool way to switch off the screen saver is to pound your desk with your fist. That jostles the mouse and deactivates the screen saver.

- ✔ Beware of downloading screen saver files from the Internet. Although some of them are legitimate screen savers, most of them are invasive ads or programs that are impossible to uninstall or remove. If you download this type of screen saver, you're pretty much stuck with it. Be careful!

- ✔ The problem the original screen savers tried to prevent was known as *phosphor burn-in*. It can still happen on monitors now, but only if the same image is displayed for months. LCD monitors are not susceptible to phosphor burn-in.

Putting the monitor to sleep

As an alternative to using a screen saver, you can take advantage of your PC's power-management abilities and simply turn the monitor off after a given amount of time. To make it happen, click the Power button at the bottom of the Display Properties dialog box, on the Screen Saver tab (refer to Figure 10-7). Doing so displays the Power Options Properties dialog box.

Look for the Turn Off Monitor option in the Power Options Properties dialog box. Set a time interval after which the PC automatically shuts off the monitor. If you don't want the monitor shutting itself off, choose Never.

Click OK to close the Power Options Properties dialog box.

- ✔ If you're using a screen saver, set the value *greater than* the time after which the screen saver kicks in.

- ✔ I forgo the screen saver and merely choose to turn off my monitor after an hour of inactivity.

- ✔ You can also get to the Power Options Properties dialog box by opening the Power Options icon in the Control Panel.

Taking a Picture of the Screen

It's possible in Windows to capture information on the screen just like taking a picture. It's technically called a *screen dump,* where dump is an ancient computer term for copying raw information from one place to another, a pouring out of the old bit bucket, as it were.

Pressing the Print Screen key takes a snapshot of the desktop. Click! All that graphical information — whatever you see — is saved as a graphics image in the Windows Clipboard. You can then paste the image into any program that can swallow graphical images, such as Windows Paint or Microsoft Word.

To see how this process works, follow these steps:

1. **Press the Print Screen key.**

2. **Start the Windows Paint program.**

   Find it on the Start panel by choosing Programs➪Accessories➪Paint.

3. **Choose Edit➪Paste in the Paint program.**

   The desktop image is pasted into the Paint program, ready for editing, saving to disk, or printing and framing.

To print the image after it's been pasted, simply use the program's File➪Print command. I know that's a lot of steps, but it finally puts meaning into the key's name, *Print* Screen.

 ✔ On some keyboards, the Print Screen key is labeled PrtSc.

 ✔ If you press the Alt+Print Screen key combination, only the frontmost, or "top," window is copied to the Clipboard.

 ✔ Note that you cannot capture a frame from a DVD movie by using the Print Screen key.

Chapter 11

The Keyboard and Mouse Chapter

In This Chapter

▶ Understanding the keyboard

▶ Using specific keys

▶ Controlling the keyboard in Windows

▶ Sitting and typing properly

▶ Getting to know the mouse

▶ Working with the mouse in Windows

▶ Fixing various mouse problems

In every great adventure story, the hero generally has a sidekick. The sidekick isn't as great as the hero, and it can be argued that the hero could easily accomplish his labors without the sidekick, but the sidekick becomes a vital part of the story. The sidekick is the plucky comic relief. The sidekick comes in handy every so often, and perhaps even saves the day, which more than justifies his contrivance as a plot device.

In the land of computers, on the mesa of Input Devices, your computer keyboard is the hero. Its sidekick is the mouse. You use the keyboard and mouse together to create interesting things, take care of business, or just tell the computer what it can do with itself. It may not be utterly heroic, but it's the subject of this chapter.

Your PC Needs Its Keyboard

Forget about talking to the computer. Yes, on those futuristic science fiction TV shows, they talk to the computer. They have to! There isn't a keyboard in sight! But, you — you have to peck away at the keys to make your intentions known to Mr. Computer.

✔ The keyboard is the computer's standard input device. Refer to Chapter 1 for more information on computer input.

✔ Okay, I lied: You can dictate to the computer. See Chapter 14 for information on computer speech recognition.

The standard PC keyboard

The typical PC keyboard layout is shown in Figure 11-1. It's known as the *Enhanced 104-key keyboard.* Yes, it has 104 keys on it. You can count them yourself, if you don't believe me and you have the time.

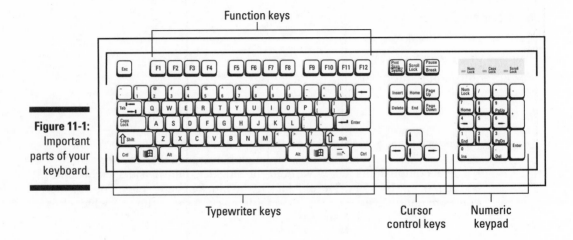

Function keys

Figure 11-1: Important parts of your keyboard.

Typewriter keys   Cursor control keys   Numeric keypad

Four main areas are mapped out on your PC's keyboard, as shown in Figure 11-1:

Function keys: These keys are positioned on the top row of the keyboard. They're labeled F1, F2, F3, and on up to F11 and F12.

Typewriter keys: These keys are the same types of keys you would find on an old typewriter: letters, numbers, and punctuation symbols.

Cursor-control keys: Often called *arrow keys,* these four keys move the text cursor in the direction of their arrows. Above them are more cursor-control keys — the six-pack of Insert, Delete, Home, End, Page Up, and Page Down.

Numeric keypad: Popular with accountants, bank tellers, and airline ticket agents, the numeric keypad contains calculator-like keys. This keypad also doubles as a cursor keypad; the Num Lock key determines its behavior.

TIP

"Must I learn to type to use a computer?"

The short answer: No, you don't need to learn to type to use a computer. Plenty of computer users hunt and peck. In fact, most programmers don't know how to type, but that brings up an interesting story: A computer software developer once halted all development and had his programmers learn how to touch-type. It took two whole weeks, but afterward, they all got their work done much faster and had more time available to break away and play those all-important computer games.

As a bonus to owning a computer, you can have it teach you how to type. The Mavis Beacon Teaches Typing software package does just that. Other packages are available, but I personally love the name Mavis Beacon.

The keyboard shown in Figure 11-1 is typical and boring. More exciting keyboard models exist, some ergonomically designed keyboards and others with *even more* buttons on them. You read about those variations throughout the following sections.

✔ The *cursor* is the blinking goober on the screen that shows you where the stuff you type appears. As though *cursor* isn't weird enough, the blinking doodad is also called an *insertion pointer.*

✔ See the section "The Lock sisters," later in this chapter, for more information on the numeric keypad's duplicity.

Shifty keys

Four keys on your keyboard are *modifier* keys. These keys work in combination with other keys to do various interesting and unbelievable things:

✔ Shift

✔ Ctrl or Control

✔ Alt or Alternate

✔ Win or Windows

You hold down a shift key and then press another key on the keyboard. What happens then depends on the shift key you pressed and how the program you're using reacts to the key combination.

✔ The Shift key is used to make capital letters or to access the punctuation and other symbols on the number keys and other keys. This is how you can create the %@#^ characters that come in handy for cursing in comic strips.

✔ The Ctrl and Alt keys are used in combination with other keys as short-cuts for menu commands. For example, if you hold down the Ctrl key and press S (Ctrl+S), you activate the Save command. Holding down the Alt key and pressing the F4 key (Alt+F4) closes a window on the desktop. You press and hold the shift key, tap the other key, and then release both.

✔ When pressed by itself, the Win key pops up the Start menu thing. Otherwise, the Win key can be used in combination with other keys to do various things on the desktop. For example, Win+E summons the Windows Explorer program, and Win+D displays the desktop.

✔ Even though you may see Ctrl+S or Alt+S with a capital *S*, it doesn't mean that you must press Ctrl+Shift+S or Alt+Shift+S. The *S* is written in uppercase simply because Ctrl+s looks like a typesetting error.

✔ Don't be surprised if these shift keys are used in combination with each other. I have seen Shift+Ctrl+C and Ctrl+Alt. Just remember to press and hold the Shift keys first and then tap the letter key. Release all the keys together.

✔ Some manuals use the notation ^Y rather than Ctrl+Y. This term means the same thing: Hold down the Ctrl key, press Y, and release the Ctrl key.

The Lock sisters

The three Lock sisters are special keys designed to change the way other keys on the keyboard behave:

Caps Lock: This key works like holding down the Shift key, but it produces only capital letters; it doesn't shift the other keys like a typewriter's Shift Lock key would do. Press Caps Lock again, and the letters return to their normal, lowercase state.

Num Lock: Pressing this key makes the numeric keypad on the right side of the keyboard produce numbers. Press this key again, and you can use the numeric keypad for moving the text cursor.

Scroll Lock: This key has no purpose in life. Some spreadsheets use it to reverse the function of the cursor keys (which move the spreadsheet rather than the cell highlight). Scroll Lock does little else that's significant or famous.

Strange keyboard abbreviations

The keys on the keyboard are only so big. Therefore, some words have to be scrunched down to fit on the key cap. Here's your guide to some of the more oddly named keys and what they mean:

Print Screen is also known as PrScr or Print Scrn.

Page Up and Page Down are written as PgUp and PgDn on the numeric keypad.

Insert and Delete appear as Ins and Del on the numeric keypad.

When a lock key is on, a corresponding light appears on the keyboard. The light may be on the keyboard or on the key itself. That's your clue that a lock key's feature is turned on.

- Caps Lock affects only the keys A through Z; it doesn't affect any other keys.

- If you type **This Text Looks Like A Ransom Note** and it looks like `tHIS tEXT lOOKS lIKE a rANSOM nOTE`, the Caps Lock key is inadvertently turned on. Press it once to return everything to normal.

- If you press the Shift key while Caps Lock is on, the letter keys return to normal. (Shift kind of cancels out Caps Lock.)

Specific keys from Any to the bizarre

Your computer keyboard is a virtual playground of buttons — some famous, some mysterious, and some non-existent. The following rundown of what's important ignores what's not:

 Ha-ha. There is no Any key on the keyboard. The old message once read, "Press Any key to continue" and the programmer thought he was being generous, but people still did look for that elusive Any key.

When the computer asks you to press the Any key, press *any key* on the keyboard. Specifically, press the spacebar.

 The Break key does nothing. Why is the key named Break? Why not call it the Brake key? Wouldn't that make sense? Who wants a computer to break, anyway?

The Break key is the same as the Pause key. In fact, Break is really the Alt+Pause key. See the Pause key description later in this section.

Know your ones and zeroes

On a typewriter, the lowercase letter *L* and the number 1 are often the same. In fact, my old Underwood upright lacks a 1 key altogether. Unfortunately, on a computer, a big difference exists between a one and a little *L*.

If you're typing 1,001, for example, don't type l,00l by mistake — especially when you're working with a spreadsheet. The computer gags.

The same holds true for the uppercase letter *O* and the number 0. They're different. Use a zero for numbers and a big *O* for big O things.

Sometimes, zero is displayed with a slash through it, like this: Ø, or maybe with a dot in the middle. That's one way to tell the difference between O and 0, but it's not used that often. A better indication is that the letter O is often fatter than the symbol for zero.

This is the keyboard's most popular key; you press Enter to end a paragraph in a word processor. In a dialog box, pressing the Enter key is the same as clicking the OK button.

A second Enter key can be found on the numeric keypad. It's there to facilitate the rapid entry of incorrect numerical values. Both Enter keys work identically.

The one key that says "Hey! Stop it!" to Windows is the Escape key, labeled Esc on your keyboard. Pressing the Esc key is the same as clicking Cancel or No Way in a dialog box. This key closes most, but not all, windows, just to keep you guessing.

Whenever you need help in Windows, whack the F1 key. F1 equals help — there's no way to commit that to memory.

Honestly, the Pause key doesn't work in Windows. Some games may use it to pause the action, but it's not a consistent thing.

This is the forward slash key. It's used as a separator and also to denote division, such as 52/13 (52 divided by 13). Don't confuse it with the backslash key.

The backslash (\) leans to the left. This character is used in *pathnames*, which are complex and not discussed in this book.

Allow me to end the mystery: This is the System Request key. It does nothing. Ignore it.

This booger is the Context key. It lives between the right Windows and Ctrl keys. Pressing this key displays the shortcut menu for whatever item is selected on the screen. It's the same as right-clicking the mouse when something is selected. Obviously, this key is next to useless.

The Tab key is used in two different ways on your computer, neither of which generates a diet cola beverage. In a word processor, you use the Tab key to indent paragraphs — just like an old typewriter's Tab key. In a dialog box, you use the Tab key to move between the various graphical gizmos.

Use Tab rather than Enter when you're filling in a form in a program or dialog box or on the Internet. For example, press the Tab key to hop between the First Name and Last Name fields.

- The Tab key often has two arrows on it — one pointing to the left and the other to the right. These arrows may be in addition to the word *Tab*, or they may be on there by themselves to confuse you.

- The arrows move both ways because Shift+Tab is a valid key combination. For example, pressing Shift+Tab in a dialog box moves you "backward" through the options.

- The computer treats a tab as a single, separate character. When you backspace over a tab in a word processing program, the tab disappears completely in one chunk — not space by space.

For those forced to do math on the computer

Clustered around the numeric keypad, like campers roasting marshmallows around a fire, are various keys to help you work with numbers. Especially if you're dabbling with a spreadsheet or other number-crunching software, you find that these keys come in handy. Take a look at your keyboard's numeric keypad right now, just to reassure yourself.

What? You were expecting a ×_or ÷ key? Forget it! This is a computer. It uses special oddball symbols for mathematical operations:

- + is for addition.

- – is for subtraction.

- * is for multiplication.

- / is for division.

The only strange symbol here is the asterisk, for multiplication. Don't use the little *x!* It's not the same thing. The / (slash) is okay for division, but don't waste your time hunting for the ÷ symbol. It's not there.

Special keys on special keyboards

If 104 keys on the keyboard just aren't enough, you can venture out and buy special keyboards that sport *even more* keys. Or, perhaps your computer came with that type of keyboard. Typically, this type has a row of buttons along the top, right above the function keys. These buttons carry out specific tasks, such as connecting to the Internet, scanning images, sending e-mail, or adjusting the computer's sound volume.

Specialty keyboard buttons are *nonstandard:* They don't come with the typical PC keyboard and must be supported by using some special program run on the computer. That program controls the keys and their behavior. If the keys don't work, it's a problem with the special program and not anything that Windows or your computer is doing wrong.

Controlling the Keyboard in Windows

When you press and hold any key on the keyboard, eventually that key repeats itself, like a machine gun. Press and hold the A key, and eventually you see a whole slew of AAAAAAAAAAAA. . . . (That's so that you can easily type dialogue when your characters are falling off a cliff.)

The pause, or delay, before a key repeats is the *repeat delay.* The rapidity at which the key's character (or function) repeats is the *repeat rate.* Both these items are set by using the Keyboard Properties dialog box (see Figure 11-2). To get there, open the Control Panel and then open the Keyboard icon.

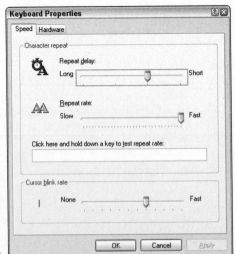

Figure 11-2:
Control the keyboard here.

Use the mouse to manipulate the sliders in the dialog box to set the rates, and then test out the rates in the text box that's provided. Click the OK or Apply button only when you're happy.

If the computer's keyboard has specialty buttons (refer to the preceding section), an extra tab may appear in the Keyboard Properties dialog box. That tab is used to assign commands or duties to the various extra buttons.

Proper Typing Attitude

Sister Mary Serious had a point about sitting up properly and not letting your wrists droop in typing class. Posture and position are important when you're using a computer keyboard, especially if you do so quite a bit. That's because many humans run the risk of something called repetitive stress injury (RSI).

Here are several things you can do to avoid RSI and keep your computing experience a pleasant one:

Get an ergonomic keyboard: Even if your wrists are as limber as rubber tree plants, you may want to consider an *ergonomic* keyboard. That type of keyboard is specially designed at an angle to relieve the stress of typing for long — or short — periods.

Use a wrist pad: Wrist pads elevate your wrists so that you type in a proper position, with your palms *above* the keyboard, not resting below the spacebar.

Adjust your chair: Sit at the computer with your elbows level with your wrists.

Adjust your monitor: Your head should not tilt down or up when you view the computer screen. It should be straight ahead, which doesn't help your wrists as much as it helps your neck.

- ✔ Ergonomic keyboards cost a little more than standard keyboards, but they're well worth the investment if you type for long hours, or at least want to look like you type for long hours.

- ✔ Some mouse pads have built-in wrist elevators. They're great for folks who use mouse-intensive applications.

- ✔ Many keyboards come with adjustable legs underneath for positioning the keys to a comfortable angle. Use these legs.

A Mouse You Can Put Your Hand On

After modem jokes, more computer mouse jokes are told than anything else. And, like the modem jokes, none of the mouse jokes is worth repeating. In fact, having a mouse with your computer is so common that the silly thing doesn't really need much explaining any more; hence, no more funny jokes about Mildred thinking that it's a foot pedal or Dave using the mouse upside down.

The PC needs a mouse

Your computer's mouse is an *input* device. Although the keyboard (another input device) can do almost anything, you need a mouse in order to control graphics and graphical whatnots on the screen — especially in an operating system like Windows.

- ✔ Your PC may have come with a specific mouse, but you can always buy a better replacement.
- ✔ The plural of computer mouse is *mice*. One computer has a mouse. Two computers have mice.

The basic, generic computer mouse

A typical computer mouse is shown in Figure 11-3, though what you see there is only one style of mouse. The variety is truly endless. Even so, nearly all computer mice have the same basic parts.

Mouse body: The mouse is about the size of a bar of soap. You rest your palm on its body and use your fingers to manipulate the mouse buttons.

The two main buttons: The standard PC mouse has a minimum of two buttons, left and right. The left button, which falls under your right hand's index finger, is the *main* button. The other button is the right button.

The wheel button: A popular addition to the standard PC mouse is the center, or wheel, button. This button can be pressed like the left and right buttons, and it can be rolled back and forth. Some wheels can even be tilted from side to side.

The mouse finds its home to the right of the keyboard (for more right-handed people). It needs a clear swath of desk space so that you can move the mouse around; an area about the size of this book is typically all you need.

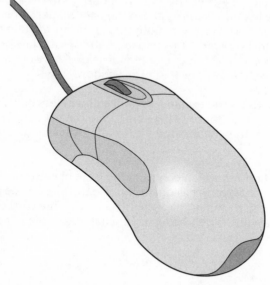

Figure 11-3:
A typical
computer
mouse.

Optical versus mechanical

You use the mouse by moving it around on your desktop. The movement is detected internally by the mouse, either mechanically or optically.

The *mechanical* mouse houses a hard rubber ball that rolls as the mouse is moved. Sensors inside the mouse body detect the movement and translate it into information that the computer interprets.

The *optical* mouse uses an LED sensor to detect tabletop movement and then send off that information to the computer for merry munching.

Of the two types, optical mice are better. They last longer and they're easier to clean. Also, optical mice don't need a mouse pad, which is necessary for a mechanical mouse's ball to get proper traction. An optical mouse can work on any nonreflective surface.

Computer gamers, always the exception, prefer mechanical mice when playing games. Mechanical mice are more responsive, whereas optical mice have a tendency to jump when moved quickly.

Cordless mice

The latest rage in computing is wireless, and computer mice have been minus their tails for years (long before the farmer's wife wielded that carving knife). There are two types of wireless mice:

The infrared (IR) wireless mouse: This type of mouse requires a line of sight to work; the mouse sends bursts of IR light to the base station, which picks up the signals the same way your TV remote transmits information to the TV set. Like the TV remote, however, if the mouse's batteries are low or something is blocking the line of sight, the remote mouse doesn't work. In that case, say "Stupid mouse!" and throw it out the window.

The radio frequency (RF) wireless mouse: Unlike IR wireless mice, the RF variation works without the mouse being able to see the base station. In fact, you can hide the base station behind the PC (or a pile of manuals and sticky notes).

Cordless mice require power, which comes in the form of batteries. They must be replaced or recharged occasionally, or else the mouse doesn't work. The best solution for this problem is a recharging cradle; the cordless mouse is stored in the cradle when it isn't being used. That makes the mouse easier to find and keeps the thing charged.

Other mouse species

Of all computer peripherals, the mouse is the chameleon. Mice come in more types than varieties of Baskin-Robbins ice cream.

The most common alternative mouse is one with more buttons on it. The extra buttons can be programmed to do specific things, such as navigate the World Wide Web or turn pages when you're reading a document. How many buttons? The typical button-ified mouse may have five buttons. The most I've ever seen, however, is 57 buttons. (I kid you not.)

A popular mouse variation is the *trackball,* which is like an upside-down mouse. Rather than roll the mouse around, you use your thumb or index finger to roll a ball on top of the mouse. The whole contraption stays stationary, so it doesn't need nearly as much room and its cord never gets tangled. This type of mouse is preferred by graphic artists because it's often more precise than the traditional "soap-on-a-rope" mouse.

Another mouse mutation enjoyed by the artistic type is the *stylus* mouse, which looks like a pen and draws on a special pad. This mouse is also pressure sensitive, which is wonderful for use in painting and graphics applications.

Finally, there are those *cordless 3D* mice, which can be pointed at the computer screen like a TV remote. Those things give me the willies.

Basic Mouse Operations

 The computer's mouse controls a graphical mouse pointer or mouse cursor on the screen. When you move the mouse around by rolling it on your desk, the pointer on the screen moves in a similar manner. Roll the mouse left, and the pointer moves left; roll it in circles, and the pointer mimics that action; drop the mouse off the table and your computer bruises. (Just kidding.)

Here are some of the more basic mouse operations:

Point: When you're told to "point the mouse," you move the mouse on the desktop, which moves the mouse pointer on the screen to point at something interesting (or not).

Click: A click is a press of the mouse button — one press and release of the main button, the one on the left. This action makes a clicking sound, which is where this maneuver gets its name. Clicking is often done to select something or to identify a specific location on the screen.

Right-click: This action is the same as a click, though the right mouse button is used.

Double-click: This one works just like the single click, though you click twice in the same spot — usually, rather rapidly. This is most commonly done in Windows to open something, such as an icon. Both clicks must be on (or near) the same spot for the double-click to work.

Drag: The drag operation is done to graphically pick something up on the screen and move it. To do that, you point the mouse at the thing you want to drag and then press and hold the mouse's button. Keep the mouse button down, which "picks up" the object, and then move the mouse to another location. As you move the mouse (and keep the button down) the object moves. To release, or drop, the object, release the mouse button.

Right-drag: This action is the same as a drag, but the mouse's right button is used instead.

Many of these basic mouse operations can be combined with keys on the keyboard. For example, a Shift+click means pressing the Shift key on the keyboard while clicking the mouse. A Ctrl+drag means pressing and holding the Ctrl key while you drag an object with the mouse.

> ✔ The best way to learn how to use a computer mouse is to play a computer card game, such as Solitaire or FreeCell (both of which come with Windows). You should have the mouse mastered in only a few frustrating hours.

✔ You don't need to squeeze the mouse; a gentle grip is all that's necessary.

   ✔ Press *and release* the mouse button to click.

   ✔ If you double-click your mouse and nothing happens, you may not be clicking fast enough. See the section "'Double-clicking doesn't work!'" later in this chapter.

Dinking with the Mouse in Windows

In Windows, the mouse is controlled, manipulated, and teased by using the Mouse icon in the Control Panel. Opening that icon displays the Mouse Properties dialog box, as shown in Figure 11-4, where you can make mousy adjustments.

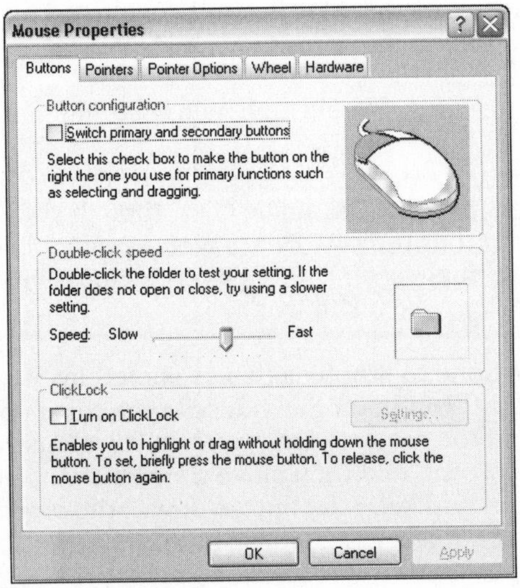

Figure 11-4:
The Mouse
Properties
dialog box.

Note that the Mouse Properties dialog box may look different from Figure 11-4 and what you see elsewhere in this book. It all depends on which mouse your PC uses. Although some tabs are generically the same, some are specific to the mouse hardware.

This section covers some of the more helpful things you can do in the Mouse Properties dialog box in Windows.

"I can't find the mouse pointer!"

The Pointer Options tab in the Mouse Properties dialog box, as shown in Figure 11-5, contains a number of options to help you locate a lonely or lost mouse pointer. These options can come in handy, especially on larger displays or when the mouse pointer is floating over a particularly busy desktop.

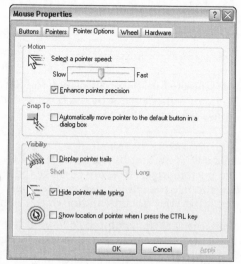

Figure 11-5:
Ways to find
a wayward
mouse.

✔ The Pointer Trails option displays a comet trail of mouse pointers as you move the mouse about. Jiggling or circling the mouse makes lots of visual racket, which allows you to quickly locate the mouse pointer.

✔ The Ctrl Key Location option allows you to find the mouse pointer by tapping either Ctrl key on the keyboard. This action makes a radar-like circle appear, by zeroing in on the cursor's location.

✔ You can also employ the Snap To option, which specifically jumps the mouse pointer to the main button in any dialog box that appears (though I find this option annoying).

"Double-clicking doesn't work!"

If you can't seem to double-click, one of two things is happening: Either you're moving the mouse pointer a little bit between clicks or the double-click *rate* is set too fast for human fingers to manage.

The *double-click rate* is set in the Mouse Properties dialog box, on either the Buttons or Activities tabs. On one tab or the other you find the Double-Click Speed area. Practice your double-clicking on the tiny folder icon off to the right. Use the Slow-Fast slider to adjust the double-click speed to better match your click-click timing.

"I'm left-handed, and the buttons are backward!"

Where is that left-handed class action suit, anyway?

In Windows, you can adjust the mouse for southpaw use on the Buttons tab, as shown earlier, in Figure 11-4. Put a check mark by the box labeled Switch Primary and Secondary Buttons. That way, the "main" mouse button is under your left index finger.

- ✔ This book and all manuals and computer books assume that the left mouse button is the main button. *Right-clicks* are clicks of the right mouse button. If you tell Windows to use the left-handed mouse, these buttons are reversed. Keep in mind that your documentation doesn't reflect that.

- ✔ Left-handed mice are available that are sculpted to fit your left hand better than all those right-hand-oriented biased mice on the market.

- ✔ No setting is available for ambidextrous people, wise guy!

Chapter 12

More than a Mortal Printer

*O*nce upon a time, computers were coupled with a common peripheral called a *printer*. The printer's job was to print, or to get that electronic stuff out of the computer and down on paper. After all, showing someone a piece of paper is far easier than lugging around your computer and monitor (or even a laptop) all day. The printer's job was simple, and it was a humble device. But that was then.

Computer printers now often do much more than just print. The current rage is the all-in-one, or a combination device that not only prints, but can also be used as a scanner, photocopier, and maybe even a fax machine. Despite its many talents, the thing is still referred to as a printer, and it's basic printing that is the subject of this chapter.

The Printer's the Thing

The basic duty of your PC's printer is to print. Yeah, it may also scan, copy, and do the dishes. But, at the heart of the thing is a gizmo that puts ink to paper and gives you what the computer nerds call *hard copy,* something you can show the world.

Printer categories

Several categories of computer printer exist, depending on how the ink gets splattered on the paper as well as on the printer's features. Here's the short list:

- ✔ Inkjet
- ✔ Laser
- ✔ Photo
- ✔ All-in-one
- ✔ Impact

The inkjet, photo, and all-in-one printers all use the same basic method for putting ink on paper: Tiny balls of ink are spewed directly onto the paper. Because the teensy-tiny ink balls stick to the paper, this type of printer needs no ribbon or toner cartridge; the ink is jetted out directly, which is how the printer gets its name.

Laser printers are found primarily in the office environment, where they can handle the high workload. The printer works like a photocopier: The difference is that the computer creates the image and etches it by using a laser beam rather than using a mirror and the magic moving bar of light you see whenever you try to photocopy your face.

Impact printers are the traditional printers of yesterday's computers. The two popular types are dot-matrix and daisy-wheel. Impact printers are slower and noisier than the other types of printers. These printers use a ribbon and some device that physically bangs the ribbon onto the paper. Because of that, impact printers are primarily used now in printing invoices or multicopy forms. They're not practical for home use.

- ✔ Inkjet printers are by no means messy. The ink is dry on the paper by the time the paper comes flopping out of the printer.
- ✔ A laser printer that can print in color is known as a color laser printer. The regular (noncolor) laser printer uses only one color of ink — usually, black.
- ✔ Low-end inkjet printers cost less because they're dumb; they contain no internal electronics to help create the image. Instead, the computer is required to do the thinking, which slows things down a tad. When you pay more for an inkjet printer, the smarts are usually included with the printer.
- ✔ High-priced printers offer a higher-quality output, faster speed, more printing options, the ability to print on larger sheets of paper, and other amazing options.

A look around your printer

Take a moment to examine your printer and look for some handy things, as labeled in Figure 12-1:

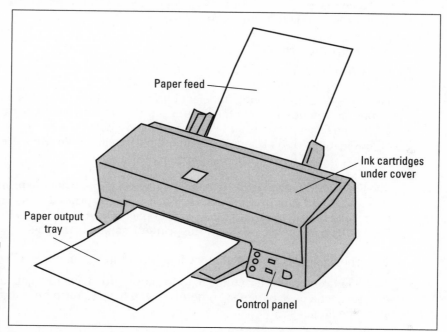

Figure 12-1:
Exciting places on the printer.

Paper feed: The paper feed is where you store the paper that the printer eventually prints on. For more information, see the section "Feeding your printer, Part II: Paper," later in this chapter.

Manual/envelope feeder: Fancier printers may have a special slot, tray, or foldout-thing used to manually feed special papers or envelopes. It may be hidden on your printer, and it's not shown in Figure 12-1, so look around a bit to see whether your printer has such a deal.

Paper output tray: The printed paper comes out and is stacked up in the output tray. If the paper comes out face up, be sure to see the section "Printing in reverse order," later in this chapter.

Control panel: Refer to the next subsection for the details.

Ink/toner replacement: Printers don't go on printing forever. At some point, you need to stuff the thing with more ink. Be sure that you know how to open the printer to find where the ink goes. Also see the section "Feeding your printer, Part I: Ink," later in this chapter.

The mighty printer control panel

Every printer has a control panel somewhere on its body. The fancy models have LCD screens that display lots of text: `Printer jammed`, `I'm out of paper`, or `You're plagiarizing`, for example. Less fancy printers may have only a couple of buttons. Either way, two important buttons to find or features to access on the control panel are

- ✔ On-Line or Select
- ✔ Form Feed

The purpose of the On-Line or Select button is to tell your printer whether to ignore the computer. When the printer is offline or deselected, the computer can't print. The printer is still on, which is good because you may need to access features or do things that you otherwise cannot do while the thing is printing.

The Form Feed button is used to eject a page of paper from the printer. For example, if you stop printing and only half a page is printed, you can use the Form Feed button to eject the rest of that page. Or, you can press the Form Feed button whenever you want the printer to spit a blank page at you.

- ✔ The computer can print only when the printer is online or selected.

- ✔ You take the printer offline if, for example, you have to unjam it or want to eject a page of paper. Sometimes, you have to turn the printer off when it jams.

- ✔ If your printer seems to lack a control panel, it's probably controlled via a software control panel in Windows. This is the printer's feature and not a part of Windows, so refer to the printer's manual for instructions.

- ✔ Printers with larger LCD control panels often use menu buttons to help you choose the online or form-feed options.

- ✔ All-in-one printers have additional buttons on the control panel for making copies and scanning, for example. A companion program in Windows probably allows for even greater control over the printer's abilities. Note that such programs are specific to your printer, and not a part of Windows itself.

- ✔ Keep your printer's manual handy. For example, I put my printer's manual right beneath the printer, where I can always find it. You may never read the manual, but if your printer suddenly pops up and displays `Error 34`, you can look up what `Error 34` is and read how to fix it. (The voice of experience is talking here.)

Feeding your printer, Part 1: Ink

This may be the 21st century, but mankind is still printing with ink and paper, just like the Chinese were hundreds of years ago. The type of ink and how it's stored depend on which type of printer you're using.

Inkjet printers, which include photo and all-in-one models, use *ink cartridges.* Laser printers use a powdery ink substance, called *toner,* that also comes in a cartridge. Either way, you spend lots of money replacing the ink in your printer.

Replace an ink cartridge by first removing the old cartridge. Carefully unwrap the foil around the new cartridge. Remove any tape or covering, per the package's instructions. Then insert the ink cartridge into the printer, again following the instructions for your specific ink printer. Put the old cartridge into the new cartridge's box and properly dispose of it or have it recycled.

Laser printers require drop-in toner cartridges. They're easy to install and come with their own, handy instructions. Just don't breathe in the toner or else you'll die. Some manufacturers sell their cartridges with return envelopes so that you can send the old cartridge back to the factory for recycling or proper disposal.

All printers use black ink or toner. Color printers also use black, plus three other inks or toners: magenta, cyan, and yellow. Photo printers add two more colors, another flavor each of magenta and cyan.

Sometimes, the colors in an inkjet printer come three to a cartridge. Yes, that means that if only one color of ink goes, you must replace the entire cartridge. That's why I recommend, in my book *Buying a Computer For Dummies* (Wiley Publishing, Inc.), getting a printer with separate cartridges for each ink color.

✔ Make a note of what type of inkjet cartridges your printer uses. Keep the catalog number somewhere handy, such as taped to your inkjet printer's case, so that you can always reorder the proper cartridge.

✔ Yes, they make money by selling you ink. That's why the printer is cheap. It's the old "give away the razor and sell them the blade" thing all over again.

✔ Several online and mail-order dealers offer cheap prices on ink and toner cartridges, better than you find locally or in an office supply superstore.

✔ If the ink cartridge has nozzles, you can refill it on your own. Refill kits are sold everywhere, and they're cheaper than continually buying new cartridges. However, the kits work best if the cartridge has nozzles. If the cartridge is just a storage bin, you're better off buying a new one.

✔ Always follow carefully the instructions for changing cartridges. Old cartridges can leak and get messy ink all over. I suggest having a paper towel handy and putting the used cartridge in a plastic baggie while you walk to the trashcan.

✔ CMYK is an abbreviation for *c*yan, *m*agenta, *y*ellow, and blac*k,* the common ink colors used in inkjet printers.

✔ You don't always have to print in color with an inkjet printer! You can also just print in black ink, which saves the (often spendy) color cartridge from running low. The Print dialog box (covered later in this chapter) often has an option that lets you choose whether you want to print with color or black ink.

✔ When the laser printer first warns you that `Toner [is] low,` you can get a few more pages from it by gently rocking the toner cartridge. Rock it back and forth the short way (not end to end), which helps redistribute the toner dust.

✔ Buy rubber gloves (or those cheap plastic gloves that make you look like Batman) and use them when changing an ink or toner cartridge.

✔ Another option for an empty laser printer toner cartridge is recharging. You can take it to a special place that cleans the old cartridge and refills it with fresh new toner. This process works and is often cheaper than buying a whole new cartridge.

✔ Never let your printer toner get low or ink cartridges go dry. You may think that squeezing every last drop of ink saves you money, but it's not good for the printer.

Feeding your printer, Part II: Paper

Next to consuming ink, printers eat paper. Fortunately, paper isn't as expensive as ink, so it doesn't bankrupt you to churn through a ream or two. The only issue is where to feed in the paper. Like feeding a baby, there is a right end and a wrong end.

The paper goes into a feeder tray either near the printer's bottom or sticking out the top.

Laser printers require you to fill a cartridge with paper, similar to the way a copy machine works. Slide the cartridge all the way into the printer after it's loaded up.

Confirm that you're putting the paper in the proper way, either face down or face up. Note which side is the top. Most printers have little pictures on them that tell you how the paper goes into the printer. Here's how those symbols translate into English:

 ✔ The paper goes in face down, top side up.

 ✔ The paper goes in face down, top side down.

✔ The paper goes in face up, top side up.

 ✔ The paper goes in face up, top side down.

This info helps you when you're loading things such as checks for use with personal finance software. If the printer doesn't tell you which way is up, write *Top* on a sheet of paper and run it through the printer. Then draw your own icon, similar to those shown above, that help you orient the pages you manually insert into the printer.

Always make sure that you have enough printer paper. Buying too much isn't a sin.

Types of paper

There's really no such thing as a typical sheet of paper. Paper comes in different sizes, weights (degrees of thickness), colors, styles, textures, and, I assume, flavors.

The best general-purpose paper to get is standard photocopier paper. If you want better results from your inkjet printer, getting specific inkjet paper works best, though you pay more for that paper. The higher-quality (and spendy) inkjet paper is really good for printing colors; the paper is specially designed to absorb the ink well.

At the high end of the spectrum are specialty papers, such as photographic papers that come in smooth or glossy finishes, transparencies, and iron-on T-shirt transfers. Just ensure that the paper you get is made for your type of printer.

✔ Some printers are capable of handling larger-size paper, such as legal or tabloid sizes. If so, make sure that you load the paper properly and tell your application that you're using a different-size sheet of paper. The File⇨Page Setup command is responsible for selecting paper size.

✔ Avoid thick papers because they get jammed inside the printer. (They can't turn corners well.)

✔ Avoid using erasable bond and other fancy dusted papers in your printer. These papers have talcum powder coatings that gum up the works.

✔ Don't let the expensive paper ads fool you: Your inkjet printer can print on just about any type of paper. Even so, the pricey paper *does* produce a better image.

✔ My favorite type of inkjet paper is *laser paper.* It has a polished look to it and a subtle waxy feel.

Setting Up Your Beloved Printer

Printers are one of the easiest devices to set up and configure. After freeing the printer from its box, and from various pieces of tape and evil Styrofoam, locate the printer's power cable. Then locate the printer cable, the one that connects the printer to the console.

A-ha! The printer didn't come with a printer-to-console cable, did it? It doesn't. You have to buy one extra. I recommend getting a USB cable if the printer is USB-happy. Otherwise, buy a standard, bidirectional PC printer cable. Refer to Chapter 3 for information on plugging things in.

Refer to the printer's instruction sheet to see whether you first need to install software before turning the printer on. Otherwise, turn the printer on. A USB printer is instantly recognized and configured by Windows.

Printers using the traditional printer cable, or network printers, require more work. See the section "Manually adding a printer," later in this chapter.

Most printers, like computers, can now be left on all the time. The printer automatically slips into a low-power sleep mode when it's no longer needed. However, if you don't print often (at least every day), it's perfectly fine to turn off your printer.

✔ I recommend placing the printer near the console, about an arm's length away.

✔ Some USB printers demand to be directly connected to the computer, not plugged into a USB hub.

✔ You can connect a number of printers to a single computer. As long as the computer has a second printer port or uses another USB port or even the network, multiple printers work fine.

Windows and Your Printer

The printing action in Windows happens inside the Printers and Faxes window (see Figure 12-2). To get there, open the Printers and Faxes icon inside the Control Panel. Or, more quickly, you can choose the Printers and Faxes command from the Start button's menu (though it may not be there).

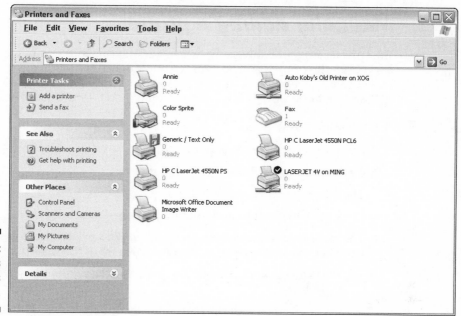

Figure 12-2:
The Printers and Faxes window.

The Printers and Faxes window lists all printing devices attached or available to your computer. Here's a smattering of what you may see:

 The default printer: This is the printer Windows uses automatically — the primary, or first, printer — which Windows calls the *default* printer. You can always spy this printer because of the check mark in a circle.

 The fax machine: This icon represents your PC's fax modem — if you have one. Sending a fax works just like printing.

 A shared printer: Printers with the sharing hand icon are connected to your PC, but are available for use by others on the network.

A network printer: Printers with plumbing beneath them exist elsewhere on the network. You can use them just like any other printer, but it's a walk to get your document after it prints.

The printer icon is generic. All printers appear in the Printers and Faxes window using the same icon, so you cannot really tell what type of printer it is by looking at its icon in the window.

Manually adding a printer

Your printer was probably set up when you first ran your computer. Windows asks about the printer, and you answer a few questions, and then it's done. But when you need to add another printer, especially a non-network or non-USB printer, more work is involved. It's not difficult — just heed these steps:

1. **Open the Printers and Faxes folder.**

   Refer to the preceding section.

2. **Choose File⇨Add Printer from the menu.**

   The Add Printer Wizard starts.

3. **Click the Next button and follow the wizard's directions.**

   The steps that follow vary, depending on your printer. Here are my words of wisdom to help you through the rest of the wizard:

   • Let the network administrator worry about connecting network printers.

   • Don't bother with the Plug and Play option; Windows has already recognized any Plug and Play printers.

   • The printer is most likely connected to the first printer port, code named LPT1.

   • If your printer came with its own CD, you may need to install programs from that CD to begin or finish the printer installation. Refer to the documentation that came with the CD.

4. **The final installation step is to print a test page on your printer.**

   When the printer is connected properly and everything is up to snuff, you see that gratifying test page print.

You can now start using that printer. Its icon appears in the Printers and Faxes window.

Setting the default printer

When your PC is connected to, or has access to, multiple printers, you can pick and choose which one you want to print on each time you go to print something. The option to choose a printer is available in any Print dialog box, as covered in the following section.

When you don't choose a printer, Windows uses what it calls the *default* printer. To set one of the printers as the default, follow these steps:

1. **Open the Printers and Faxes window, as covered earlier in this chapter, in the section "Windows and Your Printer."**

2. **Click the printer you plan to use most often.**

3. **Choose File⇨Set As Default Printer.**

The tiny check mark on the printer's icon confirms that you've set the default printer.

You can change the default printer at any time by repeating these steps.

Basic Printer Operation

Under Windows, printing is a snap. All applications support the same print command: Choose File⇨Print from the menu, click OK in the Print dialog box (see Figure 12-3), and — zit-zit-zit — you soon have hard copy.

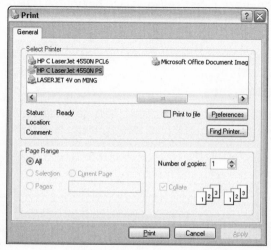

Figure 12-3:
A typical
Print
dialog box.

The Print dialog box shown in Figure 12-3 is typical for most programs. To print the entire document, just click the Print button. Otherwise, you can use the settings in the dialog box to change what and how you print.

For example, you can choose another printer from the list of available printers. Or, you can set the number of pages to print (Page Range) and the number of copies printed.

The Print dialog box may sport a Properties, Settings, or Options button that lets you set other, more specific aspects of printing and control how the printer works. For example, options to set whether printing happens in color or grayscale, determine how to render graphics, and choose which paper tray to use can be found by clicking an Options or Properties button.

- ✔ The common keyboard shortcut for the Print command is Ctrl+P.

- ✔ Rather than waste paper, consider using the File⇨Print Preview command instead. That command displays a sneak peek of what's to be printed so you can examine the printers output before wasting a sheet of paper.

- ✔ Many applications sport a Print toolbar icon. If so, you can click that button to quickly print your document.

- ✔ The Print toolbar icon doesn't summon the Print dialog box. It just prints the entire document. To summon the Print dialog box, you must use Ctrl+P or choose File⇨Print from the menu.

"Where do I set my margins?"

The Print dialog box is only concerned with printing, not with formatting. Setting margins, paper size, and other aspects of what is to be printed is handled elsewhere in a program, usually in a Page Setup dialog box, as shown in Figure 12-4.

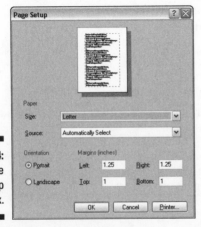

Figure 12-4:
The Page
Setup
dialog box.

To access the Page Setup dialog box, choose File⇨Page Setup from the menu. As with the Print dialog box, each application's Page Setup dialog box is different, with commands not always in the same location.

- ✔ The Page Setup dialog box is where you set things like margins, paper size, and so forth — not in the Print dialog box.
- ✔ Two options worth looking at in the Page Setup dialog box are Portrait and Landscape. *Portrait* is the normal way documents print; *Landscape* is printing "sideways," or with the long edge of the paper on top.
- ✔ Use the Page Setup dialog box to choose between Letter, Legal, and a number of other paper sizes. Be sure to stock the printer with that same size of paper as well.
- ✔ Note that printers cannot print on an entire sheet of paper. There's usually a small margin around the sheet or just on one end of the paper, where no printing can take place. That's the part of the page that's held by the printer's paper-feeding mechanism, and its size and location vary from printer to printer.

Printing in reverse order

When you have a printer that spits out its sheets of paper face up, notice that the sheets are always in reverse order. That is, Page 1 is on the bottom of the stack, and the last page is on the top. Rather than constantly reshuffle your pages, why not let the computer do the work?

Most programs give you the ability to print in reverse order. For example, in Microsoft Word, you click the Options button in the Print dialog box. In the next dialog box that appears, put a check mark by the item labeled Reverse Print Order. Click the OK button and then click the Print button to have your document print perfectly.

Printing in reverse order isn't a printer feature; it's part of the program you use. Some programs have that feature, and others don't.

Stop, printer! Stop!

The most frustrating printer experience you can have is wanting the dumb thing to stop printing. It happens. Often.

The easiest way to stop printing is to look on the printer's control panel for a Cancel button. Click that button, and all printing stops. Oh, a few more lines may print and a half-written page gets ejected from the printer, but that's it.

If you have an older printer (or just a cheap one) without a Cancel button, do this:

1. **Open the Printers and Faxes window.**

2. **Open your printer's icon.**

   The printer's window is displayed, similar to what's shown in Figure 12-5.

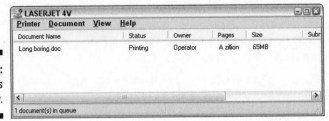

Figure 12-5:
A printer's
window.

3. **Click to select the document you want to cancel.**

4. **Choose Document⇨Cancel from the menu.**

   Or, if you want to cancel all pending documents, choose Printer⇨ Cancel All Documents.

5. **Wait.**

It may take a few moments for the last bit of text to print. But, seriously, if the printer continues to spew out pages at this point, just turn it off. Wait a few seconds, and then turn it back on again.

Chapter 13

The Mighty Morphin' Power Modem

Time was that the computer modem was an obscure peripheral. I'm not kidding! With the dawn of the Internet, and the popularity of the Web and e-mail, the once neglected modem moved from an optional extra to a vital part of every computer. The big deal is *communications*. In fact, it's the modem that brought the world of the Internet to the desktop computer, and that's what helped bring more desktop computers into homes and the workplace.

Modems are no longer considered optional components in a PC. Not only that, modems are so common that they now sport first names: dial-up, DSL, cable, and satellite. Obviously, modems are important; hence, this whole chapter covers the big deal with modems.

What Does a Modem Do?

The main reason for having a modem now is to get your computer connected to the Internet. In fact, that would be the cheap description: The *modem* is the box through which your PC yells at the Internet and from which the Internet yells back. Simple enough.

The modem's secret job, the one it would have if it were a superhero, is *translator*. What it does is transform the crude language of ones and zeroes inside the computer into something that can be sent out over the phone lines, over your cable TV wire, or even straight up into outer space. Then, at the other end of the line, another modem retranslates those signals into information the computer can understand, and — long story short — you have two computers talking with each other.

The modem does its job so well that it doesn't even have any buttons on it, other than maybe an on–off switch (if that). Modems do, however, have lights. The lights let you know that the computer is on, connected, transmitting information, and other various things.

- *Modem* is a combination of two words: *mod*ulator and *dem*odulator. No one really cares about the further, technical details.

- As with all PC hardware, you need software to control the PC's modem. Modem software is now mainly used to get the modem to connect with the Internet.

- High-speed modems don't modulate or demodulate any more. Those modems communicate entirely with digital signals.

- It's still possible to use dial-up modems as they were used throughout the early part of PC history: You can use your modem to dial into another PC, as long as that PC is set up with a modem to answer the phone and provide software to give you something to do. Various online BBS and personal systems still exist in many cities, though the number is rapidly dwindling. The telecommunications program in Windows is called HyperTerminal, and it can be found on the Start button's All Programs⇨Accessories⇨Communications menu.

Types of Modem

On TV and in the movies, they typically show the old acoustic coupler type of modem, the kind in which you would rest a telephone handset. One is shown in the popular movie *WarGames*. It's a great visual, but those modems were horrible! They picked up too many sounds from the room, and, because the phone company stopped making standard telephones, few phone handsets would fit into the old acoustic couplers. Thank goodness those days are over.

The modems of today are difficult to recognize on sight. I can't really provide a generic description. Some are expansion cards dwelling inside the computer, and others are uninspired beige or gray boxes sitting outside the computer. There are, however, two distinct modem categories:

- Dial-up
- Broadband

Dial-up is the traditional type of modem that uses the telephone system. *Broadband* includes all high-speed modems, whether they're cable, DSL, or satellite modems. These are discussed in this section.

The traditional dial-up modem

Dial-up modems are called such because they use standard telephone lines to transmit and receive information. That's the way modems worked for years, and it was the only type of modem available to personal computer users until cable and DSL came around in the late 1990s.

Nearly all PCs sold come with a dial-up modem preinstalled. The modem circuitry is either part of the chipset on the motherboard, or it dwells in an expansion slot, with its circuitry living on an expansion card. This type of modem is known as an *internal* modem because it dwells inside the PC's bosom. *External* dial-up modems are available as well, which live in a box outside the console, though they're rapidly becoming more rare.

Whether internal or external, dial-up modems assume one of the PC's serial or COM ports. That's the interface through which the modem communicates with the rest of the computer.

The advantages of a dial-up modem are that you can use them anywhere that you have telephone service. Simply plug the modem into the wall, and you can make phone calls with the computer just as you can yourself. No extra charges apply (well, other than long distance or other standard phone fees). Also, dial-up is the least expensive way to get on the Internet.

The disadvantage of a dial-up modem is that it's slow when compared to other ways of accessing the Internet.

 ✔ Computer geeks may refer to a dial-up modem as being *narrowband,* which is play on the term broadband (for faster modems).

 ✔ The plain old telephone system modem is also known as a *POTS* modem. POTS stands for Plain Old Telephone System.

Faster than a speeding phone bill: Broadband modems

High-speed modems fall under the category of *broadband* modems. These modems use a special means to connect to the Internet at top speeds. Their only downside is that you must live in an area that provides broadband service and you pay more for access than you do with a dial-up modem.

Three common broadband services are available: cable, DSL, and satellite. Each comes with its own type of modem.

Cable: This type of modem is the fastest you can buy, often faster than the computer can keep up with! The only downside is that when more of your neighbors begin using their cable modems, the overall speed decreases. But at 2 a.m., your cable modem *smokes!*

DSL: This type of modem gives you fast access by taking advantage of unused frequencies in existing phone lines. The modem hooks up to the phone line, but all other phones on that line require special filters. This type is easy to install and, next to cable, gives you the fastest connection speeds.

Satellite: Combined with an outdoor antenna and a subscription to the satellite service, this is one of the fastest modem options available. Try to get a satellite modem that provides both sending and receiving abilities. Avoid satellite service that is "download only."

Regardless of the broadband service, you pay more for the extra speed than you do with dial-up. First, you pay for the modem itself (though many are "free"). This isn't bad because DSL modems cost about $100 and most cable companies rent their modems. Satellite modems, however, are spendy because they also include the satellite dish and its hardware.

Second, you have to pay the company that provides the service: your phone company for DSL, your cable company for cable, and your satellite company for a satellite modem. They may offer various speed levels at different prices; the faster the speed, the more you pay. But if you use the Internet a lot, it's worth it!

✔ Broadband is synonymous with high-speed Internet access.

✔ DSL stands for Digital Subscriber Line. It has variations, such as ADSL and other *something*-DSL options. Your phone company knows more about this matter than I do. Basically, everyone calls it DSL, no matter what.

Modem speed

Modem speed is measured in *kilobits per second.* That's kilo*bits,* not kilo*bytes.* To give you an idea of how fast that is, 100 kilobits is about as much information as you see on a line of text in this book. If this book were appearing on

What's a null modem?

A *null modem* isn't a modem at all. In fact, it's either a tiny adapter or a cable that works like a standard serial port (COM) cable, but with its wires reversed. Also called *twisted pair,* a null modem is designed to connect two computers for direct communications.

For example, if you're moving files from an older PC to a newer system and the older system lacks network access or a CD-R (both of which make transferring files easier), you can purchase a null modem cable at an office supply store along with file transfer software and use them to send files between the two systems.

your screen through your modem, one line per second, you would have a connection that flies by at 100 *kilobits per second,* or 100 Kbps.

The slowest modem you can buy now is a dial-up model that whizzes out information at 56 Kbps. That modem can transmit approximately 14 pages of printed information every second.

The fastest modem you can buy (or rent) is a cable modem that whizzes along at 5,000 Kbps, also written as 5 Mbps (megabits per second). That's many, many pages of information per second, or enough speed to display a real-time video image with sound.

- ✔ A modem's speed rating is for comparison purposes only. Rarely do modems crank out information as fast as they're rated. It happens, but rarely. For example, a 56 Kbps dial-up modem usually chugs along at about 48 Kbps. That's normal.

- ✔ Values over 1,000 Kbps may be written as 1 Mbps, or 1 megabit per second. Sometimes, the M and K are written in lowercase: kbps and mbps.

- ✔ For dial-up modems, the connection speed is displayed by Windows whenever the modem connects. You can also point the mouse at the tiny modem icon on the system tray to see your connection speed.

- ✔ You can gauge your broadband modem speed online by visiting a site such as www.dslreports.com.

Installing a Modem

Setting up a modem is so easy that most elected officials can do it in a matter of days. You can do it faster, of course, an individual who is unused to making decisions in committee.

Connecting the modem to the console

Modems are easy to connect to the computer: Dial-up modems connect to the telephone jack on the wall; broadband modems connect to the network port, or RJ-45 jack. For more details, refer to Chapter 3.

✔ Cable, DSL, and satellite modems are external, so they all must be plugged into a wall socket somewhere. As a suggestion, I recommend plugging them into a UPS, which helps keep their signals going during intermittent power outages.

✔ Generally speaking, broadband modems are left on all the time. There's no point in turning them on or off. In fact, doing so may cause the broadband service to phone you up to see whether everything is okay.

✔ Be sure to put the filters, or "dongles," on each phone that shares the line with the DSL modem. If you don't, you have difficulty hearing phone conversations on that line.

Telling Windows about your dial-up modem

Windows automatically recognizes USB and certain internal modems. For external modems and those few unruly internal modems, you must manually set things up. That's done by opening the Phone and Modem Options icon in the Control Panel and then clicking the Modems tab.

To manually add a new modem, click the Add button on the Modems tab in the Phone and Modem Options dialog box. That runs one of the Windows wizards; work through the wizard to have it detect and install your modem.

My advice is to *not* have the wizard automatically detect your modem; just select it from the list of manufacturers and models or use the CD that came with the modem.

After installation, the modem is ready for use in Windows. Its name appears on the list of modems in the Phone and Modem Options dialog box.

- ✔ The best way to use a modem is with its own phone line. Just about every house or apartment can have a second line added without having to pay for extra wiring. If so, have your phone company hook up that line and use it for your modem. Why? Because —

- ✔ You can't use your phone while your modem is talking. In fact, if somebody picks up another extension on that line, it garbles the signal and may lose your connection — not to mention that the human hears a horrid screeching sound. Also see the section "Dialing Rules from Here to Eternity," later in this chapter.

- ✔ If Windows ever seems to lose track of your modem, restart your PC. Often, that helps Windows find a lost modem. If you have an external dial-up modem, turn it off and then on again, and Windows may suddenly find it.

Telling Windows about your broadband modem

Broadband modems are really more of a networking thing than a modem thing. As such, the broadband modem is configured when you set up your computer for the Internet. The best place to look for that information is in Chapter 18.

Dialing Rules from Here to Eternity

When you think about it, the telephone system is rather smart. Witness that there's no Enter key on your telephone. The phone system is smart enough to know when you dial a local, long distance, or even international number. It just knows!

The universal broadband modem fix

Broadband modems are fairly robust and reliable, but they do occasionally go down. An easy and simple fix is to turn your modem off, wait, and then turn it back on again. Often, that supplies the kick necessary to get the modem up and running.

A dial-up modem also needs to know about dialing local and long distance numbers. But, unlike the telephone, your modem needs to be instructed about certain things so that it can properly deal with them. This section provides some hints and helpful examples.

Setting a location for your dial-up modem

Your modem needs to know a little bit about how to dial phone numbers. Even if you don't plan to dial any other number than the one you use to connect to the Internet, it's a good idea to follow these steps:

1. **Open the Control Panel's Phone and Modem Options icon.**

2. **If no location is entered, click the New button to create a new location; otherwise, select the current location and click the Edit button.**

   Either way, a dialog box similar to the one shown in Figure 13-1 appears.

Figure 13-1:
Set dial-up modem rules here.

3. **Type a name for your location.**

   My favorite name is "In my chair," but most folks put "Home" or "Office" or "Las Vegas Office" for when they're supposed to be working but are really gambling.

4. **Fill in the rest of the material on the General tab, as necessary.**

    Choose your country or region and enter the area code for your location's phone number or the area code for the line you're dialing out on (if your locality has more than one area code).

    Optionally, enter the numbers to disable call waiting, if you have call waiting on the modem's phone line. Specify Tone or Pulse.

    If you plan to phone more than just your ISP with the modem, you may want to enter information on the Area Code Rules tab in the Location dialog box. If you plan on staying put, you're pretty much done now.

5. **Click OK.**

You need to specify only the most basic information for your dial-up modem, especially if you plan to keep the computer in one spot and only dial into the Internet.

Laptop computers are an exception to the one-location rule. For information on properly configuring a laptop computer to dial from multiple locations, refer to my best-selling tome *Laptops For Dummies* (Wiley Publishing, Inc.), available at fine bookstores all over, as well as at Barnes & Noble.

Dealing with call waiting

Call waiting is a handy feature to have for humans, but it can knock a computer's modem offline faster than you can clear a room by saying "I'm with Amway." Technically, the call waiting tone is what disrupts the modem connection.

The best way to disable call waiting is described in the preceding subsection's Step 4: Put a check mark by the item labeled To Disable Call Waiting. Then specify the proper code for your area, either *70 or 70#, or 1170 for pulse dialing.

You don't need to worry about call waiting when you're using a broadband modem.

Another way to deal with call waiting is to use software that lets you hear who's calling you while you're online. Visit www.callwave.com or www.buzme.com for more information on that type of product.

Dealing with "local" long distance

Phone companies seem to delight in forcing us to dial our own area codes for *local long distance*. To deal with this situation, use the Area Code Rules tab in the Edit Location dialog box (refer to Figure 13-1). Click the New button to display the New Area Code Rule dialog box, and then fill in the items required for dialing area codes that are required for your part of the country. That's it — well, at least until the next time they change the rules.

Chapter 14

Sounds Like

*T*he hills are alive, with the sound of PC. . . .

Way back when, computer manufacturers often debated whether their new machines should have a speaker. Even the cheapest speakers added cost to the product. In the end, the voice of the users spoke the loudest: They wanted computers that made sound!

The early PCs had speakers and simple sound-generation hardware. Later, at about the time of the multimedia craze of the early 1990s, PCs came with built-in synthesizers and quite fancy sound-generating circuitry. That's all pretty standard on PCs now, as well as quality stereo speakers and those all-important subwoofers. This chapter covers the whole spectrum of PC sound in as quiet a manner as possible.

Your PC Can Make Noise

Your PC makes noise by using a sound system composed of many parts, both hardware and software. In a way, the sound system is similar to the video system: The speakers, like the monitor, are only the external parts. Much more goes on inside the console, as discussed in this section.

Noisy hardware

A PC includes sound-generation hardware on its chipset, which comes soldered to the motherboard. The sound hardware includes the ability to process and play digitally recorded sounds, CD music, as well as an on-board synthesizer for generating music. For most folks, it's about all you really need in order to use the computer, play games, listen to music, and have some fun.

More advanced sound hardware can be added to any PC via an expansion card. This sound upgrade is necessary only for diehard audiophiles, people who are composing their own music or are using their PCs as the heart of their audio studios. Otherwise, the sound hardware that comes on the chipset is just hunky and dory for everyone.

- ✔ The standard for PC audio is the SoundBlaster series of audio cards, manufactured by Creative Labs. Nearly all PC sound hardware is now Sound Blaster compatible.

- ✔ Standard PC sound is sampled at 16 bits. All you need to know is that 16 bits is a great rate, much better than 8 bits. Yes, 32 bits are available, but are necessary only for those interested in high-end audio work.

- ✔ If your PC lacks expansion slots, you can upgrade your audio by adding an external, USB sound device, such as the Sound Blaster Audigy system. This is one way to add better sound to a laptop computer.

Speakers here and there

Most PCs come with a tiny, awful internal speaker. It's a backup. It exists just in case you don't connect external speakers to the system. That way, in an act of typical computer desperation, the thing can meekly *bleep* at you. Sad, but true.

On the other hand, your PC most likely came with external stereo speakers. If not, or if the quality was just too crude for your refined tastes, you can upgrade the speakers to include a subwoofer or maybe even surround sound. Golly! The things you can spend money on these days. . . .

Figure 14-1 illustrates a typical PC speaker setup. Note that the left and right speakers are positioned on the left and right sides of the monitor as you're facing the monitor.

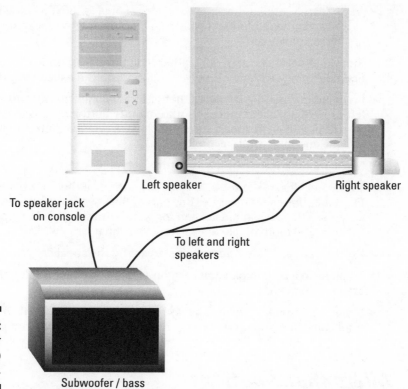

Figure 14-1:
PC speaker
setup
(maybe).

Left speaker

Right speaker

To speaker jack
on console

To left and right
speakers

Subwoofer / bass

In Figure 14-1, the sound output from the console goes first to the subwoofer and then to the left and right speakers. Sometimes the sound goes into one of the speakers first, and then into the subwoofer. And, sometimes the left speaker is wired directly to the right speaker (or vice versa). In other words, there is no standard for connecting speakers. Typical.

One step beyond the left-right-subwoofer speaker configuration is Dolby surround sound, similar to the sound setup for a home theater. In that configuration, left, right, *and* center speakers are by the computer. Behind it, you have left and right surround speakers. A subwoofer completes the system.

The Dolby surround sound is necessary only when both the PC's hardware and software support it. There are two standards: Dolby 5.1, which supports five speakers and one subwoofer; and Dolby 6.1, which adds a sixth speaker, rear-center.

✔ Any cheap-o set of stereo speakers works on a PC. If you enjoy listening to music on the computer, I would pay more and get a nicer set of speakers and a subwoofer.

✔ Run your speakers electrically rather than through batteries. If your speakers didn't come with an AC power adapter, you can usually buy one.

✔ I recommend getting speakers that have a volume control, either on the left or right speaker. Another bonus: a mute button on the speaker. Note that some high-end speaker systems have a remote control that has the volume and mute buttons on it.

✔ Speakers built into the PC's monitor are typically terrible.

✔ *Subwoofer?* It's a speaker box, typically sitting on the floor beneath your PC. It amplifies sounds at the low end of the spectrum. Subwoofers give oomph to the bass in music, and for games, they truly add emphasis to the horde of football players sacking your quarterback.

✔ Refer to Chapter 3 to find out where exactly the speakers plug in.

✔ If you have a DVD expansion card on your PC, be sure to plug the speakers into that card.

✔ Refer to my book *Troubleshooting Your PC For Dummies* (Wiley Publishing, Inc.) if you're having trouble hearing sounds from your PC.

Microphone options

Any cheesy microphone works on a PC. If sound quality is important to you and you're using your PC as a digital audio studio, you have to spend money on microphones and mixers and all that. But if that's not you, any old microphone does the trick.

✔ Two popular types of microphones are used on a PC: condenser and dynamic. *Condenser* mics can be plugged right into the PC's mic jack. *Dynamic* microphones require amplification and may work when plugged into the Line In jack, but may require a pre-amplifier for them to work best.

✔ If you plan to use voice over the Internet or dictation, get a microphone-headset combination. That way, you can chatter without having to mess with holding the microphone or setting up a mic stand near your PC.

Having Fun with Sound in Windows

If you have time to waste, you can turn your serious business computer into a goofy business computer by adding sounds to Windows. This is one area where you can waste eons of time. Of course, keep in mind that this is Important Computer Configuration, not something you're having fun with.

The types of files that contain noise

Sound recorded on a computer is merely raw data — digital information recorded on a hard drive as opposed to analog information you find on a cassette tape. Like other data, sound is kept in a file. Three primary types of audio files are used for the PC: WAV, MP3, and MIDI.

WAV: This is a basic *wave,* or audio, file, which simply contains a digital sound sampling. Most sounds you hear in Windows, or even sounds you record yourself, are WAV files, pronounced "wave" files.

MP3: These special compressed WAV files take up less space on disk. A typical MP3 file occupies 1MB of disk space for every minute of sound contained inside. These files contain mostly audio tracks from CDs or other sound sources; any type of sound can find its way into the MP3 format.

MIDI: This synthesized music file format doesn't contain sound. Instead, the MIDI ("MIH-dee") files contain instructions that are read by the sound hardware's synthesizer, which then plays back the song as a musician would read sheet music.

You can find other sound file formats, such as AU and AIFF and too many more to mention. The three in the preceding list are the most popular with Windows.

- ✔ Windows keeps its sound files in the My Music folder, which you find inside the My Documents folder. See Chapter 21 for more information on folders.

- ✔ MIDI stands for Musical Instrument Digital Interface. It's the standard for electronically generated music.

- ✔ Software exists to record sounds as well as convert the sounds from one file format to another. One useful and free program I can recommend is Audacity, a free digital audio editor:

```
http://audacity.sourceforge.net/
```

- ✔ By the way, sound files take up huge amounts of room on a disk. That's why most digitized sounds are limited to short bursts, like golf swings and grunts.

Playing sounds in Windows

Playing any sound file in Windows is easy: Just double-click to open the file. The sound plays in the Windows Media Player program. Use the controls in Media Player to start, stop, and repeat the audio files you open. Media Player works just like a stereo or CD player, and the buttons are labeled the same.

✔ See Chapter 24 for information on creating playlists of music in Media Player.

✔ A great alternative to Media Player is the MUSICMATCH Jukebox program, available from `www.musicmatch.com`.

The Windows sounds playground

You can assign sounds to various events, actions, or things you do inside the Windows operating system. The playground where that happens is the Sounds and Audio Devices Properties dialog box, found on any Control Panel near you:

1. **Open the Control Panel's Sounds and Audio Devices icon.**

2. **Click the Sounds tab.**

   The dialog box sports a scrolling list of events, which are various things done by Windows or your applications. You can apply a specific sound to any of those events so that when such-and-such an event takes place, a specific sound is played.

   For example, the Critical Stop event — a bad one in Windows — is highlighted in Figure 14-2. The sound associated with that event appears on the Sounds drop-down list as `Windows XP Critical Stop.wav`. That's the WAV file that plays when Windows stops critically.

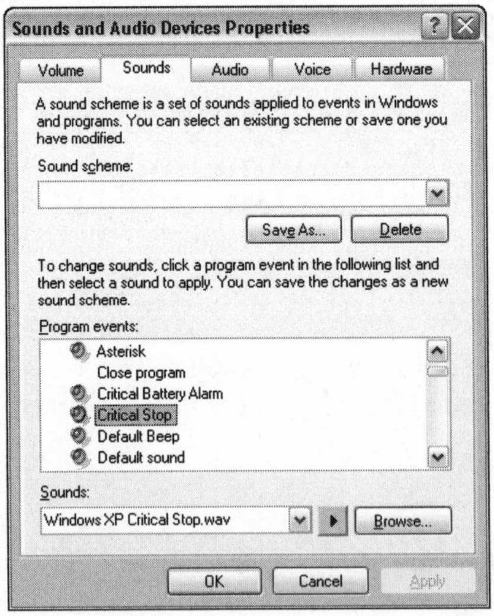

Figure 14-2:
Assigning sounds to events.

3. **Select an event to assign a sound to.**

   For example, select the New Mail Notification, which is the sound that plays when Outlook Express picks up new e-mail.

4. **Test the current sound, if any.**

To test the sound, click the Play button.

5. **Assign a new sound.**

To assign a new sound to an event, click the Browse button. That lets you "go out on disk" to seek out a specific sound.

You can also choose from one of the preselected sounds on the Sounds drop-down list (where `Windows XP Critical Stop.wav` appears in Figure 14-2).

6. **Click the OK button when you're done assigning sounds.**

Windows comes with various sound schemes. Each one has a whole set of assigned sounds, specific to the theme of the sound scheme. That way, you can select a whole symphony of sounds at one time by choosing a scheme from the Scheme drop-down list.

You can create your own, personalized sound scheme by saving your particular favorite sounds as their own scheme. To do this, after assigning your individual sounds, click the Save As button in the Sounds and Audio Devices Properties dialog box, on the Sounds tab. Give the scheme a name and then click OK. That way, you can instantly recover your favorite sounds by choosing that same scheme again.

✔ To remove a sound from an event, choose (None) from the top of the Sounds drop-down list.

✔ If you can't find an event on the list, you cannot assign a sound to it.

✔ The Sounds and Audio Devices Properties dialog box is used to assign *sounds* to events — specifically, WAV files. Windows isn't equipped to play MIDI or MP3 files for certain events.

✔ The best source for sounds is the Internet, where you can find Web page libraries full of sound samples. Go to Google (`www.google.com/`) and search for "Windows WAV file sounds" to find them.

✔ See the section "Recording Your Own Sounds," later in this chapter, for more information about recording sounds.

Adjusting the volume

Determining how loud your PC plays sounds is done in two places. The first place is a hardware place: the sound volume knob on your PC's speakers or on the subwoofer — though that's only when such a knob exists.

The second spot for adjusting the volume is the Volume icon, found on the system tray. It looks like a tiny speaker.

To set the volume, click the Volume icon once. Use the slider in the pop-up window to increase (up) or decrease (down) the volume. Or, just click the slider bar to get an idea of how loud the sound is set now.

To mute the sound, click to put a check mark in the Mute box.

Click anywhere else on the desktop to make the pop-up window go away.

If the Volume thingy doesn't appear on the system tray, open the Control Panel's Sounds and Audio Devices icon. Click the Volume tab and click to put a check mark next to the option labeled Place Volume Icon in the Taskbar.

Using the master volume control

To specifically control the volume or individual sound-producing devices, you need to use what I call the master volume control, as shown in Figure 14-3. It's where you can set the volume for various types of sound sources in Windows, mute specific sources, or adjust stereo settings. It's powerful and mysterious, like that special flavor ingredient that makes you crave KFC.

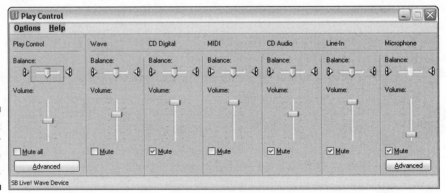

Figure 14-3:
The master volume control.

The master volume control displays a whole window full of squeaking and squawking things in Windows, each with its own volume setting slider and Mute button. Set things individually as you see fit.

For example, if you detest having MIDI music play while you're on the Internet (or anywhere), just mute that one item. All other sounds in your system continue to play, but MIDI sounds are muted.

✔ Yes, I know that the window is named Play Control in Figure 14-3, but I prefer calling it the master volume control. Someday, Microsoft will see the light and agree with me on this subject.

✔ Use the Options⇨Properties command to set which sound-producing devices in your PC appear in the volume master control window.

Recording Your Own Sounds

Thanks to the sound input jacks on the PC's console, you can use your computer to record any type of sound. All you need is a *patch cable* to connect a sound-producing device to the audio inputs on your PC.

✔ To record your own voice, plug a microphone into the Mic In or amplified line-input jack.

✔ To record from any other device, plug it into the Line In or unamplified input jack.

On the software side, you need a program that lets you record from the sound circuitry inputs. I recommend the Audacity program (mentioned earlier in this chapter). Windows also has a silly little program that does this, named Sound Recorder.

Recording software on the computer works just like using a tape recording in the real world. To record, you prepare the sound source or get ready at the microphone, and then you click a Record button on the screen (generally, a red dot). To stop recording, click the Stop button (a black square). To hear the sound, use the Play button (a triangle).

Save your work to disk by choosing the File⇨Save As command, just as you would with any file in any application.

✔ I say that Sound Recorder is silly because it lets you record only one minute of sound at a time. To record for longer than a minute, refer to this Web page: www.wambooli.com/help/pc/sound_recorder/.

✔ Sound files are huge! Although playing and collecting sounds is fun, be aware that they occupy lots of disk space.

Getting the PC to Talk and Listen

Sound. Speakers. Microphone. Perhaps the day you can actually yell at the PC and have it be moved by your passion isn't too far away. Until then, consider this section on the state of the PC's cybernetic mouth and ears.

Can it talk?

Your PC is more than capable of speaking. The sound card can be programmed to emulate the human voice, usually by running some voice utility that came with the sound card. Sadly, if your PC lacks such a program, few other good alternatives are available.

Windows XP comes with a speech program named Narrator. Rather than a toy, however, Narrator is designed to be a tool to assist the visually impaired with using a computer. To run Narrator, from the Start panel choose the Programs command and then Accessories➪Accessibility➪Narrator. The program starts, and begins by immediately reading the window it starts in. To close Narrator, keep closing its windows until it's gone.

Does it listen?

Some programs let you talk to your PC. You talk, and the program fairly accurately interprets your speech as text right on the screen. The technology has been available for about 10 years now, yet it's still crude, in my opinion.

Eats till Vera crew din Maya pinion.

The biggest problem with dictation is that you must train the computer to understand your voice. It requires — at minimum — three hours of reading aloud into the computer while it analyzes your speech patterns. (That's a long time; keep a glass of water handy.) On the plus side, the more you train the PC, the better it gets at interpreting your speech. Do you have the time to invest?

- ✔ Speech recognition software is included with Microsoft Office XP and Office 2003. The programs add two new icons on the Control Panel: Speech and Text Services. Each one controls how the PC communicates, either by reading text or accepting audio input.

- ✔ Another popular dictation package is Dragon Naturally Speaking, at www.scansoft.com.

- ✔ Dictation works best with a headset microphone.

- ✔ People who get the most from dictation software spend at least 9 to 12 hours training the computer to understand them.

- ✔ For a fast typist, such as myself, talking software doesn't really work. I find talking mode and typing mode to be two different things. Also, I change my mind a lot, which means that I'm always editing my own text as I write it, something the dictation software is rather poor at.

Chapter 15

Even More Hardware!

The success of the original IBM PC was due to its openness. The PC's software and hardware documentation were available to anyone who wanted it. By publishing the "specs," IBM encouraged lots of folks to make new hardware and write new software for its fledgling machine. The results paid off, and the PC has since become the most popular computer hardware and software platform ever.

The PC's expandability continues to this day. Thanks to its internal expansion slots and versatile expansion ports, like USB, you can continue to add new goodies to your basic computer system. This chapter covers some of the more popular options, or peripherals, that you can have on your PC.

The Wide, Wide World of Peripherals

Peripheral refers to anything outside the main. For example, the peripheral nervous system is made up of all the nerves in your body outside your brain (which is called the central nervous system). Peripheral vision includes things you can see without looking directly at them. And, peripheral nervous vision is what first-time buyers get when they enter the computer store. On a computer, however, a *peripheral* is any accessory or auxiliary equipment you may buy and connect to the computer.

The variety of peripherals you can buy for your computer is endless. Common peripheral items include scanners, disk drives of all types, digital cameras, videocameras, and numerous other toys you can connect to the typical PC.

- ✔ All peripherals are hardware.

- ✔ Many devices that were once considered peripheral are now considered part of the basic computer system: The mouse and modem, for example, were once optional peripherals.

- ✔ Peripherals enable you to expand your computer system without having to buy a totally new computer. You can add these extra hardware devices yourself or have a guru, computer consultant, or some other overpaid individual do it for you.

- ✔ Although the word *peripheral* refers to things outside a computer, you can also add peripherals *internally* — inside the PC's console. (In a way, peripheral refers to anything beyond what comes standard in the computer.)

Installing a peripheral

The hardware side of adding a peripheral is cinchy. Most peripherals sit outside the PC. All you need to do to connect them is find the proper hole and plug the thing in.

Granted, you need to follow other instructions when adding a peripheral, but plugging the thing into the proper port is usually part of the action.

Because peripherals can also live inside the PC, installing one may involve opening the console and plugging in an expansion card. Again, this process isn't that tough, but it's not the sign of a PC wimp if you pay someone else to do it.

- ✔ Most peripherals plug into standard connectors on the back of every PC. Refer to Chapter 3.

- ✔ USB peripherals are the easiest by far to install. You don't even need to turn off your PC: Just plug in the cable, and you're on your way. Refer to Chapter 7 for the details.

Telling Windows about your new hardware

The yin and yang of your computer are hardware and software. You normally cannot add hardware to the computer without having to do some kind of software addition or adjustment as well. Fortunately, with Windows XP, the software is the easy part; Windows often instantly recognizes new software and sets things up for you automatically.

Regardless of Windows automatic detection, please read the installation instructions that come with any new hardware. Sometimes, nothing else is required, and sometimes, you need to first install special software. How do you know for certain? Read the instruction sheet!

 ✔ The Windows capability to instantly recognize new peripherals is known as *plug and play.*

 ✔ The software that controls your hardware is a *driver.* When someone says "Windows needs a new driver," he's not insulting you as the computer operator.

"Windows is stupid and doesn't recognize my new peripheral!"

In some cases, Windows plays dumb and refuses to recognize new hardware. It could mean that the hardware wasn't properly set up, that the hardware is broken, or, most likely, that you're installing something that doesn't grab the computer's attention directly, such as an external dial-up modem.

 When Windows refuses to recognize the new hardware, you should run the Add Hardware Wizard. Open the Control Panel and then double-click the Add Hardware icon to run the wizard.

As the wizard runs, read the screen. It's important advice! Click the Next button or select options as necessary. In mere moments, your new hardware should be up and running, and everything is groovy.

The Big Decision point in the Add Hardware Wizard is whether to let Windows look for the new hardware or select it yourself from a list. Sometimes, it's tempting to taunt Windows: "Go ahead! Find that hardware! I dare you to find it! I double-dog dare you!" At other times, plucking the device from a list on your own is easier and quicker.

Popular Peripherals

With each edition of this book, the list of popular peripherals grows shorter. It's not that fewer peripherals are being made, it's that more and more things that were once considered peripherals are now standard features on most computers.

For peripheral motivation, you need go no further than your local computer or office supply store. There, you find inspiration lining the aisles, and if not, you can peruse the remaining sections of this chapter for enlightenment.

External disk drives

You can easily expand your system's storage: Just plug in another disk drive! Adding a CD-R, CD-RW, hard drive, DVD, media card reader, or multiple combinations of each one is a snap.

The best way to add external storage is via the USB port. (If your PC lacks a USB port, buy a USB expansion card for $20 and you're in business!) With the USB port, you can add as many external storage devices as your credit card can afford.

One major bonus for external storage devices is that they can survive your current computer setup. For example, my external FireWire hard drive may outlive my current computer and end up plugged into next year's model. That way, I don't have to copy over my software; instead, I just plug in the FireWire drive.

It's live, and it's living on top of your monitor!

An interesting toy to add to your PC is a videocamera. These little mechanical eyeballs perch near your PC, usually on top of the monitor. You can use them to record movies or single images or to send live images over the Internet — it all depends on the software that comes with the camera.

 ✔ If you want one of those cameras that sends pictures to the Web, you want a *Webcam*. I have such a device in my office, which you can view by visiting www.wambooli.com/fun/live/.

 ✔ Note that a difference exists between a cheap little monitor-top videocamera and a digital videocamera used to create movies. I'm not sure what the technical differences are, but pricewise, one is about $50 and the other is about $200 (and up).

 ✔ Make sure that the software you need is included with the camera. For example, videoconferencing is possible only with the proper software. The camera is just a device; you need software to play with it.

Scan this, Mr. Spock!

Scanners are nifty little devices that work like photocopiers. Rather than make a copy, the scanner converts the image into a graphics image that's then stored in your computer. From there, you can modify the image, save it

"I have some money, and I want to upgrade my hardware"

Your computer should last you a good four to six years. At that time, the components start to go: First, the hard drive, and then other things as well. Also, after that length of time, the new technology that's available is so much better than your current computer that it just makes sense to buy something new. In the meantime, you can upgrade some of your computer's components — if you have the money.

The first thing to upgrade is memory. Adding more memory to a PC improves its performance no matter how much memory you have already. Computers just love memory, and the bottom line is always "more is better."

The second thing to upgrade is the hard drive. Rather than replace your PC's existing hard drive, install a second internal drive or add an external USB drive. The extra capacity can be used for storing greedy files, such as music, video, and graphics.

The last thing to spend money on is the microprocessor. Though you can upgrade most PCs' microprocessors, it's not really cost effective. Again, the price of a new computer is often better than forking over a paycheck for the CPU alone.

For more information on upgrading, refer to my book *Buying a Computer For Dummies* (Wiley Publishing, Inc.). That book not only tells you how to upgrade your computer, but also explains how to buy a computer correctly in the first place so that you don't have to worry about upgrading it later.

to disk, add it to a document, or send it off as an e-mail attachment. That's the big picture.

Figure 15-1 illustrates the typical computer scanner, not because you may be unfamiliar with what it looks like, but more because I really like that illustration.

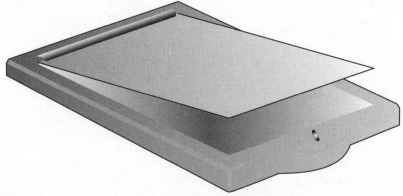

Figure 15-1: A typical scanner.

You should consider a few important points when getting a scanner. Here's the short list:

- Scanners are judged by their *resolution,* which is measured by the number of dots per inch (dpi) the scanner can read. The higher the dpi resolution, the better the scanned image.

- If you plan on scanning film negatives or transparencies, be sure to get a scanner with a negative/transparency adapter.

- Scanners come with software. You usually get three packages. The first is a utility that lets you use the scanner to scan in an image. The second is typically some type of photo-editing program, such as Adobe Photoshop Elements. The third is an OCR program, which is used to translate written documents into editable text.

- OCR stands for *optical character recognition.*

- Typical scanner prices range from $50 to more than $1,000. You pay more for higher-quality scanners, but those are used mostly by graphics professionals. Also, high-priced scanners contain options like sheet feeders (for law offices or other outfits that need to scan in large quantities of text).

- Don't let anyone fool you into believing that adding a scanner can turn your PC into a photocopier. True, you can scan an image and then print that image. But the process takes more time than it would to drive to the copy store and make a few copies. (Well, maybe not that long, but scanning and printing aren't the fastest things the PC does.)

Everyone say "megabyte!" (Digital cameras)

The latest PC craze is the digital camera. These wonderful toys not only have come down drastically in price, but the quality of the images they take is also rivaling traditional cameras.

Digital cameras range in price from you-don't-want-it cheap to well over $1,000 for professional setups. The average price for a decent digital camera is between $200 and $800.

Look for three things in a digital camera: resolution, image storage, and how the image gets transferred from the camera to your computer.

Resolution: The ready gauge of a digital camera's resolution is the *MP,* or *megapixel.* For example, a 3MP camera can shoot high-quality images that can be enlarged to the photo-quality 8 x 10 inches. Higher MP values can shoot higher-resolution images that can be enlarged even more. Lower MP values, although they can take pictures okay for e-mail, just don't look good when they're enlarged.

Image storage: For "digital film," most cameras use a digital media card capable of storing many megabytes of pictures. You can remove and replace the card — just like film — which allows the camera to take an infinite number of pictures.

Beaming the image to the computer: The most important thing to consider when selecting a digital camera is how the image is transferred from the camera into the computer. Most cameras use a special cable (such as a USB cable) that you use to send the images to the computer. Or, they may employ a device that reads the memory card and mounts it like a disk drive on your PC.

Here are some other digital camera points to ponder:

- ✔ Avoid any digital camera with a resolution of less than 3MP. Likewise, unless you're a professional, don't bother paying for anything over 6MP.

- ✔ Most cameras use LCD viewfinders, which means that you must hold them away from your face to get an image, like those camcorders that have LCD viewfinders — same thing.

- ✔ Beware of digital cameras with too many confusing and poorly labeled dials and buttons.

- ✔ I prefer using a digital camera that operates using standard batteries. That way, I can find extra batteries easily. Cameras that use special rechargeable batteries don't have such a fast turnaround time (but may save on battery cost in the long run).

- ✔ Buy a few digital media cards so that you always have a spare or three.

Part III
Networking Nonsense

"You know, Jekyll, this is a single log—on ID system. There's no need for multiple identities anymore."

In this part . . .

'T was not long ago that the realm of networking was best left to those geeks at the office who were *paid* to know such things. They knew the wires. They knew the gizmos. They knew the secret commands and could find the printers and connect to the hard drives. Their white lab coats were their priestly robes; their clipboards, sacred tablets. Their utterings were hallowed, their time was precious. Offerings were made, of chips and pizza. All praise the network geek! Om!

Networking today isn't the big deal it once was. Sure, the office may still have networking mysteries, such as "Where is the Exchange server, what is it, and why do I need it?" But, for basic networking, well, Grandma had to do that when she hooked up the Internet to her wireless DSL router and surprised everyone after she sent e-mail from the back porch while watching *Dr. Phil*. If Grandma can do it, so can you. The chapters in this part of the book explain how it's done.

Chapter 16

Basic Painless Networking

Computer networking is just like kindergarten: It's all about learning to share with others. You can color in kindergarten, and with a computer network, you can share a color printer. You may also learn about your ABCs in kindergarten, and when you share disk drives on a network, you use letters of the alphabet — all the way up to Z!

Networking makes no sense when you have only one computer. If you have only one computer and you use a broadband modem — you need to network! Otherwise, most folks find that they have more than one computer in the home or office. It just makes sense to use a network so that those computers, like kids in kindergarten, can share stuff and be nice to each other — well, at least share stuff.

This chapter provides an overview of basic computer networking using PCs and Windows.

The Big Networking Picture

Computer networking is about communications. More than that, it deals with sharing resources. That sounds good. But, what is a resource?

A *resource* is something a computer uses to get work done. Just about any component in the computer can be viewed as a resource, but the main resources are computer memory and disk storage. From reading this book, you may know that having enough of each one is ideal for any computer.

What networking brings to the PC table is the ability to share certain resources between several computers. By using a network, you can share these resources:

- ✔ Disk storage
- ✔ Printers
- ✔ Modems (Internet access)

Regardless of where the disk drives are located, and which computer is connected to the printer or modem, networking allows all those resources to be shared equally by each computer connected to the network.

The network itself, like everything else in the computer, is a combination of hardware and software. The hardware is what physically connects the computers and allows communications to take place. The software controls the hardware, by giving the operating system access to the network and giving *you* access to those resources on other computers.

Here are some important network terms to familiarize yourself with:

Ethernet: Many types of networks are available, in different hardware and software varieties. The networking done on PCs, and described in this part of the book, is referred to as *Ethernet.* This networking standard dictates that a certain type of hardware be used and that certain software rules be obeyed. The specifics of Ethernet aren't really important to understanding the whole networking ball of wax. Just be sure that you say it properly: "EE-thur-net."

LAN: When you connect a group of computers to form a network, it's called local area network, or LAN. You pronounce LAN like *land,* but without the *d* at the end, like how Aunt Minnie pronounced "Land sakes!"

Peer-to-peer network: A network that simply connects computers together is known as a *peer-to-peer network.* In that scheme, no single computer is in charge; each computer is "on the network," just like any other computer. Peer-to-peer contrasts with another scheme called *client-server.* In that setup, there's one main computer, called the server (or a computer that merely runs special server software). Servers aren't typically found on peer-to-peer networks, and this book doesn't cover using servers or installing server software.

Networking Hardware

You need, on the hardware side, three different pieces to create the physical network. Each computer must have a networking adapter, you need wires in order to connect the adapters, and there's a central location, or *hub,* where all the wires are connected to complete the network. Figure 16-1 illustrates how the network looks; this section provides the details.

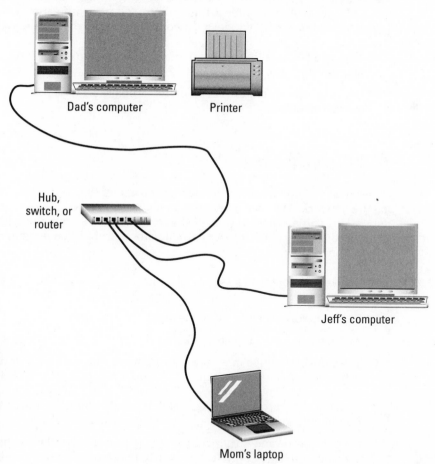

Dad's computer   Printer

Hub,
switch, or
router

Jeff's computer

Figure 16-1:
The net-
working
picture (not
drawn to
scale).

Mom's laptop

Saint NIC

To connect your PC to the network, it must have proper Ethernet networking hardware. That hardware is called a *network information card,* or *NIC.* It may also be known as an Ethernet card or a network adapter. The circuitry may indeed be on a separate expansion card, but on most newer PCs, the hardware comes as part of the chipset on the motherboard.

There are two types of NICs. The first is the traditional one, which uses the RJ-45 adapter. (Refer to Table 2-1, in Chapter 2, for identification.) The second type is the *wireless* NIC. Wireless networking is covered in Chapter 19.

- ✔ Adding a NIC to a PC is easy; they're cheap, and you can find one at any office supply store.

- ✔ Get a NIC that configures at 10 or 100 Mbps (megabits per second). The faster, the better.

Network hoses

Unless you go wireless, you need wires to connect the computers, thus creating the network. The wire you use is a cable known as CAT 5, or Category-5, networking cable. One end of the cable plugs into your computer, into the NIC, and the other plugs into a central location, or hub (covered in the next subsection).

- ✔ Cat 5 cable comes in a variety of lengths and in several bright and cheerful colors.

- ✔ Cat 5 networking cable contains eight different wires.

- ✔ You can also use Cat 5 networking cable with your telephone system.

- ✔ You can get creative in wiring your home or office with networking cable. I crawled under my house to wire it all up, and I used the attic and outside walls. You can also buy "raceways" and connectors and boxes if you don't want to tear up your walls. (Unless you're into such things, though, I recommend having an electrician do it for you.)

- ✔ It's possible — and rather convenient — to run networking cable through your home's heating ducts. If you choose to do it this way, be sure that you buy special high-temperature cable, rugged enough to stand being inside a heating duct. It's called *plenum cable,* and it ain't cheap.

- ✔ Yes, heating ducts are filthy.

- ✔ If wiring drives you batty, be smart and go with a wireless type of network, as described in Chapter 19.

Hubs, switches, and routers

All the network wires from each PC's NIC shoot back to a central location, the heart of the network. At that location is a box into which all the network wires plug, effectively connecting all the computers. That box is known as a *hub,* as shown earlier, in Figure 16-1.

A hub is basically a dumb box that contains the proper wiring to allow your computer's networking hardware and software run the network. Sure, you could just try tying all those cables into one huge knot, but that has been proven not to work. And, soldering all the wires together seriously slows down network speed. No, a hub is the thing.

For a bit more money, you can buy a smarter version of a hub, called a *switch.* It does the same thing as the hub, but it contains more brains and allows your networking to run faster and more efficiently.

The smartest type of hub you can buy is a *router.* It's quite sophisticated and has the brains to not only manage hundreds of networked computers but also deal with Internet traffic.

Which should you get? Easy: If you have only two computers and speed isn't an issue, get a hub. If you want better performance, get a switch. If the network is connected to the Internet, a router is a must.

The Software Side of Networking

Fortunately, Windows XP has the best networking software of any version of Windows, especially with regard to setting up and configuring the basic peer-to-peer network, as discussed in this book. Thankfully, there's nothing else you need to buy.

The NIC software (driver)

If you've just installed networking hardware in your PC, refer to the documentation that came with the NIC. You may need to install some software, to help the computer recognize and use the NIC. Or, there may be software that's used to diagnose and troubleshoot. In any event, that software must be installed before you configure the network on your computer.

If the NIC came with your PC or the software is on the motherboard, you're ready to go.

Setting up the network configuration

Windows most likely has automatically configured networking for you. Just to be sure, why not check on things in the Network Connections window? To get there, open the Control Panel and then open the Network Connections icon. The screen you see may look something like Figure 16-2.

Figure 16-2:
The
Network
Connections
window.

If you see a Local Area Connection icon in the window, as shown in Figure 16-2, you're all set up and ready to go — though I recommend that you continue reading the next several subsections, to better familiarize yourself with some networking jargon and to know where the bodies are buried. That helps you out later, if the need arises.

If you don't see a Local Area Connection icon or you see only dial-up connections, you need to configure the networking software in Windows. Locate the area on the left side of the screen that says Network Tasks. Then click the link in the area that says Set Up a Home or Small Office Network. That runs a wizard or two; follow the directions on the screen.

When you're done, the network should be running. Note that for a network to be working, you must have at least *two* computers connected properly and on speaking terms. See the section "Testing the Network," at the end of this chapter, for more information.

  ✔ If your PC has more than one network adapter (NIC), you see an icon for each connection in the Network Connections dialog box.

  ✔ If you have any dial-up connections, they appear in a separate area in the Network Connections window and are dial-up.

  ✔ Note the helpful Network Troubleshooter in the See Also pane.

A networking connection's Properties dialog box

To get your hands dirty with the software side of networking, you need to see the Properties dialog box for your Network Connection icon. This is the place to go for confirming network settings and for changing the network's configuration. Especially when you first set up a network, it's a good idea to know where and how to see this particular Properties dialog box. Here's the skinny:

1. **Open the Network Connections window.**

   Refer to the preceding subsection.

2. **Right-click your networking icon.**

   The icon is shown in the margin.

3. **Choose Properties from the pop-up menu.**

   You see a Properties dialog box, as shown in Figure 16-3. Here's a reference to what's what:

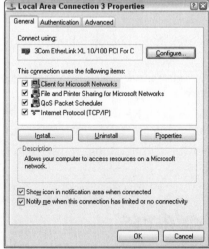

Figure 16-3: A connection's Properties dialog box.

- The official name for your NIC appears atop the General tab.

- Three types of items are listed in the middle of the dialog box: Clients, Services, and Protocols.

- The Client for Microsoft Networks is what allows you to do peer-to-peer networking with other Windows computers on the network. It's necessary.

- The File and Printer Sharing for Microsoft Networks service lets you access and share network disk drives and printers.

- The Internet Protocol (TCP/IP) thing governs Ethernet. It's a set of rules and such.

- I recommend putting a check mark by the item Show Icon in Notification Area When Connected. See the subsection "The little networking guys," later in this chapter.

4. **Close the Properties dialog box when you're done poking around.**

Generally speaking, you rarely need to mess with the settings in the Properties dialog box, but it's good to know where the thing is in case the need arises — especially for troubleshooting. The following subsection also makes use of the dialog box.

The little networking guys

 If you heeded my advice earlier in this chapter, you notice the Little Networking Guys icon on the system tray part of the taskbar. Those guys appear when the network is connected, and they flash during periods of network activity.

✔ Point the mouse at a connection, and a pop-up bubble gives you a quick network summary.

✔ You can click the Little Networking Guys icon to see the connection's Status dialog box (see the next subsection).

✔ Right-click the icon and choose Open Network Connections from the pop-up menu to see that window displayed.

✔ Note that if you have two network connections, you see two networking guys, one for each connection.

Checking your IP address

Just as every house on your street as its own, unique street address, each computer on the network must have a unique IP address. Two houses with the same address would lead to confusion, like on the TV show *Desperate Housewives*. Ditto for your network, but without the gratuitous sex.

The IP address can be either manually entered or assigned by a single computer on the network or a router. To check the IP address, follow these steps:

1. **Open the Network Connections window.**

2. **Double-click to open your Network Connections icon.**

   The connection's Status dialog box appears. The General tab tells you some information about the connection. Primarily, you can determine that the network is up and good because it says `Status: Connected` and the Activity area indicates information both sent and received.

3. **Click the Support tab.**

   On the Support tab, you find the IP Address listed. It's one of those dotted numbers, like `10.0.1.1` or something similar. You also find two other important values listed:

   - The subnet mask, which helps Ethernet find local computers on the network.

   - The default gateway, which is required when your LAN is also connected to the Internet. The gateway is usually the IP address of the router.

4. **Click the Close button.**

IP addresses that start with `192.168` or `10.0` are used for the local network only. Other IP addresses are used on the Internet and can be assigned only by an ISP or some outfit with the authority to assign those numbers. Otherwise, the IP address you see with starts out with `192.168` or `10.0`.

Manually assigning an IP address

In most situations, the IP address is assigned for you automatically, or *dynamically*. This happens when you use a router to connect your network and the router has been configured to deal out IP addresses. It also happens when you use Internet connection sharing, as covered in Chapter 18. It may also happen if you just have one computer connected to a broadband modem. When it doesn't happen, you must manually assign an IP address to each computer in the network.

To manually assign an IP address, you use the network connection's Properties dialog box. Here's the nitty and the gritty:

1. **Open the Network Connections window.**

2. **Right-click your networking icon and choose the Properties command from the pop-up menu.**

3. **On the General tab, click the item labeled Internet Protocol (TCP/IP).**

4. **Click the Properties button.**

   The TCP/IP Properties dialog box appears, as shown in Figure 16-4.

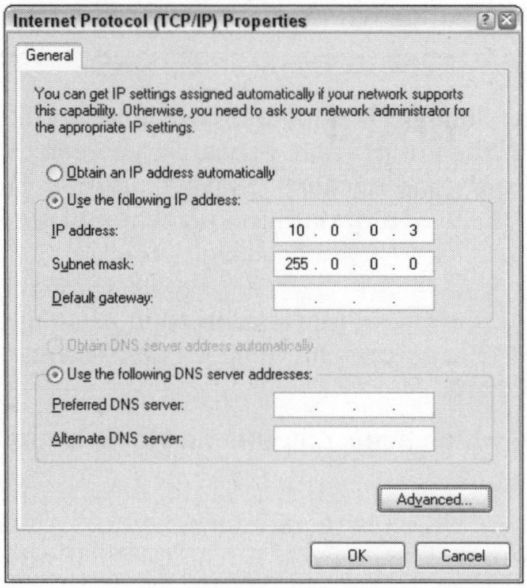

Figure 16-4:
The TCPI/IP
Properties
thing.

If you have a network computer that hands out IP addresses or you're using Internet connection sharing (see Chapter 18) or you have a router that assigns IP addresses or you have a computer running the DHCP program, you can choose the option labeled Obtain an IP Address Automatically; skip to Step 8.

5. **Type an IP address for the computer. Type** 10, **press Tab, type** 0, **press Tab, type** 0, **press Tab, and then type a number.**

   Each PC on your network must have a unique IP address.

6. **Enter** 255.0.0.0 **as the Subnet mask.**

7. **Leave everything else alone.**

8. **Click OK and close any other open dialog boxes or windows.**

The most important part of these steps is to ensure that no two PCs on the network use the same IP address. If they do, the network doesn't work.

Setting Your Computer's Network Name and Workgroup

All computers on the network must have a network name. For Windows peer-to-peer networking, they must also all belong to the same workgroup.

Getting the MAC address

Along with a computer's IP address, another unique number given to each computer using Ethernet is something called the MAC address. Unlike the IP address, however, the MAC address is a unique number assigned to your networking hardware, the NIC. No two NICs have the same MAC address, which is done primarily as a security measure.

To view the MAC address used on your PC's NIC, open the Network Connections window and double-click to open the Network Connections icon. Click the Support tab and then the Details

button. The Network Connections Details box lists the MAC address as the "physical address." It shows up as six pairs of values separated by hyphens. Values include the numbers 0 through 9 and the letters A through F.

You may need to know this value when you're configuring a router or doing other networky things.

MAC stands for Media Access Control, or it could be short for McCarthy, depending on whom you know.

Here's how to check or assign the computer's name as well as the work-group name:

1. **Right-click the My Computer icon on the desktop.**

2. **Choose Properties from the pop-up menu.**

3. **Click the Computer Name tab.**

4. **Type a description for your computer in the Computer Description text box.**

   The description helps further identify the computer when its icon is shown in a networking window.

5. **Click the Change button.**

6. **Enter or change the computer's name (if necessary).**

7. **Enter a new workgroup name.**

   I use single names, all caps. The name must be the same in order for all computers in a workgroup to see each other. Changing this name also affects other computers on the network that are connected to your PC.

8. **Click OK to set the new names in the Computer Name Changes dialog box.**

9. **Click OK to close the System Properties dialog box.**

For a small network, names are just for show. Even so, it helps to know which computer you're dealing with on a network. That's why I gave my computers names rather than silly numbers or cryptic things that only I would understand.

- ✔ The computer's network name cannot be the same as another computer on the network.

- ✔ Workgroups are just a way to divide a large network into more manageable chunks. Even if you have a dozen computers, it's okay to keep them all in the same workgroup.

- ✔ After you assign your computer a name, don't change it. That could screw up connections made by other computers on the network.

- ✔ Don't bother messing with multiple workgroup names if you're networking PCs only in your house or small office. Trust me — it's too much of a hassle.

Testing the Network

The network is working when your computer can "see" other computers on the network. To view them, open the My Network Places icon on the desktop. The My Network Places icon may also exist on the Start button's menu.

In the My Network Places window, locate on the left side the pane that says Network Tasks. On the list, you find text that reads "View workgroup computers." Click that text to see all the other computers on the network and in your workgroup. They should appear similar to what you see in Figure 16-5.

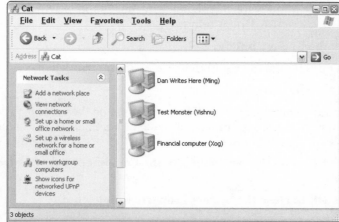

Figure 16-5: Other computers in the workgroup.

Note that the name of the window is the same as the workgroup name. In Figure 16-5, the workgroup is named Cat. Three computers are present. The computers are listed by their description first and then by the computer name in parentheses.

If you don't see any computers listed, check the following:

✔ Ensure that each PC has its own unique IP address.

✔ The subnet mask for each PC needs to be the same as well.

✔ All PCs need to be in the same workgroup.

✔ Check the network connections.

✔ Ensure that the hub, switch, or router is turned on.

✔ Go to another computer and check its My Network Places window to see whether the problem is one way or both ways.

✔ Restart Windows.

✔ Run the Network Troubleshooter, as mentioned in the section "Setting up the network configuration," earlier in this chapter.

Chapter 17

Abusing the Network

· ·

· ·

*H*ooking your PC into a network expands greatly the fields on which you can compute. No more are you limited to using your own PC's resources. Remember how Ed vanished into his office with the new color printer? Well, as soon as that sucker was up and on the network, *everyone* could use it. Poor Ed! Ha!

Networking is about communications and sharing resources. After the network is up and running, it's resource shopping-spree time. Windows provides ample tools for using resources on the network, for grabbing and using network disk drives and printers, as well as for sacrificing your PC's own disk drives and printers. This chapter tells you how all that is done.

Networky Places in Windows

Windows has several ways of letting you peek at the network and view which network resources are available. This section tells you what's what and where the bodies are buried.

Shared files in the My Network Places window

The main networking window thing in Windows is called My Network Places. It's an icon on the desktop, or on the Start button's menu, that opens a window also called My Network Places, as shown in Figure 17-1.

Figure 17-1:
The My
Network
Places
window.

When your PC first starts, Windows goes out on the network and identifies all other Windows computers on the network. It then gathers a list of shared resources that are available on each network computer. The My Network Places window shows you a summary of any shared folders on those computers.

The shared folders appear as folder icons, but with "plumbing" below them. The shared folder name is then given, followed by the word *on* and then the network computer's description. The network computer's name appears in parentheses.

Opening a shared folder allows you to view and access files inside that folder — just like in Windows — but the files actually exist on another computer on the network.

  ✔ Windows XP automatically puts all shared folders up for display in the My Network Places window. Any new resources that are made available appear in the window as though by magic.

✔ Shared folders on your own computer also show up in the My Network Places window. They appear as regular folder icons, minus the plumbing.

✔ You can assign a drive letter to any shared folder, to make that folder part of your own PC's disk system. See the section "Mapping in a network drive," later in this chapter.

✔ You can open the icons in the My Network Places folder. Opening an icon for a folder causes Windows to access the network and then report the contents of that folder. But, on your computer, you see the folder's contents displayed just as though it were a folder on your own computer.

✔ The View Network Connections item in the Network Tasks panel opens the Network Connections window, another handy networking place in Windows. Refer to Chapter 16 for more information.

✔ You can save favorite Internet locations — specifically, FTP sites — in the My Network Places window. This is done by clicking the Add a Network Place link on the Network Tasks panel, on the left side of the window. That's all I have to say about that here.

✔ The My Network Places folder is named the Network Neighborhood in other versions of Windows. Both terms refer to the same thing.

Shared printers

In addition to looking for shared folders on the network, Windows scourers the network for any printers marked "up for grabs." Unlike the folders, however, the shared printers don't show up in the My Network Places window. Instead, they show up in the regular Printers and Faxes window, as shown in Figure 17-2.

Figure 17-2:
Shared printers show up here.

To view the Printers and Faxes window, open the Control Panel and then open the Printers and Faxes icon.

Printers elsewhere on the network appear as printer icons with network plumbing beneath them. Printers directly attached to your computer also show up, but without the plumbing (refer to Figure 17-2).

- ✔ Refer to Chapter 12 for more information on printers and printing.
- ✔ See the section "Sharing a printer," later in this chapter, for information on sharing printers attached to your computer. See the section "Using a network printer," near the end of this chapter, for info on using network printers.

Network computers and their shared resources

Windows lets you see only those resources available for sharing on the network, and you don't have to share anything you don't want to. To get a quick view of what's available from each computer, you can use the My Network Places window to browse through the computers on your workgroup and see what's available for sharing. Follow these steps:

1. **Open the My Network Places icon on the desktop.**

2. **Locate the Network Tasks area, on the left side of the window.**

3. **Choose the View Workgroup Computers task.**

   A window appears that lists all computers in the workgroup. For most small offices and home networks, that should include all computers on the network (refer to Chapter 16).

4. **To see which resources are being shared on a specific computer, double-click to open that computer's icon.**

   For example, Figure 17-3 shows the resources being shared from the computer Ming on the network; three folders and one printer are being shared. Those aren't the entire contents of that computer's hard drive — just what the user has elected to have shared.

5. **Click the Up button on the toolbar to return to the workgroup window.**

   The window now shows all computers up on the network in the same workgroup.

Figure 17-3:
Folders and
printers
shared on a
network
computer.

6. **Click the Up button again.**

   The topmost network level is the Microsoft Windows Network level. On this level, all workgroups on the network appear. That should just be one workgroup for a small or home office.

7. **Click the Up button one last time.**

   The final location is called Entire Network and includes some globe-and-mouse icons. I have no idea what they are and how they're used.

8. **Close the window.**

   Wise move.

Doing Network Things in Windows

Here's a list of fun things you can do on a PC network. Keep in mind the basic network mantra as you review these sections: "Networking is about sharing."

- ✔ Several of these subsections assume that you know about finding specific places in Windows: Refer to Chapter 5 for finding some locations.

- ✔ See Chapter 21 for information on folders if the concept is new to you.

- ✔ The only thing you can share that's not mentioned here is a modem or high-speed Internet connection. Refer to Chapter 18 for information specific to that chore.

Sharing a folder on the network

If you want others on the network to have access to a folder on your computer, you *share* the folder. This makes the folder — and its contents (all files and subfolders) — available to all other computers on the network. Here's how to share a folder:

1. **Select the folder you want to share.**

    Click the folder's icon once to select it.

2. **Choose File⇨Sharing and Security.**

    The Sharing tab in the folder's Properties dialog box appears, similar to what you see in Figure 17-4.

Figure 17-4:
A disk drive's Properties dialog box.

3. **Click to put a check mark by the option labeled Share This Folder on the Network.**

4. **Optionally, click the item labeled Allow Network Users to Change My Files.**

    Checking this item allows full access to the folder and its files. If you don't check this item, the folder appears as read-only to other users on the network.

5. **Optionally, change the share name.**

   The *share name* is the same as the folder's name, but remember that it can be vague; I have many folders named book on my computer. In this case (refer to Figure 17-4), I would change the share name from book to the specific name of the book that its contents represent.

6. **Click OK.**

   The folder is now shared.

 Icons for shared folders appear with the graphical "sharing hand" beneath them, as shown in the margin. On other computers on the network, the shared folder appears in the My Network Places window or can be seen by opening your computer's icon inside the workgroup folder.

   ✔ Don't share an entire disk drive. This is a security risk; Windows warns you when you try to do so.

   ✔ If you're unable to share a folder, it may be protected. You see a check mark by the option labeled Make This Folder Private in the folder's Properties dialog box (refer to Figure 17-4). Remove that check mark to share the folder.

   ✔ If you cannot remove the Make This Folder Private check mark (it's dimmed), check the parent folder's Properties dialog box, and so on and so on, until you find the main folder that was originally marked as private. Removing that private status allows the subfolders to be shared.

   ✔ Windows XP uses the Shared Documents folder for things that really need to be shared on the network. My advice is to merely share that folder and then copy into it things you want shared on the network. To share the Shared Documents folder, open the My Computer icon on the desktop. The Shared Documents folder can be found inside.

Sharing a printer

Sharing a printer connected to your PC works just like sharing a folder:

1. **Open the Printers and Faxes folder.**

   It's inside the Control Panel.

2. **Click to highlight the printer you want to share.**

3. **Choose File➪Sharing from the menu.**

   The printer's Properties dialog box appears, with the Sharing tab selected.

What about network printers?

Network printers, or printers with their own networking cards, don't need to be connected directly to any PC. To access the network printer, however, you must have software installed on each computer by using the installation program that came on a CD with the printer. Unlike printers directly connected to Windows XP computers, network printers don't have the brains to announce their presence and share their drivers.

---

4. **Click to select the item labeled Share This Printer.**

5. **Optionally, give the printer a name.**

   For example, name it Color Laser to let everyone know that you're finally sharing your darn precious color laser printer.

6. **Click the OK button.**

 As with sharing a folder, the printer's icon appears with the sharing hand beneath it. In other Printers and Faxes windows all across your network, that shared printer appears, ready to roll. (Unlike in previous versions, Windows XP automatically locates shared printers and instantly installs their drivers.)

Accessing a network folder

You access a folder elsewhere on the network just as you would access any folder on your PC's disk system. The difference is that you need to browse to the folder, which takes some extra steps.

The key to browsing to a network folder is My Network Places. Either open that icon on the desktop or choose it from a drop-down list in a folder window or in the Open or Save As dialog boxes.

After displaying the contents of the My Network Places window, you can then choose any folder window shared on the network. Figure 17-5 shows the window's contents as seen from an Open dialog box. The folders shown there are all shared folders from other computers on the network.

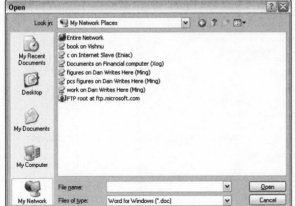

Figure 17-5:
Finding a
shared
folder.

✔ You can also get to the My Network Places window by clicking the icon on the left side of most Open or Save In dialog boxes (refer to Figure 17-5).

✔ After you open a shared folder from the My Network Places window, you see its contents just as you would in a local folder on your own hard drive.

Mapping in a network drive

If you find accessing a folder on another computer (as described in the preceding subsection) tedious, you can opt instead to *map* that folder to your local disk drive system. This choice provides easy, quick, and consistent access to the folder's contents, just as though the folder were another disk drive inside your PC.

To map a folder, follow these steps:

1. **Open the My Computer icon.**

   You can pull this trick in any folder; I chose the My Computer folder because that's where the mapped folder's drive icons show up.

2. **Choose Tools⇨Map Network Drive.**

   The Map Network Drive dialog box shows up, as depicted in Figure 17-6.

Figure 17-6:
The Map
Network
Drive dialog
box.

3. **Choose a drive letter for the networked drive.**

   You can give the network drive any unused drive letter. Be clever here. For example, if you mapped in a folder full of MP3 files, give it drive letter M. Otherwise, the drive letter choice doesn't really matter.

   The drive letter you assign is personal to your computer. It doesn't affect any other computer on the network.

4. **Select the network folder to map to that letter.**

   If you have recently accessed the folder, you can choose it from the Folder drop-down list. Otherwise, use the Browse button, which opens a special window to My Network Places, where you can select a network folder.

5. **Ask yourself, "Do I always want to use the network drive?"**

   If so, put a check mark by the item labeled Reconnect at Logon. That way, Windows always maps in the folder to that specific drive letter every time you start your computer. Otherwise, the mapping is forgotten when you log out.

6. **Click the Finish button.**

   Windows opens that folder and shows you its contents.

 Back in the My Computer folder, however, you see the mapped folder as a disk drive icon, complete with plumbing (as shown in the margin). Accessing that network folder is as easy, and the same as, using the drive letter on your own PC.

Using a network printer

Because Windows XP automatically spies and loads network printers, all you have to do to use one is choose it from the drop-down list in a Print dialog box. Refer to Chapter 12 for more information on printing.

Unsharing a folder

To remove the magical sharing properties from a folder, repeat the steps in the subsection "Sharing a folder on the network," earlier in this chapter. This time, however, remove the check mark to share the folder on the network. Click OK, and the folder is unshared and the sharing hand vanishes from beneath its icon.

Disconnecting a mapped network drive

To remove a mapped network drive, open the My Computer window and click to select Mr. Disk Drive with Plumbing. From the menu, choose File⇨ Disconnect. The drive is unmapped.

Unsharing a printer

Unsharing a printer is as simple as sharing one: Repeat the steps in the subsection "Sharing a printer," a little earlier in this chapter, but click to choose Don't Share This Printer. The little hand goes away, and the printer is, once again, all yours!

Chapter 18

Your Network and the Internet

*I*t probably surprised you, as it surprises most people. When you get a high-speed modem — cable, DSL, satellite, or other broadband connection — even though you may have only one computer, you need networking hardware to hook up the thing. That's because the *net* part of Internet stands for *networking*. The Internet itself is merely a huge network of computers, all of them hooked up with hardware and using software in nearly the same way as a local area network (LAN) in a small business or home office.

You can also use, beyond the broadband modem thing, your existing local area network to share a single dial-up modem and that computer's network connection. It's very similar to the broadband Internet connection, which is why both those things are covered in this single chapter.

The Broadband Internet Connection

You've seen the advertisements where they compare the various high-speed, or broadband, Internet connections. There's the one that claims how DSL is slower than cable. That's true, but what they don't tell you is that cable's speed is *not* guaranteed. Whatever. My point is that one thing they universally don't tell you is that in order to connect to the broadband modem, you need a PC with a networking card.

They say that it takes a minimum of 20 minutes for any Windows computer connected to the Internet to be attacked by a worm or virus. Trust me, the bad guys are really out there, and they aggressively want to take over your computer, especially if you have a broadband connection.

You can do two things to protect yourself. The first is to use a router and con-figure it as described in this chapter. The second thing to do is configure and use firewall software, also described in this chapter. Don't wait! Do it now!

Types of broadband modems

Three popular types of broadband modems are available:

- ✔ Cable
- ✔ DSL
- ✔ Satellite

Cable: This option is the fastest and cheapest. If you live in an area serviced by a TV cable company, you should check into its Internet offerings. The cable modem plugs into the cable jack on the wall — just like you plug in a TV.

For speed, cable cannot be beat. The downside, however, is that the speed isn't guaranteed. If more folks in your neighborhood start using their cable modems, your speed rapidly decreases. Fortunately, that rarely happens, which means that cable is still the best deal around.

DSL: The Digital Subscriber Line, or DSL, connection is the second-fastest option available for a high-speed Internet connection. The speed you get is chosen ahead of time and is offered in given increments, such as 128 Kbps, 384 Kbps, 512 Kbps, and other, faster speeds.

The speed values used by a DSL connection are listed twice. The first is the sending speed, and the second is the receiving speed. So, you can pay for a connection that has a slower sending speed and a higher receiving speed if you don't plan on sending lots of information.

The DSL speed available to you depends on your location; DSL connections can be made reliably only within a certain radius of the telephone company's main office. Yes, you pay more for the higher speeds.

Satellite: The satellite connection is the only broadband connection available for remote locations. It's not as popular as cable or DSL, plus you have more equipment to buy. It's really only an option when you need speed and nothing else is available.

I would recommend a bidirectional satellite connection. Avoid those that are download-only and require a dial-up connection for uploading.

Broadband connection options you don't want to read about

An up-and-coming broadband option, soon to be popular all over the world (or so they say), is *wireless*. This isn't the current type of wireless networking you get at Starbucks. Nope, it's wide-area wireless networking. It means that you don't even need a modem to connect to the network — just a wireless NIC and all the right passwords and stuff. Chapter 19 has more information on wireless networking.

The other, remaining broadband options are the scary ones used mainly by businesses. The T1 line, or fractional T1, is where a networking connection is wired directly into your home or office from the phone company's network. The speed is guaranteed, but it's not as fast as cable, and it's terribly expensive. Even faster and more terrible and awfully more expensive is the T3 line. And then you can mix in fiber optic connections, and pretty soon you start getting into telepathy and subspace and technologies not yet invented. These issues are addressed in this book's publishing contract, but not anywhere in reality.

Above all, be sure to check in the Yellow Pages under *Internet* for additional high-speed Internet connections not listed here, but that may be offered in your area.

- Modem speed is measured in kilobits per seconds, or Kbps. Refer to Chapter 13 for more information on modem speed.

- Some cable companies may offer minimum speed guarantees — at a premium price.

- A DSL connection with the same sending and receiving speeds is called *bidirectional*. If you have a 768 Kbps bidirectional DSL line, you're both sending and receiving information at 768 Kbps.

- DSL is a generic term. Specific types of DSL connections are denoted by a letter prefixing DSL. For example, there's ADSL, VDSL, and SDSL. No need to know the specifics.

Connecting the broadband modem to your PC

Some broadband modems are available at the computer store along with dial-up modems, paper shredders, and, occasionally, computer books written by Dan Gookin. Other modems are available from broadband service providers. Sometimes you rent them, sometimes you buy them, and sometimes the phone company forgets to bill you.

If the cable or phone company doesn't install your broadband modem for you, you have to do it. The instructions come with the modem, and it's really a simple thing to do.

Before installing your DSL modem, you need to attach your dongles! The *dongle* is a line filter — a gizmo. You attach it to the phone jack on the wall and then plug your telephone, fax machine, dial-up modem, answering machine, caller ID box, or anything *but* the DLS modem into the dongle. You must do this, or else the feedback from the DSL modem makes using your telephone difficult.

Cable modem users don't have to worry about the dongle.

If the modem came with specific setup instructions, follow them first. Otherwise, use these directions as a guide:

1. **Plug the modem into the cable connector for a cable modem; for a DSL modem, plug the modem into any standard phone jack.**

2. **Plug the modem into the networking jack on the back of your PC.**

   If you have a local area network, things hook up differently. See the section "Sharing the broadband connection," later in this chapter.

   Some modems plug into an Ethernet-to-USB adapter, and the USB adapter then plugs into the computer.

   If you're following my advice and using a router, plug the modem into the router, and then plug your PC into the router. See the sidebar "Advice for setting up a router," later in this chapter, for more information.

3. **Plug the modem into the wall socket.**

   I highly recommend that you plug the modem into a UPS to keep it powered on during brief outages. Refer to Chapter 3 for more information on UPS (the power supply, not the delivery company).

4. **Turn the modem on, if possible.**

   Some modems don't have power switches; plugging them in is the same as turning them on.

Check the lights on the modem after you turn it on. The lights are good for telling you that

- ✔ The modem is on and receiving power.
- ✔ The modem is receiving a signal from the Internet.
- ✔ The modem is sending or receiving information.
- ✔ The modem isn't screwed up.

Refer to the modem's guide for more information on what the lights mean. Note that it may take a few moments for the lights to provide proper feedback; don't be to quick to assume that something is wrong.

✔ Yes, leave a broadband modem on all the time.

✔ Refer to Chapter 4 for information on leaving the PC on all time.

✔ Don't put a dongle between the DSL modem and the telephone wall jack! The DSL modem doesn't work if you do so.

✔ If you have two or more phone lines, the dongles need to go on only the phone line that shares the DSL connection.

Telling Windows about the broadband modem

The best way to complete the software side of your broadband modem setup is to refer to the information sheet or CD provided by your Internet Service Provider (ISP). It's specific.

When you're using a broadband connection with an existing local area network in your home or office, see the following subsection. Otherwise, if it's just you, your PC, and the broadband modem, follow these general steps:

1. **Open the Network Connections window.**

   You can get to this window by choosing Network Connections from the Start button's menu or by opening the Network Connections icon in the Control Panel.

2. **On the left side of the Network Connections window, in the Network Tasks area, click the link labeled Create a New Connection.**

   The New Connection Wizard appears.

3. **Click the Next button.**

4. **Choose Connect to the Internet and then click the Next button.**

5. **Choose Set Up My Connection Manually, unless you have a CD from your ISP, and then click the Use the CD I Got from an ISP option.**

   If you have a CD, skip to Step 8.

6. **Click the Next button.**

7. **Choose the option required for your connection, depending on whether you need to log in.**

   Some broadband connections require you to log in, and others are "on" all the time. Choose the proper option on the screen.

8. **Continue with the wizard until you eventually find and click the Finish button.**

After the wizard is done, you see your broadband connection appear in the Network Connections window. You can close the window now.

That's pretty much it — except for one more important thing you must do
and do quickly: Get a firewall. See the section "The Importance of a Firewall,"
later in this chapter.

Sharing the broadband connection

There's no reason that only one computer on your network should have
access to the broadband modem. After all, aren't networks about sharing and
love and all that?

Here's the secret: Broadband modems can plug directly into your network hub,
switch, or router, to make the modem instantly and equally accessible to all
computers on the network. Figure 18-1 illustrates how simply this can be done.

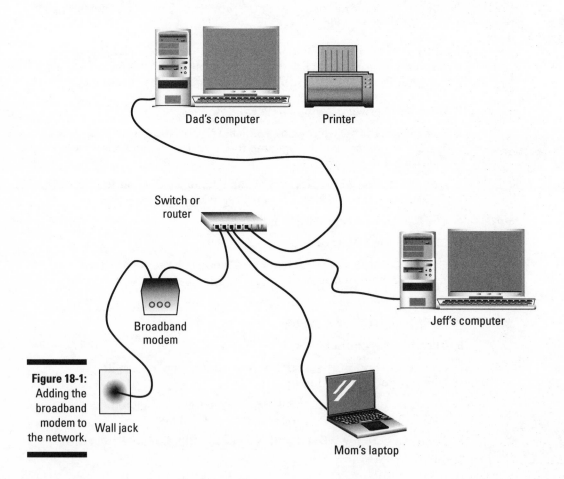

Dad's computer   Printer

Switch or
router

Jeff's computer

Broadband
modem

Figure 18-1:
Adding the
broadband
modem to   Wall jack
the network.

Mom's laptop

Advice for setting up a router

A *router* is a smart type of Ethernet hub, one that helps make decisions regarding where information goes and offers protection from the wiles of the Internet for computers on a local area network. My advice is to use a router even if you have only one computer connected to a broadband modem.

As a bonus, consider getting a router with firewall protection. That fixes two problems with one solution. There are many such routers. I personally use the NETGEAR line.

Routers are often configured by accessing the router's Web page. (Yes, it has its own Web page.) From the Web page, you can further configure the router or assist in its automatic configuration. You want to tell the router to block unwanted incoming traffic while still allowing the computers on your local network to access and use each other's resources.

Also direct the router to assign local IP addresses to each computer on the network. (Refer to Chapter 16 for information on IP addresses.) It's usually done via a feature named DHCP. That's a good thing!

Take note of the router's own IP address. You want to enter it in each PC's network setup window, by entering the router's IP address as the gateway for your network. If you have difficulty with this part, call your ISP's tech support line, and someone there can help you. (After all, you pay the ISP for this type of support.)

Most of what a router does is technical, so don't let it bother you if you can't understand half the options. Most of the time, the default or standard setup is best.

Plug the broadband modem into the hub, switch, or router, just as you would plug in any computer. For fastest results, use a switch, not a plain old dull hub. My best advice is to use a router; see the nearby sidebar, "Advice for setting up a router," for important details. Also, if you use a hub or a switch, you need to run the Internet Connection Sharing Wizard on all your computers. This step isn't required when you use a router.

After setting things up, run the New Connection Wizard as described in the preceding subsection. This must be done for each computer on the network, but, fortunately, it needs to be done only once.

Sharing a Dial-Up Internet Connection

Though a dial-up connection isn't as spiffy as a broadband connection, you can still share that Internet access with other PCs on your computer network. For one, you needn't worry about dialing out on a line already used by someone else in your house. If the line is in use, the second computer simply "piggybacks" onto the modem through the network and accesses the Internet.

To share a dial-up connection, follow these steps on the Windows XP computer with the dial-up modem and existing dial-up Internet connection:

1. **Open the Network Connections window.**

2. **Click to select a dial-up connection to share.**

3. **Choose File➪Properties from the menu.**

4. **Click the Advanced tab in the connection's Properties dialog box.**

5. **Put a check mark by the option labeled Allow Other Network Users to Connect through This Computer's Internet Connection.**

6. **Put check marks next to the two options below that one.**

   These items together allow other computers on the network to access and control the Internet connection.

7. **Click OK, and the connection is now shared.**

Other Windows computers on the network (not Windows XP systems, but, rather, earlier versions of Windows) need to configure the Internet Connection Wizard so that they know to use another PC's modem to dial out and connect to the Internet. After that's all set up, whenever another computer tries to access the Internet, it forces the shared modem computer to dial out, make the connection, and then share the connection throughout the network.

Windows XP computers automatically sense a shared Internet connection.

Note that privacy is still enforced with a shared connection. Despite getting information into one computer through another, the first (sharing) computer cannot access or interpret the information that's flowing through.

To disable sharing, reverse the steps to uncheck the check box. To temporarily disable the connection, you can simply unplug the modem from the phone line.

Testing the Internet Connection

To see whether the Internet connection you've set up is working, simply run an Internet program. For example, start the Internet Explorer Web browser. Type the address for Yahoo! on the Address bar:

```
http://www.yahoo.com/
```

Press Enter, and within seconds you should be able to see the Yahoo! home page on the Internet. If not, or if you get some error message, something is wrong with the connection. Phone up your ISP for technical support.

The Importance of a Firewall

A firewall is a safety device. For a building, the firewall is created from special slow-burning material, rated in hours. For example, a three-hour firewall theoretically takes three hours to burn through — and that helps protect a building from burning down before the fire department shows up.

On a computer with an Internet connection, a *firewall* is designed to restrict Internet access, primarily to keep unwanted guests out. The firewall effectively plugs holes through which bad guys could get in and mess with your PC.

✔ The Internet wasn't designed with security in mind. Back in the original days, scientists were open about their systems and didn't feel the need to protect their computers from other Internet users.

✔ Especially if you have a broadband connection, your PC is most vulnerable to attack. You must get a firewall.

✔ The best firewall protection is the *black hole*. That is, a computer on the Internet can probe your broadband modem and get the same response as though no computer were attached to the modem. To test for this condition, as well as test for weaknesses in your firewall, use ShieldsUP, from Gibson Research:

```
http://grc.com/
```

Installing the Windows XP firewall

Windows XP comes with limited firewall security, available through your Internet connection. Follow these steps to set it up:

1. **Open the Control Panel's Network Connections icon.**

2. **Right-click your ISP's or dial-up Internet connection icon and choose Properties from the pop-up menu.**

3. **Click the Advanced tab in the Properties dialog box.**

4. **Click the Settings button to access the Windows Firewall dialog box.**

   The Windows Firewall dialog box appears.

5. **Click to select On (recommended).**

6. **Click the Exceptions tab.**

   The Exceptions are things you want to allow through the network — stuff that's okay. Normally, the firewall blocks everything — which is secure, but not very efficient or friendly.

7. **Put a check mark by File and Printer Sharing.**

   That step allows other computers to access your computer to share files and the printer.

8. **Put a check mark by SmartFTP.**

   That action allows you to use the FTP program to send and receive files on the Internet.

9. **Remove all other check marks.**

   Only if you really know what a program does or use it enough should you put a check mark there.

10. **Click OK, and the firewall is set.**

The Windows firewall isn't that bad, especially if you have Windows XP SP 2 release. If you don't, or you're reluctant to update, get a third-party firewall. In fact, you can disable the Windows firewall if you use a third-party firewall. Unlike other things in the PC, you get no benefit from running two firewalls at once.

Third-party firewalls

The advantages of a third-party firewall are that, well, they're far more robust and capable than what Windows offers. For example, Zone Alarm, from Zone Labs, monitors *both* incoming and outgoing requests for the Internet and offers e-mail protection. I highly recommend it: www.zonelabs.com.

Other third-party solutions exist. If you enjoy the Norton stuff, consider getting the Norton Personal Firewall or the Norton Internet Security programs (www.symantec.com). Another fine firewall is available from Kerio Technologies (www.kerio.com).

✔ The key to running a firewall is to forbid access to your PC from random computers on the Internet while still allowing computers on the local network full access. That may be tricky to set up, but it's the configuration you want.

✔ Windows may tell you that "no firewall is detected" when it starts, despite the fact that you have a third-party firewall installed. Ignore those messages.

✔ You have no reason to run a third-party firewall if you're using a router that has built-in firewall protection. A single firewall is enough.

✔ Your ISP can be a great resource if you want more information or recommendations on this subject.

Chapter 19

Look, Ma: No Wires!

*I*f the entire 20th century was about getting everything wired, the 21st century is beginning to undo that trend. The buzzword everywhere is *wireless.* Wireless keyboard and mouse. Wireless phones. Wireless this and that. At the top of the heap is wireless computer networking, which has been heralded as the biggest improvement to computers since the switch from steam to electrical power in the late 18th century.

Hardware-wise, wireless networking is a piece of cake; no wires means an easier setup. The software side? Ha! Configuring your wireless network is, well, *different,* as you discover while reading through this chapter.

✔ This chapter refers to some basic networking concepts common to both wireless and wired networks. Refer to Chapter 16 for more information on networking basics.

✔ The information in Chapter 17 (and somewhat in Chapter 18) on using the network applies equally to wireless and wired networks.

✔ Wireless networking is a Big Issue with PC laptops. For details on that topic, please see my book *Laptops For Dummies,* published by the same malicious people who brought you this friendly tome.

Wireless Basics

It's true that shouting at someone is a type of wireless technology. But, as you've probably learned, shouting at a computer does little or no good. Wires virtually guarantee that a signal gets through. But, wireless?

If you understand the basics of computer networking, wireless networking isn't all that different. You have some terms to know, standards to obey, and various ritual dances and chants. This section discusses those and other wireless networking basics.

The ABGs of wireless networking

Computers would just go nuts without standards. There are acronym standards, number standards, standards with cute names, plus various fruit-flavored standards. For networking, the standard is Ethernet. For wireless networking, the standard is 802.11, which is properly pronounced, "eight oh two dot eleven," or, to save time you can omit the *dot:* "Eight oh two eleven."

At this point, there are two versions of the 802.11 standard, called B and G and written as 802.11b and 802.11g, respectively. The 802.11b standard is older and more common. The 802.11g standard is newer and faster and becoming more common every day.

What happened to 802.11a? Well, you may see that standard listed on some wireless networking adapters, but it's really an antique now. Letters C through F also existed at one time, but they never caught on. You're left with only 802.11b and 802.11g.

What's the point?

The point is — and this is important — that for all your wireless networking hardware to work, it must all be on the same standard.

For example, if the wireless networking adapter on all your computers, laptops, and routers is 802.11b, you're okay. If they all use 802.11g, you're still okay. But, if they mix it up between 802.11b and 802.11g, you're screwed.

✔ Some wireless networking adapters cover both popular standards. This is often specified as 802.11b/g. The adapter costs more, but you get an adapter that works in just about any wireless networking situation.

✔ The multiple standard wireless adapters may also be compatible with the old 802.11a standard, in which case they're labeled as 802.11 a/b/g.

✔ The long name of 802.11 is IEEE 802.11, the same IEEE group that created the 1394, or FireWire, port.

✔ There are also 802.11h and 802.11i standards, though they're not commonly implemented or available as wireless networking adapters.

Behold, the wireless NIC

Wireless networking requires its own wireless NIC, or network information card. This card is either an expansion card you add to your PC's motherboard or a special adapter that plugs into the USB port.

The wireless networking card adheres to one or more of the wireless networking standards, either 802.11b or 802.11g, or both. As long as that standard matches all the other computers and wireless networking apparatuses in your home or office, you're set!

✔ I recommend getting a wireless adapter with an external antenna. For some reason, the antenna makes picking up the wireless signal all the more easier — especially if the antenna is directional (can be moved).

✔ Laptops equipped with built-in wireless networking rarely have an external antenna; the antenna is there — it's just inside the laptop's case.

✔ Yes, you can have both a wireless and standard NIC inside your PC.

The wireless network setup

Setting up a wireless network is done just like setting up a wired computer network. Each computer must be equipped with a wireless networking adapter, and all adapters must support or use the same standard, either 802.11b or 802.11g.

At the center of the network is a wireless hub, or router, also known as a *base station*. It serves the same function as a hub does in a wired network: The base station is responsible for receiving the wireless transmissions and sending them on to the other computers in the network.

Figure 19-1 shows a sample wireless network setup, which looks disturbingly like Figure 18-1, over in Chapter 18, mostly because the only real difference is the lack of wires. Note that most wireless hubs or routers have the ability to let you connect wire-based networks as well, so you can share your network between existing wired connections and wireless ones.

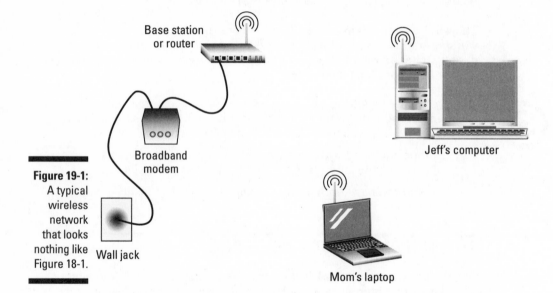

Figure 19-1:
A typical wireless network that looks nothing like Figure 18-1.

To connect broadband Internet to your wireless network, simply plug the broadband modem into the wireless router. Most routers come with a connection specifically designed for the broadband modem, so making this addition is a cinch.

What's left over is making the connection on the software side. See the section "Hooking into a Wireless Network," later in this chapter.

Setting up the base station

The wireless base station requires a little more setup than a wired base station. Here are some things you may want to configure on the base station, per the instructions that came with it and using the base station's controlling program installed on your PC:

✔ Set a Service Set Identifier, or SSID, for your wireless network. This is the name by which the wireless network is known.

✔ You have the option of making the SSID name visible or invisible. If security is an issue, make the name invisible. That way, the base station doesn't broadcast the name, and only computers that know the name can connect to the wireless network.

✔ Set the encryption for the network, known as the WEP, or Wired Equivalent Privacy. Make sure that you note the password! It's a long string of numbers and letters, and you must enter it exactly to access the network.

✔ You may hear or read that the password is optional. My opinion: It's not. Don't compromise your network by omitting the password. In fact, Windows XP may not even connect to a wireless network that lacks a password.

✔ Optionally, configure the base station to allow connections only from known computers. You specify this by listing the MAC address of the wireless Ethernet adapter in each PC. Refer to Chapter 16 for information on getting the MAC address.

✔ Tell the wireless router to provide IP addresses dynamically for all computers on the network. This is also known as DHCP; refer to Chapter 16 for information on configuring the NIC to accept a dynamic IP address.

✔ If the base station offers firewall abilities, enable them.

✔ The base station may also serve as a router. Refer to Chapter 18 for more information.

The most important pieces of information you need are the wireless network's SSID or name and the long, cryptic password you need in order to access the network. I recommend that you write those things down and keep them in a safe place.

"How far does the signal go?"

The 802.11 wireless networking standard uses radio signals to send and receive information. Because of that, you don't need to set up your network so that all the computers have a direct line of sight to the base station. It's completely possible to have the wireless hub in one room and use a wireless computer in another — though there are exceptions.

The key to the wireless network is the base station. Your PC's wireless NIC must be able to access the base station directly in order for that computer to be on the network. The base station may advertise that it can broadcast its signal up to 300 feet away — but that's only under ideal conditions, like on the barren wastes of the moon.

Amazingly enough, things like walls can greatly decrease the reception of a base station's wireless signal. In fact, a standard wood-and-plaster wall can cut a wireless networking signal in half — or more. If the walls are brick or metal, no signal may get through at all.

If you're having any problem with your wireless signal, try moving either the PC or the base station. Also, adjusting the directional antenna on the base station or PC may help.

✔ Most offices that use wireless networking keep a base station in every room that has wireless computers. The base stations are then hard-wired together to help build the network.

✔ I mount my base stations high up, either near or on the ceiling where there is little interference from other things in the room. Even setting a book down in front of a base station may disrupt the signal enough to disconnect a remote computer from the network.

Hooking into a Wireless Network

You have to be deliberate when you use wires to connect a network. One wire can go into only one plug at a time. But, with wireless networking, you often have a choice of which wireless network you want to connect to.

For example, if you're in a high-tech yet densely populated part of town, you may discover that dozens of wireless networks are set up, each of which is detected by your computer. Some are closed or password protected, and others may be open. This section tells you how to scan for a wireless network or how to hook into one specific network, if that's all you want to do.

Connecting to your own wireless network

Follow these steps to connect your wireless PC to a wireless network. Remember that what you're really connecting to is the base station that provides the central access point for all the other wireless computers in the network. Here's what you do:

1. **Open the Network Connections window.**

   You can get there by double-clicking the Network Connections icon in the Control Panel.

2. **Right-click the wireless network connection's icon.**

3. **Choose View Available Wireless Connections from the pop-up menu.**

   The Wireless Network Connection dialog box shows up, as depicted in Figure 19-2. This dialog box lists any and all wireless networks that are within range of your laptop and compatible with your wireless networking protocol.

Figure 19-2:
Desperately
scanning for
available
wireless
networks.

If your wireless networking gear supports more than one protocol, you see every matching protocol appear in the window.

In Figure 19-2, one network shows up as available. Its name is KITTY, which is the network's SSID.

4. **Select the wireless network's name (if you have more than one).**

5. **Enter the password twice.**

   You should have written down the password when you first configured the wireless base station. Or, if you're in a cybercafé or other remote location, the password is provided for you. Yes, you have to type that sucker twice, which can be a real pain, especially for those 128-character passwords.

6. **Click the Connect button.**

   If everything goes well, you see the little networking buddies appear in the notification area, plus a pop-up bubble alerting you to the wireless networking connection (see Figure 19-3). You've made it!

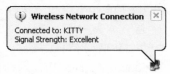

Figure 19-3:
A wireless
network
connection
has been
made.

If the preceding steps don't work, you can try a back-door approach to finding
and accessing any available wireless networks. In the Network Connections
window, right-click your Wireless Network Connection icon and choose
Properties from the pop-up menu. Then click the Wireless Networks tab in
your network connection's Properties dialog box, as shown in Figure 19-4.

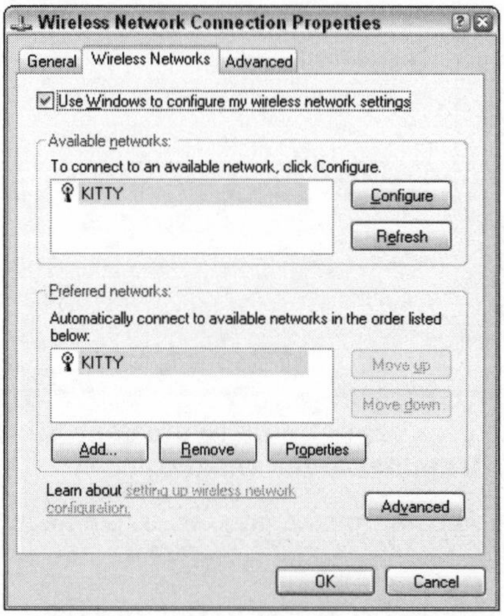

Figure 19-4:
Manually
doing the
wireless
thing.

Using the Wireless Networks tab may be necessary when switching from one
wireless connection to another. The bottom part of the dialog box (labeled
Preferred Networks) is used to store connection information about various
networks so that you don't have to toil with the same connection information
again and again.

Scanning for wireless networks

Your wireless network adapter came with a host of software, most of which
you can cheerfully ignore. One program that's quite handy and often comes

What is Bluetooth?

Bluetooth is the name of a wireless gizmo standard, which can be confused with wireless networking, although the only similarity between the two is the wireless part.

The Bluetooth standard allows for various gizmos or PC peripherals to wirelessly communicate with each other over short distances. For example, you could buy a Bluetooth expansion card and allow your PC to talk wirelessly with compatible Bluetooth peripherals, such as a keyboard, a mouse, a printer, or even a monitor. Theoretically, you could use a Bluetooth MP3 music player with your PC and then take it into your Bluetooth-enabled car and hear the music in the car.

Although Bluetooth has been around a while, it's not really popular on the PC. Someday, it may be an interface worth knowing about and using, but for now it's just one of many wireless solutions for adding peripherals to your PC.

All Bluetooth devices sport the Bluetooth symbol, which I would illustrate in this book if computer companies weren't so uptight about their trademarks.

with the wireless NIC is a scanning tool. Often, this tool is much better than the simple, primitive programs Windows offers.

Figure 19-5 shows a network scanning tool that came with my laptop PC's wireless networking hardware. It shows five available networks. Two are suppressing the SSID, or network name. The two Linksys networks have no password; encryption is disabled. (Such a thing is typical when people set up wireless networking: They forget to rename the wireless hub, and they don't apply password protection.)

Figure 19-5: All available wireless networks.

Wireless utilities, such as the one shown in Figure 19-5, can also be used to scan for and connect to available wireless networks. Often, these utilities are far easier to manage than what Windows offers.

✔ These wireless scanners usually sport an icon in the notification area. The icon generally offers feedback regarding the signal strength of the wireless network.

✔ Scanning for unprotected wireless networks is known as *war driving,* often because a guy in a car with a laptop can do it and get free Internet access when unprotected wireless networks are found.

Part IV
The Soft Side of Computing

The 5th Wave   By Rich Tennant

"Oh, look, this must be one of those PCs that are assembled by prison inmates. It came bundled with a homemade shank in the mousepad."

In this part . . .

Mighty hardware may get all the attention, but it's *software* that sits on your PC's throne. Know the software side of your computer, and the hardware side just follows, like an obedient pup. Yes, this is primarily a hardware book. Even so, consider that understanding software is the key to getting the most from your PC. Besides, you may have read some 300 pages of hardware yackety-yak. It's time for software to have its day in the sun.

Chapter 20

Files: The Key to Understanding Software

*E*very day, millions of people sit down at a computer and go about their work. They do e-mail. They process words. They browse the Internet. They play games. Some work may be done. Because computers have become easier to use over the past few years, it's relatively easy for anyone to sit down at a computer and do *something*. Even so, the computer remains a mysterious and often frustrating device for most people.

The problem with computers is that the software is so easy to use that no one bothers taking that extra bonus step of *understanding* how things work. Despite your ability to get work done, you really need to know a few software basics to get the most from your computer. I'm serious! It all starts with the knowledge unfolded in this chapter, the nucleus of all software: the file.

Do You Know What a File Is?

I would guess that 80 percent of everyone who uses a PC doesn't have the slightest idea what a file is. Yes, there is a File menu. You save files to disk and you open files on disk. But, only when you truly understand what a file is can you begin to really appreciate your computer and start to take control of the beast.

Presenting the file

A *file* is a chunk of information stored in a computer. The word *file* is used because, in an office setting, information is traditionally stored on paper and those papers are grouped into files, stored in a file cabinet. The same analogy applies to computer files, though I don't think that the comparison has been successful.

When you think of a file, don't think of a paper file at all. Instead, the file is a container. The container can be very small or very large. Unlike a printed sheet of paper, a file can contain a variety of stuff. The container keeps that stuff together and separate from other containers, which also contain stuff separate from other containers.

> ✔ A file is really nothing more than a container, a place to hold a chunk of information stored in a computer.

> ✔ I think *file* is a bad choice for describing something stored in a computer. Had I been one of the computing pioneers, I would have called it a *container* or *holder* or even made up a word using flowery Greek or Latin. The problem with *file* is that it's ambiguous and doesn't adequately describe the nature of the "container o' stuff" inside a computer. Also, as with many computer terms, *file* is used as both a noun and a verb.

What's in a file?

On the atomic level, all the information in a file is *binary*, or just a series of ones and zeroes, like this:

```
1100010011011110111001011010010110111001100111100001
```

Boring! Computers can do miraculous things with ones and zeroes, however, so — categorically speaking — there are really three types of files:

> ✔ Documents
> ✔ Programs
> ✔ Data files

These types describe the contents of the file, or how the ones and zeroes are interpreted by the software you use.

A *document* includes any file you've created. It can be a true text document, such as a to-do list, a chapter of a novel, or a note to Jimmy's teacher explaining that his skin condition isn't contagious. Documents can also be sound files, graphics images, or any other type of information the computer can create, store, or seize from the Internet.

Program files contain instructions for the computer's microprocessor; they tell the computer what to do. Note that programs are also files. Even the operating system, which is a program, is also a file. In fact, the operating system consists of many files.

Data files include all other files on disk that aren't exactly programs or documents. These include support files for programs, temporary files, and other random stuff that must be saved inside the computer.

Everything stored inside the computer is a file. There are files you create, program files you buy, program files that are part of the operating system, and data files that make up just about everything else. Everything is a file!

Describing a file

Just as people are different, so are files. People are described by how they look and act and by their given names. People also have birthdays and live in certain places. The same is almost entirely true for files, though files don't usually get moody or care whether other files think that they're fat.

All files stored inside the computer have various *attributes,* or specific ways of describing the files and keeping each file unique and separate from the other files. Five of these attributes help you not only identify what the file is but also keep each file unique:

- ✔ Name
- ✔ Size
- ✔ Date and time
- ✔ Type
- ✔ Icon

All files have a name, or *filename.* The name describes the file's contents or gives you a clue to what the file will be used for. The name is given to the file when it's created. This is true for all files.

Files have a physical size. They occupy storage space inside memory, and they also occupy storage space on disk. Some files are tiny, some can be quite large.

When a file is created, the operating system slaps it just like a doctor slaps a human baby. But a file doesn't breathe, and it lacks a butt, so what's slapped on it is a date-and-time stamp. This stamp helps keep your files organized and allows you to sort through your files based on their creation dates and times. A second date-and-time stamp is applied to a file whenever it's updated, changed, or modified. (The original creation date and time remain the same.)

Finally, each file has a type, which is closely related to the file's icon you see in Windows. The file type depends on the file's contents, and each program that creates a document assigns that file a specific type and related icon. This is a big topic, so it's covered later in this chapter, starting with the section "File Types and Icons."

- ✔ The size of a file is measured in bytes, just like memory. Refer to Chapter 9 for more information on bytes.

- ✔ A file can be zero bytes in size, in which case the file exists, but lacks any contents.

- ✔ The largest a file can be is 4GB. Rarely, however, do files get that big.

- ✔ The date-and-time stamp is one reason that the PC has an internal clock. It also explains why it's important to keep the PC's clock up to date. Refer to Chapter 6 for more information on setting the clock.

- ✔ Additional attributes are used to describe files — for example, whether a file is a system file, hidden, read-only, compressed, archived, and a bunch of other trivial things. The operating system keeps track of all that stuff.

Files dwell in folders

Another description of a file, missing from the list in the preceding section, is that files are all stored on disk in containers called *folders*. Again with the file cabinet metaphor! Will they ever learn?

The folder helps keep files organized, which allows you to separate files into groups for similar things. Using folders is one key way to keep from going insane when you use the computer — just as using a closet or cupboard is a way of keeping stuff around the house organized.

Folders are a big part of organizing and using files, so they're covered by themselves, in Chapter 21. That chapter also covers the Windows Explorer program, mentioned in this chapter.

Slap a Name on That File

All files need to have names, and it's good that the computer affords you the opportunity to name your files. If things were up to the computer, files would be named like car license plates, but without the optional wildlife or historical themes.

Because the computer lets you, the human, name the files, you can get as flowery and creative as you were when you named the dog or your motorcycle or that comet you discovered. Have fun! Be playful! This section reviews the basics for naming files.

Choosing the best name

Be clever when you name a file! Naming stuff is one thing humans are good at. I'm referring to older humans, of course. If 2-year-olds were in charge of naming things, all animals would be called "dog."

You name a file when you're saving it to disk, which happens in the Save As dialog box (see the section "Using the Save As dialog box," later in this chapter). When naming a file, be brief and descriptive. Try using only letters, numbers, and spaces in the name. For example:

```
Agenda
Chapter 16
Trip to Branson
2006 May Expense Report
Places in Town to Dump Toxic Waste
```

Each of these examples is a good filename, which properly explains the file's contents.

- ✔ Upper- or lowercase doesn't matter. Although capitalizing Pocatello is proper, for example, Windows recognizes that filename the same as pocatello, Pocatello, POCATELLO, or any combination of upper- and lowercase letters.

- ✔ Though case doesn't matter in a filename, it *does* matter when you're typing a Web page address.

- ✔ The file's name reminds you of what's in the file, of what it's all about — just like naming your car Ticket Magnet tells everyone what the car is all about.

- ✔ You can rename a file at any time after it has been created. See Chapter 22 for information on the Rename command.

- ✔ All the rules for naming files in this and the following subsections also apply to naming folders, though folders are covered in Chapter 21.

Official file-naming rules

Here's the law when it comes to naming files in Windows. All this stuff is optional reading; as long as you stick with the simple rules in the preceding subsection, this stuff is merely trivia.

Characters: Files can be named using any combination of letters and numbers, plus a smattering of symbols.

Length: Technically, you can give a file a name that's over 200 characters long. Don't. Long filenames may be *very* descriptive, but Windows displays them funny or not at all in many situations. Better to keep things short than to abuse long-filename privileges.

Forbidden characters: Windows gets angry if you use any of these characters to name a file:

```
* / : < > ? \ | "
```

These symbols hold a special meaning to Windows. Nothing bad happens if you attempt to use these characters. Windows just refuses to save the file — or a warning dialog box growls at you.

Use periods sparingly: Although you can use any number of periods in a filename, you cannot name a file with all periods. I know that it's strange, and I'm probably the only one on the planet to have tried it, but it doesn't work.

Spaces: Filenames can contain spaces. Try not to start a filename with a space, though, because it's difficult to see. It's common in computerland to use the underscore (or underline) character rather than a space.

Numbers are okay: Feel free to start a filename by using a number. You can even use symbols, though not the forbidden characters just listed. I mention this because there are rumors out there about not starting a filename with a number. Poppycock.

File Types and Icons

Who knows what evil lurks inside a file? Well, honestly, no one does! A file by itself knows nothing of its contents. In fact, the best the operating system can do is to *guess* about a file's contents. Most of the time, it makes a good guess. The system used to determine the stuff of a file's guts, however, isn't that solid.

The key is something called the *filename extension*. That extension is used by Windows to help identify not only the file's contents (it's type), but also which program created the file and which icon is displayed on the screen. This section mulls all this over.

The supersecret filename extension

The filename *extension* is a secret bit of text added to a filename when the file is first created. The filename extension is applied by the program used to create the file. It tells the operating system three things:

- ✔ The type of file that's created — document, graphics, or sound, for example
- ✔ The program that created the file
- ✔ Which icon to use to represent the file

It's the extension that offers a clue to what's inside a file, and the operating system relies heavily on that extension.

Filename extension details

The filename extension is the last part of a filename, usually hidden from view. It starts with a period, which is then followed by one to four characters. For most files, the extension is three characters long.

For example, the .doc filename extension is used by Microsoft Word to identify Word documents. The extension is pronounced "dot dock," with the dot or period followed by DOC, which is short for document.

Web page files use the .HTM or .HTML filename extension.

Graphics files have a number of filename extensions, depending on the graphics file type: JPG, GIF, TIFF, and PNG, for example.

Note that it's common to write the extension without the leading period, though in a filename the period and extension are there. For example:

```
Chapter 20.DOC
```

The name of this chapter's document file on disk is Chapter 20.DOC. You may see only Chapter 20 on the screen, but the DOC part is there.

- ✔ There are gazillions of common filename extensions.
- ✔ Most program files in Windows use the EXE extension, where EXE stands for *exe*cutable file.

> ✔ A full list of filename extensions is maintained on the Internet, at this Web page:
>
>   www.filext.com

> ✔ A filename extension is created by the program used to create the file. The extension is added automatically, and it's necessary in Windows. As the computer operator, it helps if you know about extensions, but beyond that, don't mess with them.

How to see or hide a filename extension

You can tell Windows whether you want the filename extension displayed when you view a list of files. Most beginners prefer to hide the extension; old-time PC users like to see the extension. Either way, showing or hiding the extension is done in the same place. Abide by these steps:

1. **Open the My Computer icon on the desktop.**

   The window you see displayed is the Windows Explorer program, which is used to examine files and stuff stored in your computer. (Read more on that in Chapter 21.)

2. **Choose Tools⇨Folder Options.**

3. **Click the View tab in the Folder Options dialog box.**

4. **Locate the item on the list that says `Hide extensions for known file types`.**

5. **Put a check mark there to hide the extensions, or remove the check mark so that Windows displays the extensions.**

   Or, if the item is already set the way you like, you're just dandy.

6. **Click OK to close the Folder Options dialog box.**

7. **Close the My Computer window.**

If you elect to show the extension, refer to the next subsection for important information on renaming extensions.

Keep in mind that it's Windows job to maintain filename extensions. You should really never mess with them, whether you see them or not.

Don't rename the extension

If you have configured Windows to display filename extensions (refer to the preceding subsection), be careful when you assign a file a new name by using the Rename command: You must not rename the extension!

The filename extension is just an extra appendage on a filename. It's utterly possible to rename the extension — or delete it. But, when you do so, you deny Windows the opportunity to know what's really in the file. It really messes things up!

Fortunately, Windows warns you when it comes time to rename a file and you either forget to keep the same filename extension or type a new one. When that happens, use the Rename command again, and carefully edit the name so that you keep the file's original extension.

See Chapter 22 for more information on renaming files.

Icons

Windows is a graphical operating system, and, as such, it uses *icons,* or tiny pictures, to represent files. The picture supposedly relates directly to the type of file as well as to the program that created the file. After reading the previous subsections, you should recognize that both those attributes are directly related to the filename extension.

Figure 20-1 shows a file as Windows displays it; a graphical icon representing a Word document appears, along with the full filename, including the .DOC extension.

Figure 20-1:
A file with
an icon,
a name,
and an
extension.

Chapter 1.doc

Each filename extension, or file type, sports a unique icon in Windows, as you discover while you use Windows.

Creating Files

Files are created by using programs — software. Specifically, the software that creates stuff is called an *application.* For example, you use the word processing application Microsoft Word to create text documents, brochures, novels, plays, and left-wing manifestos.

The good news is that it's easy to create things with a computer and the proper software. The bad news is that the computer happily and repeatedly loses anything you create — until you save that something to disk.

Saving to disk is important! Nothing is truly created until you save!

It doesn't matter how long you worked to create the thing — the document, image, or whatever: Until you've used the Save command, that information exists only in the wispy gossamer of the computer's fickle imagination (also known as RAM). Pull the plug and — *POOF!* — that stuff is gone for good.

To avoid disaster you must save your stuff to disk. Your tool for doing so is the Save command.

The Save command

Windows has two Save commands: Save and Save As. Both exist on the File menu.

The first time you save your stuff to disk, the Save As command is used (even if you choose File⇨Save). Save As directs Windows to give the file a name and save it on a specific disk drive and in a specific folder. The Save As command *creates* the file.

After your stuff is saved to disk with Save As and the new file is created, you use the plain Save command to update the file. So, after initially saving, you work a little bit, and then you use the Save command, File⇨Save, to update the file on disk. It works this way until you're done, when you save one last time before quitting the program.

✔ The Save command can also be accessed from the Save button on a toolbar or by pressing Ctrl+S on the keyboard.

✔ If your stuff hasn't yet been saved, using the Save command is the same as the using Save As command.

✔ You can also use the Save As command specifically to save a file with a new name or in a new location.

✔ After a file has been saved, the file's name appears on the title bar (at the top of the window).

Using the Save As dialog box

The first time you save your stuff to disk, a Save As dialog box appears. The purpose of this dialog box is, obviously, to save your precious work to disk, or permanent storage. That way, you always have a copy of your stuff handy for future use.

The Save As dialog box is also the place where you assign your stuff a file name and set the file in a specific folder on a specific disk drive. (Folders are covered in Chapter 21.)

Figure 20-2 shows the typical Save As dialog box. It contains a lot of controls specifically designed to baffle the new computer user. What you need to find specifically is the text box, near the bottom, labeled File Name. That's where you type the name of the file you're saving.

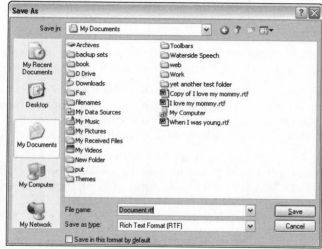

Figure 20-2:
The typical
Save As
dialog box.

Here's how the Save As dialog box works on the simplest level:

1. Type a name for your file.

Refer to the file-naming rules earlier in this chapter. Be clever. Be descriptive. Be brief.

2. Click the Save button.

The file is safely stored on your hard disk.

Trust me: The file is saved to disk. There's no need to confirm this. Had there been an error, Windows would promptly inform you.

If the Save button doesn't work, you probably used a forbidden character in the filename or used the name of a file that has already been saved. The more polite programs tell you specifically the booboo you've made. Ruder programs just don't let you click the Save button.

Additional controls in the Save As dialog box allow you to select a specific disk drive and folder for your stuff. I recommend that you read Chapter 21, on folders, before you attempt to do that.

✔ The Save As dialog box appears only the first time you save your stuff to disk; from that point on, the Save command merely resaves a file to disk.

✔ Not every Save As dialog box looks like the one shown in Figure 20-2. Some are very complex, depending on the program. Also, when saving some types of files, additional dialog boxes may appear and prompt you for more input about the file being saved.

✔ To save the file in a specific folder, open that folder in the main part of the Save As dialog box. (Open the folder by double-clicking with the mouse.)

✔ You can also choose a specific folder (or disk drive) from the Save In drop-down list.

✔ Click the New Folder button to create a new folder for your stuff. Refer to the section "Let There Be Folders," in Chapter 21, for more information.

✔ If you've directed Windows not to display the filename extension, you don't see the extension used in the Save As dialog box. On the other hand, if the extensions are visible, you see them as shown in Figure 20-2, where it says (in very tiny letters) ".rtf" after the filename.

✔ The Save As Type drop-down list directs the program to save the file as a specific file type. This tool can be used to override the program's normal file type and save your stuff in a specific type. For example, you can use this option to save a Word document in the plain text (TXT) file type. Mess with the option only when you know that you want to save the file as a different type.

Chapter 21

Organizing Your Compu-Junk

. . . .

In This Chapter

▶ Knowing what a folder is

▶ Discovering the root folder

▶ Understanding folder lingo

▶ Visiting popular folders

▶ Using the Windows Explorer program

▶ Opening folders

▶ Using the tree structure

▶ Creating new folders

▶ Working in the Open dialog box

. . . .

Stuff happens, and on your PC, you soon discover that it happens quite a bit! If you do any work at all with your computer, you soon discover yourself buried hip deep in files. Files everywhere! Files you created, files you downloaded from the Internet, and files that seem to grow like freckles on a redhead. What to do, what to do?

The solution to the file flood is a wee bit of organization. It comes from the concept known as a *folder,* which is the first step in organizing your stuff. Even programs and Windows itself use folders for organizing things, which makes the folder the equivalent of the California Closet or extra bonus garage shelving — what everyone with a lot of stuff needs. This chapter explains how it's all done.

The Folder Story

Folders exist to organize your files, which continues with the office metaphor that computers use — the one I totally dismiss in Chapter 20. *Folders* are merely containers for files. Folders keep files of similar types together, or they allow you to organize files by project, date, or however you want to use them to keep your stuff sane.

Yes! Sanity is the key! Without folders, files would litter the hard drive like pieces of a casino after a Las Vegas demolition. The typical PC hard drive now stores between 10,000 and 50,000 files. Imagine finding your one file! Heck, it would take you a week to scroll through the list. I won't even go into the madness of duplicate filenames and how sluggish the computer would behave any time you saved or opened anything on disk. Yech!

No, folders are the key to organizing files on your computer's hard drive. Windows uses them. You should use them as well.

✔ A folder is a storage place for files.

✔ Refer to Chapter 20 for information on files. It's very important! Understanding files is the key to using software on your computer.

✔ All files stored on your computer's hard drive are kept in folders. The folders keep files together — like barbed wire keeps prisoners, vicious animals, and kindergartners from wandering off.

✔ Folders appear in Windows using the folder icon, as shown in the margin. To open the folder, double-click it with the mouse. This action displays the folder's contents in a window — the folder window.

✔ Folders hold files. They can also hold other folders. Folders within folders! Just like those Russian matryoshka dolls.

✔ Folders may also be referred to as *directories*. This term is merely a throwback to the old days of DOS (which is a throwback to the days of Unix, which King Herod used).

Famous Folders throughout History

Whether you like it or not, all your computer's disk drives are organized into folders. Disk drives exist to store files, and files *must be* stored in folders. Beyond that, some specific and aptly named folders are available on your PC when you run the Windows operating system. This section mulls over the lot of them.

The root folder

Every disk — even the stupid floppy disk — has at least one folder. That one folder — the main folder on the disk — is the *root folder*. Like a tree (and this isn't a dog joke), all other folders on your hard drive branch out from that main, root folder.

The root folder doesn't have a specific icon. Instead, it uses the icon for the drive that the root folder is on. So, the root folder on drive C has the same icon as drive C. You can see those icons in the My Computer window.

✔ The root folder is simply the main, or only, folder on a disk drive.

✔ The root folder is like the lobby of some grand building: It's merely a place you pass through to get to somewhere else. Where else? Why, other folders, of course!

✔ The root folder may also be called the *root directory*.

The subfolder

When one folder exists inside another, it is said to be a *subfolder*. This term has nothing to do with underwater naval vessels or hoagy-like sandwiches.

For example, you may be told to open the My Documents folder. Then, you may be told to open the My Pictures subfolder. That simply means that My Pictures is the name of a folder within the My Documents folder — a folder within a folder.

✔ In addition to holding files, folders can hold more folders.

✔ No limit exists on the number of subfolders you can create. You can have a folder inside a folder inside a folder, and so on. If you name the folders well, it all makes sense. Otherwise, it's just like a badly organized filing cabinet, though without the smell of booze.

✔ A subfolder can also be called a *child* folder.

✔ The *parent* folder is the folder that contains the subfolder. So, if Windows is a folder inside the root folder, the root folder is the parent folder and Windows is the child folder.

✔ Yes, parent folder and child folder are terms rarely used. And the people said "A-men!"

The My Documents folder

The root folder is for the computer itself; humans don't use it. Instead, Windows offers a place for your stuff on the computer (a home plate, as it were), where you can save the files you create or make numerous new folders to keep your stuff organized. That place, that famous folder, is the My Documents folder.

The My Documents folder is your personal folder in Windows, where you can freely and wantonly store your stuff.

Because the My Documents folder is so important, you have many easy ways to get to the folder and display its contents: You can open the My Documents icon on the desktop; choose My Documents from the Start button's menu;

click the My Documents button on the left side of any Open or Save As dialog box; plus many, many more wonderful and confusing ways.

- ✔ Use the My Documents folder as the main place for storing the stuff you create or collect in your computer.

- ✔ Also make use of folders to organize your stuff within the My Documents folder. This topic is covered throughout the rest of this chapter.

- ✔ The My Documents folder is generally found on drive C, where Windows dwells. If your PC has other hard drives, you can also use them to store your stuff. In that case, it's okay to use the root folder on those drives.

Oh, my — my folders

The My Documents folder contains some pre-made folders to help you get into the notion of organizing your stuff. Here's a sampling of some of the other folders — subfolders — you may find there:

 My Pictures: This is the folder where many graphics applications yearn to save the images you create. See? It's organization in action, and you haven't even done anything yet!

 My Music: This folder is used by many audio programs — specifically, Windows Media Player — for storing the various music files you save on your PC.

 My Videos: Getting the hint? The My Videos folder is used to store video files on a computer. Already, you can smell the organization happening: If you want to save a video file, you choose the My Documents folder, open the My Videos folder, and then save the file there. Celebration organization!

My Goodness: During the course of your Windows travels, you may find other folders created in the My Documents folder, either by some program or by yourself. Use the folders for the specific documents they describe. And, if things don't go into folders, consider creating the popular Misc or Junk folder.

Famous Yet Forbidden Folders

In addition to needing folders for your stuff, your computer needs folders for the stuff Windows uses and folders for your applications. These are what I call the forbidden folders; don't mess with them!

- ✔ Though you may someday poke around inside a forbidden folder, don't mess with anything there.

> ✔ Use the My Documents folder, or any of its subfolders, to store your stuff. Don't store your stuff in a forbidden folder.
>
> ✔ Delete only those folders you created yourself, such as any folder in the My Documents folder. Don't mess with anything elsewhere, such as in the Windows or Program Files folders.
>
> ✔ Mess with a forbidden folder only if you're *specifically* directed to do so.
>
> ✔ The root folder of the hard drive is considered forbidden.

The Windows folder

Windows itself lives in the Windows folder, which may be named WINNT on some computers. This folder contains many files and a heck of a lot of sub-folders, all of which comprise the Windows operating system and its support programs. *Touch ye not the files that lurketh there!*

You may occasionally hear the Windows folder (and its subfolders) referred to by their official corporate name, the *system folders.*

The Program Files folder

The software you use on your PC also has its own home plate, called the Program Files folder. Within that folder are numerous subfolders, one each for the various programs installed on your computer — or perhaps one general folder for all programs from a specific vendor. Oh, bother — why not take a look?

1. **Open the My Computer icon on the desktop.**

2. **Open the drive C icon.**

   This step displays the root folder for drive C.

3. **Open the Program Files folder.**

   The Program Files window appears and shows you all the folders for all the software installed on your PC.

   Look, but don't touch.

4. **Close the Program Files window.**

See how each program lives in its own folder? Those folders may even have subfolders for further organization. For example, the Adobe folder may contain a subfolder for the Adobe Acrobat Reader program and then another folder for some other Adobe product you may have on your PC.

Other folders, mysterious and evil

The computer's C drive is chock full of folders. What do they do? I don't know! I don't think anyone knows, but that's not the point. The point is to use only the My Documents folder and those subfolders you create inside My Documents. Any other folder is considered hands-off.

Don't mess with any folder you didn't create yourself! You can look, but don't do anything else!

The Windows Explorer Program

One of the duties of an operating system is to help you organize the stuff you create. It's Windows job to put files on the hard drive, organize the files into folders, and keep track of all that stuff. Furthermore, Windows presents the file and folder information to you in a simple manner, which allows you to control your files and folders without the necessity of a second brain. The tool you use to help manipulate those files and folders is a program called Windows Explorer.

Note that Windows Explorer isn't the same program as Internet Explorer, though they're both similar in appearance.

Running the Windows Explorer program

Windows Explorer is one of the easiest programs to run. My favorite way to start it is to press Win+E on the keyboard. You can also right-click the My Documents or My Computer icon on the desktop and choose Explore from the pop-up menu. The Windows Explorer program is shown in Figure 21-1.

In Figure 21-1, Windows Explorer displays the files and folders found in the My Documents folder. You can see My Documents up on the title bar, which tells you which folder you're viewing. The contents of the folder appear on the right; toolbars and other information are on the top and left sides of the window.

If you don't see the toolbar in the Windows Explorer window, choose View⇨ Toolbars⇨Standard Buttons. You may also want to choose Address Bar from the Toolbars submenu.

Current folder   Toolbar

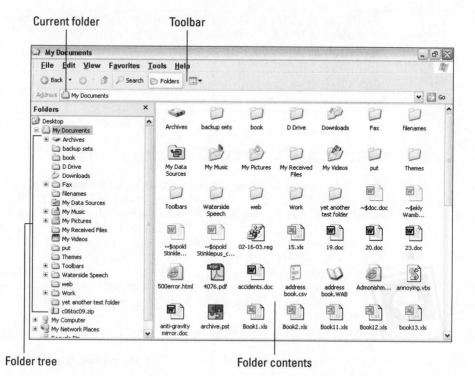

Figure 21-1:
Windows
Explorer
shows you
the tree
structure.

Folder tree   Folder contents

Opening a folder

Any time you double-click a folder icon, the Windows Explorer program runs
and displays the contents of that folder, as shown in Figure 21-1.

When you open a file, also by double-clicking it, the program that created the
file runs and displays the file's contents. Well, it may not be exactly the program that created the file: For example, graphics files may be displayed in a
"viewer" program, not the exact program that created the image.

When you open a program file, the program runs.

Opening a folder inside a folder window displays that folder's contents; the
window changes to reflect the opened folder's contents. You can configure
Windows so that each folder opens into its own folder window. To do so,
heed these steps:

1. **In the folder window, choose Tools⇨Options.**

    The Folder Options dialog box appears.

2. **On the General tab, click to choose the option labeled Open Each Folder in Its Own Window.**

3. **Click OK.**

Don't forget to close all those open folder windows when you're done with them.

Viewing the tree structure

The whole mess of folders on your hard drive is organized into something the computer nerds call the *tree structure*. It can be seen on the left side of the Windows Explorer window, titled Folders, as shown in Figure 21-1. If you don't see that list, click the Folders button on the Explorer toolbar. Or, you can choose View⇨Explorer Bar⇨Folders from the menu.

You manipulate the tree structure by using the mouse to quickly navigate to a specific folder in your computer system — if you know where to go. Just click a folder to display its contents on the right side of the window.

You click the + (plus sign) by a folder to open it up and reveal any subfolders.

Click the – (minus sign) by a folder to close that "branch" of the tree structure.

Not viewing the tree structure

When the Folders panel is hidden, the Windows Explorer program displays a list of tasks for your files and folders, as shown in Figure 21-2. These tasks provide links to things to do with the files in the folder, other places to go, and similar tasks.

The tasks that are displayed vary, depending on the type of folder that's viewed or whether a file is selected and what type of file it is.

  Note that each task panel can be displayed or hidden by clicking the up or down chevrons (see the margin).

Viewing the files in a folder

 The Views button, on the far right side of the Windows Explorer toolbar, displays a menu that controls how icons are displayed in the window:

Filmstrip: Best for previewing graphics files (available only in folders configured for viewing graphical images).

Thumbnails: Also good for viewing graphics files; previews the images inside the files in a tiny window instead of displaying the file icon.

Tiles: Displays large icons to represent the files stored in a folder.

Icons: Displays smaller icons to represent files.

List: Displays files in a list, with a very small icon and then the filename.

Details: Allows you to see detailed information about the files in a folder, displayed in columns.

If you have oodles of time to waste, click the button and choose a different view. (I like Large Icons view, but my friend Julia detests it.)

- ✔ These options can also be chosen from the View menu.
- ✔ Details view is best for finding out information about the files in a folder. It lists information such as file size, date and time, file type, and other bonus goodies.

Figure 21-2:
Folder tasks, things to do, places to go.

Let There Be Folders

I can't leave the folder chapter without a few key words on creating folders. Hopefully, this task will be something you do routinely as you organize the stuff on your PC's hard drive.

Creating a folder is easy. Remembering to use the folder is the hard part. The following steps create a folder named Stuff in the My Documents folder on drive C:

1. **Double-click the My Documents icon on the Windows desktop.**

   If the folder appears messy, choose <u>V</u>iew⇨Arrange <u>I</u>cons⇨By <u>N</u>ame from the menu. This step alphabetizes the folder's contents.

2. **Choose <u>F</u>ile⇨<u>N</u>ew⇨<u>F</u>older.**

   The new folder appears. Its name is New Folder, but note that the name is *selected*. It means that you can type a new folder name immediately.

3. **Type Stuff.**

   The folder is named Stuff, which is what you type at the keyboard. That name replaces the insipid New Folder as the folder's name.

4. **Press Enter to lock in the name.**

   The new folder is ready for use.

You can double-click the new folder's icon to open it. A blank window appears because it's a new folder and has no contents. See Chapter 22 for information on copying or moving files into the folder.

- Be clever with the name! Remember that this folder will contain files and possibly other folders, all of which should relate somehow to the folder's name.

- Generally speaking, folders are manipulated like files. After creating a folder, you can rename it, move it, copy it, delete it, or make a shortcut to the folder. See Chapter 22 for those details.

- A special type of folder is the *compressed* folder, also known as a zip file. For more information on that type of folder, refer to my Web site and look for the E-Doc on archiving:

  `http://www.wambooli.com/e`

Using the Open Dialog Box

As you use your computer, you often find yourself digging through folders with the Open command, off to fetch a file somewhere on disk. For example, you want to open that document you worked on yesterday, the one that contains the secret plans for invading Finland.

 To retrieve a file formerly saved to disk, you use the Open command. It's on the File menu, or you can click an Open command button on a toolbar (if such a button is available). The keyboard shortcut is Ctrl+O — O for Open. The Open command displays the Open dialog box, which is used for fetching files formerly saved to disk.

Figure 21-3 shows a typical Open dialog box, used by most programs in Windows. The following steps explain how this dialog box is used:

Figure 21-3: The typical Open dialog box.

The main part of the Open dialog box lists files — just like a Windows Explorer window. In fact, you can even change the view (refer to the section "Viewing the files in a folder," earlier in this chapter).

If you see the file you want in the main part of the Open dialog box, click it with the mouse. That selects the file and highlights it in the dialog box. Then, you click the Open button. Windows obeys your command by fetching the file you selected from disk and opening it in a window on the screen. You can then do whatever you want with the file's contents: look, edit, modify, print — whatever.

When you don't see the file you want, you use various gizmos in the dialog box to browse through other disk drives and folders. I recommend doing these things to help hunt down that wayward file:

- ✔ Click the My Documents button (on the left side of the Open dialog box), which displays the contents of the My Documents folder.

- ✔ Double-click to open any folder displayed on the file list.

- ✔ If you want to go back up to the preceding folder, click the handy Up One Level button (as shown in the margin).

- ✔ Choose another folder from the Look In drop-down list, at the top of the dialog box.

- ✔ Choose another disk drive from the Look In drop-down list and start browsing through folders on that drive.

When you find your file, open it!

I hope that now you can appreciate properly naming files and folders — and using those folders to organize your stuff. Don't sweat it if you've misnamed things. You can easily rename files and folders, as covered in Chapter 22.

- ✔ At the bottom of the dialog box is a drop-down list, labeled Files of Type. It helps you narrow the kinds of files displayed on the Open dialog box's list. For example, in Figure 21-3, All Picture Files is selected, so any graphics file appears on the list. To narrow the list, a specific file type can be chosen.

- ✔ Note that not every program can open every type of file. Programs work best on the files they create themselves.

- ✔ The Browse dialog box is similar to the Open dialog box. It appears whenever you click a Browse button to hunt down a file for Windows.

- ✔ When you're really stuck finding a file, use the Windows Search command. See Chapter 22.

Chapter 22

File Control

*Y*our files represent the stuff you create on your computer. As such, they're very important to you. The operating system understands this, and it gives you a smattering of tools to control, manipulate, and maintain your files. Control is the issue here! Like nuclear fuel or a room full of kindergarteners, your files must be contained. This chapter describes the tools you need to use to control your files.

Working with Groups of Files

Before you can mess with any file, you must select it. As with clogging, you can select files individually or in groups.

To select a single file, click its icon once with the mouse. This step selects the file, which appears highlighted onscreen, similar to what's shown in Figure 22-1. The file is now ready for action.

Figure 22-1:
The icon (file) on the right is selected.

✔ Clicking a file with the mouse *selects* that file.

✔ Selected files appear highlighted in the folder window.

✔ File manipulation commands — Copy, Move, Rename, and Delete, for example — affect only selected files.

Selecting all the files in a folder

To select all the files inside a folder, choose Edit➪Select All from the menu. This command highlights all files in the window — including any folders (and all the folders' contents), and marks them as ready for action.

You can also use the Ctrl+A keyboard shortcut to select all files in a folder.

Selecting a random smattering of files

Suppose that you need to select four icons in a folder all at once, similar to what's shown in Figure 22-2. Here's how to do that:

1. **Click to select the first file.**

   Point the mouse at the file's icon and click once.

2. **Press and hold the Ctrl key on the keyboard.**

   Either Ctrl (control) key works; press and hold it down.

Figure 22-2:
A random smattering of files is selected.

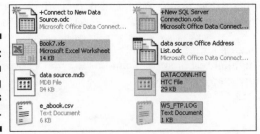

3. **Click to select the next file.**

   By holding the Ctrl key, you can select as many files as your clicking finger desires. (Otherwise, by clicking one file, you would unselect anything already selected.)

4. **Repeat Step 3 until you have selected all the files you want.**

   Or, until your clicking finger gets sore.

5. **Release the Ctrl key when you're done selecting files.**

Now you're ready to manipulate the selected files as a group.

To deselect a file from a group, just Ctrl+click it again.

Selecting a swath of files in a row

To select a queue of files, such as those shown in Figure 22-3, pursue these steps:

1. **Choose View⇨List from the menu.**

2. **Click to select the first file in your group.**

3. **Press and hold the Shift key.**

   Either Shift key on the keyboard works.

Name ▲	Size	Type	Artist
Bach's Brandenburg Concerto...	142 KB	MIDI Sequence	
Back to the Future.mid	39 KB	MIDI Sequence	
Beethoven's 5th Symphony.rmi	91 KB	MIDI Sequence	
Beethoven's Fur Elise.rmi	21 KB	MIDI Sequence	
bewitched.mid	9 KB	MIDI Sequence	
bigtop.mid	30 KB	MIDI Sequence	
bjs-ming.mid	6 KB	MIDI Sequence	
bohemian rhapsody.mid	51 KB	MIDI Sequence	
brunes.mid	47 KB	MIDI Sequence	
Bumble Bee.mid	14 KB	MIDI Sequence	
bumble.mid	21 KB	MIDI Sequence	
bwv538f.mid	25 KB	MIDI Sequence	
bwv538t.mid	36 KB	MIDI Sequence	
bwv948.mid	14 KB	MIDI Sequence	
Can't do that sum.mid	11 KB	MIDI Sequence	
CANYON.MID	21 KB	MIDI Sequence	
cartoons.mid	5 KB	MIDI Sequence	
Classical Gas.mid	8 KB	MIDI Sequence	
Dance of the Sugar-Plum Fair...	21 KB	MIDI Sequence	
Debussy's Claire de Lune.rmi	28 KB	MIDI Sequence	
doom1.mid	18 KB	MIDI Sequence	
elvis.mid	16 KB	MIDI Sequence	
EURYDICE.MID	90 KB	MIDI Sequence	
figaro.mid	38 KB	MIDI Sequence	

Figure 22-3: A group of files in a row is selected.

4. **Click to select the last file in your group.**

   By holding down the Shift key, you select all the files between the first click and second click, as shown in Figure 22-3.

5. **Release the Shift key.**

The files are now ready for action.

This file selection technique works best in List view. It works in other file views as well, though not as predictably.

You can take advantage of various file sorting commands to arrange the files in the list. Use the View↔Arrange Icons By submenu to choose how the files line up. For example, you can sort the files alphabetically, by size, by date, or by flavor.

Lassoing a group of files

Another way to select files as a group is to lasso them. Figure 22-4 illustrates how to do it by dragging over the files with the mouse.

Figure 22-4:
Lasso a
group of
files with
the mouse.

To lasso the files, start by pointing the mouse above and to the left of the icon horde you want to rope. Holding down the mouse button, drag down and to the right to create a rectangle surrounding ("lassoing") the file icons, as shown in Figure 22-4. Release the mouse button, and all the files you have lassoed are selected as a group. A vocal "Yee-ha!" is considered appropriate in this circumstance.

Selecting all but a single file

This handy trick is one I use all the time. For example, if I want to select all files in a folder except for one file (or folder), here's what I do:

1. **Click or Ctrl+click to select the file or files you *don't* want selected.**

2. **Choose Edit⇨Invert Selection from the menu.**

   Now, all the selected files are unselected, and all the unselected files are selected — and ready for action!

This trick beats having to select all the files and try to hunt for those you didn't want selected in the first place.

Mixing selection techniques

Working with groups of files is something you do often, so one of the techniques in the previous subsections can, hopefully, help you select files fast and easily. If not, keep in mind that you can mix and match techniques.

Suppose that you need to lasso two groups of files. If so, lasso the first group and then press and hold the Ctrl key to lasso and include the second collection.

You can Shift+click to select a swath of files in a row and then go back and Ctrl+click to remove specific files from that list.

Or, you can lasso a group of files you don't want to select and then choose Edit⇨Invert Selection to unselect those files and select everything else.

When you select a folder, you're selecting all the files and subfolders within that folder. Be careful!

Unselecting stuff

To unselect a file, simply click anywhere in the folder (but not on an icon). That action unselects any and all selected files in the folder. Or, you can close the folder window, in which case Windows immediately forgets about any selected files.

Files Hither, Thither, and Yon

Files don't stand still. You find yourself moving them, copying them, and killing them off. If you don't do those things, your hard drive gets all junky and, out of embarrassment, you're forced to turn off the computer when friends come over.

Moving or copying files to another folder

Files are moved and copied all the time. *Moving* a file happens when you transplant it from one folder to another folder. *Copying* happens when you duplicate a file, by keeping the original in its place and making an exact copy elsewhere.

Windows has about a dozen different ways to copy and move files. It may have more, but I've lost count. Rather than bore you with every possible alternative, here's the way I prefer to move or copy a file or group of selected files:

1. **Select the files or folders you want to move or copy.**

2a. **For moving, choose Edit⇨Move to Folder from the menu.**

2b. **For copying, choose Edit⇨Copy to Folder from the menu.**

   The Move Items or Copy Items dialog box appears. Both work similarly, though only the Move Items dialog box is shown as an example in Figure 22-5.

Figure 22-5:
The Move Items dialog box.

3. **Choose the destination folder from the scrolling list.**

   The scrolling list works like the tree structure thing, as covered in Chapter 21.

4. **Click the Move or Copy button.**

   The files are moved or copied from their current location to the folder you selected.

The Copy command makes file duplicates, and the Move command moves the files.

   ✔ If the destination folder doesn't exist, you can create it: Click to select the parent folder and then click the Make New Folder button. Give the new folder a name and then choose it as the destination.

   ✔ To move or copy files or folders to another disk drive, simply choose that drive's letter from the list.

   ✔ Moving folders moves all the files and subfolders inside that folder. Be careful when you do this: Windows may lose track of the documents previously opened in those folders.

   ✔ The popular My Documents folder is at the top of the list of folders in the dialog box.

   ✔ Rather than copy a file, consider creating a shortcut instead. See the section "Creating shortcuts," later in this chapter.

Moving or copying files with cut-and-paste

In Windows, where everything is like kindergarten anyway, you cut and paste files to move or copy them.

Moving a file is a cut-and-paste operation.

Copying a file is a copy-and-paste operation.

Here's how it's done:

1. **Select the files you want to move or copy.**

2a. **To move the files, choose Edit⇨Cut.**

2b. **To copy the files, choose Edit⇨Copy.**

If you cut, the files appear dimmed in the window, which means that they have been chosen for cutting. Nothing is wrong; keep moving on with the next step.

3. **Open the folder where you want the files moved or copied.**

4. **Choose Edit⇨Paste.**

The files are moved or copied.

Windows remembers which files were cut or copied until you cut or copy something else — so be methodical here. Don't put off pasting!

✔ You can also use the handy keyboard shortcuts: Ctrl+C for Copy, Ctrl+X for Cut, and Ctrl+V for Paste.

✔ To cancel the operation, simply press the Esc (escape) key before you paste the files. This action restores the cut files to a nondimmed state.

✔ Don't eat the paste.

Moving or copying files can be such a drag

Perhaps the easiest way to move or copy a file is to have both the file's window and the destination window open on the desktop at the same time. To move, simply drag an icon from one window to the other. To move a group, select the icons and then drag them from one window to the other.

Copying files involves dragging their icons, but when you do, press and hold the Ctrl key on the keyboard. You notice a small + (plus sign) appear by the mouse pointer as you drag the icons. It's your clue that the files are being copied (duplicated).

When you're dragging between folders on different disk drives, Windows always elects to copy rather than move the files. To override this, press the Shift key as you drag the files; the Shift key enforces the move operation, by moving the files rather than copying them.

Duplicating a file

To make a duplicate, simply copy a file to its same folder. Use any of the techniques for copying files that I cover earlier in this chapter.

The duplicate is created with the prefix `Copy of` and then the rest of the file-name. That's your clue that the file is a duplicate of the original stored in the same folder.

Copying a file to a removable disk

For some reason, people have a hang-up with copying files to a floppy disk or to any removable disk. It's quite simple to do. Here's how:

1. **Ensure that a disk is in the drive, ready to accept the file.**

   Or, in the case of a digital memory card, ensure that the drive is mounted in the card reader.

2. **Select the files to copy.**

3. **Choose File⇨Send To, and select the removable disk from the sub-menu.**

   The Send To submenu lists all available removable disk drives to which you can send the file — even a recordable CD or DVD, if your PC is blessed with such hardware.

   The files are copied to the drive as soon as you choose the command.

Always make certain that a disk is in the drive and that the disk is ready to accept files before you copy.

- ✔ Do not remove the disk until the files have all been copied!

- ✔ Note that the options on the Send To submenu may be subtly different on your computer; scan the menu carefully for your removable disk drive.

- ✔ To copy files to another hard drive, use the Move or Copy commands, covered earlier in this chapter.

- ✔ Be sure that you properly unmount a digital media card before you remove it from the drive. Refer to the section "Removing a USB device," in Chapter 7.

- ✔ See Chapter 24 for more information on writing disks to a CD-R.

Creating shortcuts

A file *shortcut* is a 99 percent fat-free copy of a file. It enables you to access the original file from anywhere on a computer's disk system, but without the extra baggage required to copy the file all over creation. For example, you can create a shortcut to Microsoft Word on the desktop, where you can always get to it — much quicker than using the Start panel.

Making a shortcut is done the same way as copying and pasting a file, as discussed in the section "Moving or copying files with cut-and-paste," earlier in this chapter. The difference is that, rather than use the Paste command, you choose Edit⇨Paste Shortcut.

- ✔ To quickly create a shortcut on the desktop, right-click an icon and choose Send To⇨Desktop (Create Shortcut) from the pop-up menu.

- ✔ If no Edit⇨Paste Shortcut command is available, right-click the mouse on the destination. When a Paste Shortcut item appears on the pop-up menu, use it.

- ✔ A shortcut icon has a little arrow in a white box nestled into its lower-left corner (see the margin). This icon tells you that the file is a shortcut and not the real McCoy.

- ✔ Shortcuts are often named `Shortcut to`, followed by the original file's name. You can edit out the `Shortcut to` part, if you like. Refer to the section "Renaming files," earlier in this chapter.

- ✔ Have no fear when you're deleting shortcuts: Removing a shortcut icon doesn't remove the original file.

Deleting files

Part of maintaining the disk drive closet is the occasional cleaning binge or spring-cleaning bustle. This task involves not only organizing files and folders by moving and copying them, but also cleaning out the deadwood — removing files you no longer want or need.

To kill a file, select it and choose File⇨Delete. Or, you can press the Delete key on your keyboard to delete any selected files. Or, if you can see the Recycle Bin icon on the desktop, drag the files with the mouse and drop them right on the Recycle Bin icon. Phew! The file is gone.

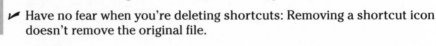

- ✔ Windows may warn you about deleting a file. Are you *really* sure? You probably are, so click Yes to delete the file. (Windows is just being utterly cautious.)

- ✔ You can delete folders just like files, but keep in mind that you delete the folder's contents — which can be dozens of icons, files, folders, jewelry, small children, widows, and refugees. Better be careful with that one.

✔ Never delete any file or folder unless you created it yourself.

 ✔ Programs aren't deleted in Windows, they're uninstalled. See Chapter 23.

Undeleting files (Files of the Undead!)

If you just deleted the file — and I mean *just deleted* it — you can choose the Edit➪Undo command (Ctrl+Z). That gets it back.

If Edit➪Undo doesn't do it, or undo it (or whatever), take these steps:

1. **Open the Recycle Bin on the desktop.**

2. **Select the file you want recovered.**

3. **Choose File➪Restore from the menu.**

   The file is magically removed from Recycle Bin limbo and restored afresh to the folder and disk from which it was so brutally seized.

4. **Close the Recycle Bin window.**

Windows has no definite time limit on how long you can restore files; they can be available in the Recycle Bin for months or even years. Even so, don't let the convenience of the Recycle Bin lull you into a false sense of security. Never delete a file unless you're certain that you want it gone, gone, gone.

 ✔ Choose View➪Arrange Icons➪by Date Deleted from the Recycle Bin's menu to display files in the order they departed (by date). That way, it's cinchy to find any recently deceased files you may want back.

 ✔ Files deleted by pressing Shift+Delete on the keyboard are permanently deleted. They aren't stored in the Recycle Bin and cannot be recovered. That's why you should use only the Shift+Delete command to seriously remove files you no longer want.

Renaming files

Windows lets you rename any file or folder at any time. You may want to do this to give the folder a better, more descriptive name, or you could have any number of reasons to give an icon a new name. Here's how it's done:

1. **Click the icon once to select it.**

2. **Choose File➪Rename from the menu.**

   The file's current name is highlighted or selected — just like selected text in a word processor.

3. **Type a new name or edit the current name.**

4. **Press the Enter key to lock in the new name.**

Note that all files *must* have a name. If you don't give the file a name (you try to leave it blank), Windows complains. Other than that, here are some file renaming points to ponder:

✔ Before pressing the Enter key (refer to Step 4), you can press the Esc key to undo the damage and return to the file's original name.

✔ Windows doesn't let you rename a file with the name of an existing file; no two items in the same folder can share the same name.

✔ If you have hidden the filename extensions, it may appear that two files share the same name. Note, however, that such files are of two different types and have two different icons.

✔ You can undo the name change by pressing the Ctrl+Z key combination or choosing Edit⇨Undo from the menu. You must do it *immediately* after the booboo occurs in order for it to work.

✔ The keyboard shortcut for renaming files is F2. I prefer using this key to choosing the menu item because my hands need to be on the keyboard to type the new filename anyway.

Windows lets you rename a group of icons all at once. It works the same as renaming a single icon, though when the operation is completed, all the selected icons have new names plus a number suffix. For example, you select a group of icons and choose the File⇨Rename command or press the F2 key. Type **Picture** as the group filename. Each file in the group is then given the name Picture (1), Picture (2), and so on, up to the last file in the group, Picture (24), for example.

Finding Wayward Files

Losing track of your files in Windows is no big deal. Unlike losing your glasses or car keys, Windows sports a nifty Search Companion. Lost files are found almost instantly. Even the Amazing Kreskin couldn't find things faster!

To find a file in Windows, use the Search Companion, which is part of any Windows Explorer window. To use the Search Companion, abide by these steps:

1. **In any folder window, click the Search button.**

Or, choose View⇨Explorer Bar⇨Search. The Search Companion appears on the left side of the window.

2. **Click to select the item titled All Files and Folders.**

   The other options sound good, but this choice gives you the most flexibility, as shown in Figure 22-6.

3. **Type all or part of the file's name.**

4. **Type a word or phrase in the file.**

   Don't bother filling in the Word or Phrase box if you're searching for a graphics file, an audio or MP3 file, a video file, or a program.

5. **Select the folder to look in.**

   To search all your computer's hard drives, choose Local Hard Drives from the list.

   To search only one hard drive, select it from the list.

   To search a specific folder, such as the Windows or My Documents folder, select it from the list.

   The rest of the settings, hidden in Figure 22-6, are optional. You're now ready to search.

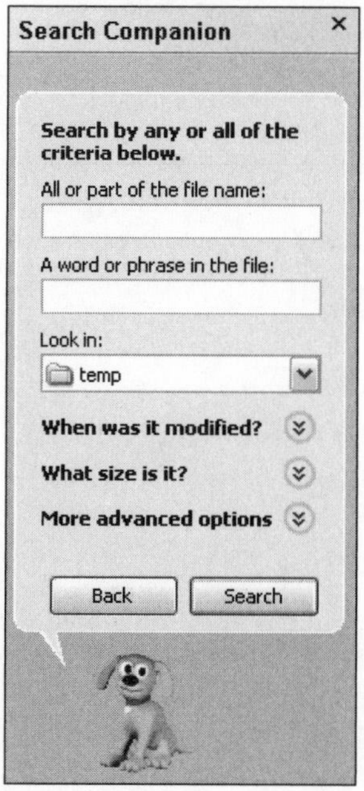

Figure 22-6:
The Search
Companion.

Search Companion

Search by any or all of the
criteria below.

All or part of the file name:

A word or phrase in the file:

Look in:

temp

When was it modified?

What size is it?

More advanced options

Back   Search

6. **Click the Search button.**

This action sends Windows off on a merry chase to locate the file you have requested. One of two things happens when it's done:

No dice: A message tells you that there are no results to display. Oh, well. Try again: Click the Back button.

Eureka! Any files matching your specifications are listed on the right side of the window.

The found files appear on a list. You can double-click a found file to open it. Or, if you want to know which folder the file was hiding in, right-click the file's icon and choose Open Containing Folder from the pop-up menu.

Be sure to close the Search Results window when you're done.

✔ If your keyboard has a Windows key, you can press Win+F, where the F means Find. This action summons the Search Companion window.

✔ In any folder window, you can press Ctrl+E to display the Search Companion.

✔ The book *Troubleshooting Your PC For Dummies* (Wiley Publishing, Inc.) contains many more Search Companion options and variations for finding just about any file based on its type, size, or date.

Chapter 23

Software, Programs, Applications

· ·

In This Chapter

▶ Installing new programs

▶ Starting programs

▶ Quickly running recent programs

▶ Accessing popular programs

▶ Creating desktop shortcuts

▶ Removing software

▶ Updating your programs

▶ Keeping Windows up to date

· ·

*T*he PC hardware may be dumb, and the operating system may be in charge, but to get any work done on your computer, you need software. Specifically, you need those workhorse applications that transform your whimsical musings into something substantial, by using the power of the computer's hefty I/O muscle to convert your keystrokes and mouse movements into something wonderful and new — or stagnant and rotten, depending on whether you love your work.

I find the main problem with software to be the terminology. Just how many words are there for a computer program? *Software* is the big term. *Computer program* is technical, though more technical is *executable*. Then there are the applications and the software suites. No matter what jargon, this chapter covers the job of setting up and using those programs on your PC.

Software Installation Chores

Software is what makes your computer do the work. But the program itself doesn't magically jump from the mostly empty software box and into your computer. It requires work on your behalf. This isn't anything technical. In fact, it's so easy that few software boxes even bother to contain instructions. When that's the case, you can start reading here:

1. **Open the software box.**

   You need a knife or scissors to remove the shrink wrap and potential transparent seal over the box flap.

   Try not to rip up the box. You want to keep it intact, either for long-term storage or in case the store lets you return the software. Most stores don't. When they don't, you can try reselling the software on eBay.

2. **Savor the smell of the industrial plastic odor of the box's insides.**

3. **Locate the installation disc or discs.**

   If you have more than one, note in which order they're used; the discs should be numbered, and you want to start with the first disc, which should also be labeled INSTALL.

   Sometimes, a DVD is included, which means that if your PC has a DVD drive, you can use that single DVD, rather than multiple CDs, to install the program.

   In addition to the installation disc, you may have other discs, bonus programs, supplements, and libraries of clip art. You don't need to install everything, but you should find the Install disc.

4. **Scour the box for printed information.**

   Specifically, you want to find a _Read Me_ sheet or _Getting Started_ booklet.

   You may have a manual in the box. It's a joke. Gone are the days when computer software came with manuals. The manual is now "on the disk," in the form of a help file, which isn't very helpful.

   If installation instructions are in the box, follow them.

5. **Insert the installation disc into the drive.**

6. **Start the installation program.**

   If you're lucky, the installation program runs automatically when you insert the CD into the CD-ROM drive.

   If the installation program doesn't start automatically, you need to run it yourself. You can do this by opening the Add/Remove Programs icon in the Control Panel. Use the dialog box that's displayed to help you hunt down your program.

7. **Obey the instructions on the screen.**

   Read the information carefully; sometimes, they slip something important in there. My friend Jerry (his real name) just kept clicking the Next button rather than reading the screen. He missed an important notice saying that an older version of the program would be erased. Uh-oh! Poor Jerry never got his old program back.

How do I quit all other programs?

Many installation programs ask you to "quit all other programs" before you proceed with installing the new software. The reason is that installation is monitored to make uninstalling easier. Having other programs run "in the background" can disturb this process. Also, because some programs require the computer to be reset after installation, if you haven't yet saved your data, you're out of luck.

To make sure that no other programs are running, press the Alt+Tab key. If Windows switches you to another program or window, close it. Keep pressing Alt+Tab until the only program you see is the installation program. That way, you're assured that all other running programs have closed. (And there's no need to close any background applications or other processes.)

8. **Choose various options.**

   The software asks for your name and company name, and maybe for a serial number. Type all that stuff in.

   Don't freak if the program already knows who you are. Windows is kinda clairvoyant in that respect.

   When you're asked to make a decision, the option that's already selected (the *default*) is typically the best option. Only if you know what's going on and *truly care* about it should you change anything.

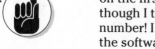

   You can find the serial number inside the manual, on the CD-ROM case, on the first disc, or on a separate card you probably threw away even though I told you to keep everything in its original box. Don't lose that number! I usually write the serial number down inside the manual or on the software box itself.

9. **Files are copied.**

   Eventually, the installation program copies the files from the installation disc to your hard drive for full-time residence.

   If asked, replace one CD with another. This process may go on for some time.

10. **It's done.**

    The installation program ends. The computer may reset at this point. That's required sometimes when you're installing special programs that Windows needs to know about. (Windows is pretty dumb after it starts.)

    Start using the program!

Granted, the preceding steps are vague and general. Hopefully, your new software comes with more specific instructions. Refer to the sidebars nearby for important information on some commonly asked installation questions.

How do I disable my antivirus software?

The better antivirus programs constantly monitor your computer to check for new viruses. So, whenever you install new software, the antivirus software may stand up and say "What a minute!" and prevent the installation. The only way around this problem is to temporarily disable the antivirus software.

The easiest way to disable antivirus software is locate the antivirus program's tiny icon on the

system tray. Right-click that icon and choose the Disable command from the pop-up menu. After doing so, you may proceed with installation. Remember, however, to reenable the antivirus software after installing the new program. One way to do that is to restart Windows, which most new programs require after installation anyway.

 You must have administrator privileges to install new software on your computer. This is fine; most users set themselves up as administrators anyway. Also, if more than one person uses your computer, be sure that you install the software for everyone to use.

Running a Program

After the software gets into your PC, the next thing you want to do is run that program. As with other things in Windows, there are many different, strange, and potentially useful ways to run your programs in Windows. This section describes some of the more popular methods.

Finding a program on the Start menu

All new software you install should set itself up on the Start button's menu, on the All Programs submenu. In fact, if the software did things properly, Windows displays a pop-up bubble on the Start button that says "New software installed" (or something similar) and highlights the new program's location.

To run your program, obey these steps:

1. **Click the Start button.**

2. **Choose All Programs to pop up the All Programs menu.**

3. **Click your program's icon on the menu.**

   This step runs the program; the Start menu thing goes away, and your program's window appears on the screen.

4. **If the program cannot be found, locate the program's submenu and then go back to Step 3.**

   Some programs may be buried on submenus and even more submenus. It all depends on how the All Programs menu is organized.

Yeah, the All Programs menu can be a mess! You can organize that menu, but that's really the topic of another book.

Be careful when you use the mouse to navigate through the various submenus; they can get "slippery."

It's possible to accidentally move a submenu or program icon from the All Programs menu. When this happens, *immediately* press Ctrl+Z on the keyboard. That's the Undo command's keyboard shortcut, and it should restore whatever damage you have done.

The program itself isn't installed on the All Programs menu. What you see there is merely a *shortcut* icon, or tiny copy of the program. The program itself is most likely located in its own subfolder in the Program Files folder on drive C. (Refer to Chapter 22 for more information on shortcut files.)

Accessing recent programs

Every time you run a program in Windows, it appears on the Start button's menu, on the left side, in an area I cleverly refer to as the Recently Used Programs list. Figure 23-1 shows you where the list is, and keep in mind that this is my kids' computer, which explains why the list is full of games.

Choose any program on the list to immediately run it again — no wading through the All Programs menu required! Note that programs fall off that list as you run new programs.

To set the number of recently run programs appearing on the Start menu, follow these steps:

1. **Right-click the Start button.**

2. **Choose the Properties command from the pop-up surprise menu.**

   The Taskbar and Start Menu Properties dialog box whisks into existence.

Pin-on area

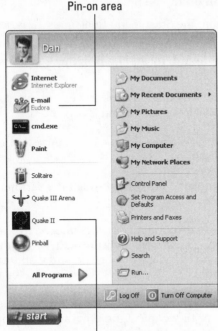

Figure 23-1:
Programs
found on
the Start
button's
menu.

Recently Used Programs list

3. **Click the Customize button.**

   I'm assuming that you have selected the Start menu option, not the Classic Start menu, which is used only by people with bad body odor problems.

   The Customize Start Menu dialog box appears.

4. **Enter the number of recently used programs to appear on the list (in the middle of the dialog box).**

   Setting the number to zero eliminates the list.

5. **Click OK, and then click OK again to close the other dialog box.**

Putting your program in the pin-on area

If you prefer to have your program appear right on the Start menu, where it's most handy, consider adding the program to the pin-on area, as shown in Figure 23-1. Programs "pinned" to the Start button's menu stay there come hell or high water or so-called computer expert nephews visiting from Ohio.

To add any program to the pin-on area, right-click the program's icon and choose the Pin to Start Menu command from the pop-up menu.

You can click any program icon, even a program on the Recently Used Programs List or a program icon found on the All Programs menu. *Remember:* Right-click.

Creating a desktop shortcut icon

When a program installs itself on your computer, it sets up a command or even a submenu full of commands on the Start button's All Programs menu. The program may also create a shortcut icon on the desktop, which allows you even faster access to the program. Well, it allows access any time you see the desktop.

If you enjoy having shortcut icons on the desktop, you can add any program (or folder or file) to the desktop as a shortcut. Here's how:

1. **Locate the file you want to place on the desktop.**

   It can be a shortcut icon or the original file, program, or folder. It can even be a program on the All Programs menu.

2. **Right-click the file's icon to display the pop-up shortcut menu.**

3. **Choose Send To⇨Desktop (Create Shortcut).**

   The shortcut file is created, and its icon appears on the desktop.

Putting an icon on the Quick Launch bar

Another handy place to put frequently used programs is on the Quick Launch bar, which is where the Quick Launch bar gets its name. If it were the Quick Lunch bar, you would put sandwiches down there, not program icons.

The easiest way to put a program icon on the Quick Launch bar is to drag the program's shortcut icon from the desktop and onto the Quick Launch bar. Refer to the preceding subsection for information on creating a desktop shortcut icon.

Uninstalling Software

To remove any newly installed program, you use an uninstall program. This program isn't a feature of Windows. Each software program comes with its own uninstall feature. Or, at least you hope it does.

Uninstall programs are usually on the Start button's All Programs menu, right by the icon used to start the program. For example, in Figure 23-2, you see a trio of icons installed on a submenu when I added the IconCool Editor program to my PC. The command to uninstall that program is called, remarkably, Uninstall. This type of setup is common for most programs.

Figure 23-2:
An uninstall program on an All Programs submenu.

If your software lacks an obvious uninstall program, you can attempt to use Windows to rid yourself of it: Open the Control Panel's Add or Remove Programs icon to witness for yourself the glory that is the Add or Remove Programs Properties dialog box, proudly depicted in Figure 23-3.

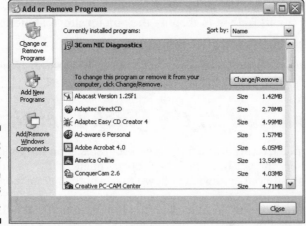

Figure 23-3:
The Add or Remove Programs dialog box.

The list of programs that Windows knows about and can uninstall is listed in the dialog box (refer to Figure 23-3). Click one of those programs, the one you want to uninstall, and then click the Change/Remove button. Continue reading instructions on the screen to uninstall the program.

✔ Do not attempt to uninstall any software by deleting it from your hard drive. You should never delete any file you did not create yourself. (You can, however, delete any shortcuts you create.)

✔ Some stubborn programs don't fully remove themselves. If you have tried everything, feel free to remove the program by deleting its icon or folder. Do not, however, delete any program or file installed in the Windows folder or any of its subfolders.

Updating Your Software

After a novel is written, it's finished. Subsequent reprints correct a few misspellings, but that's about it. Software, on the other hand, is *never* finished. It's too easy to change. Most software packages are updated about once every year or two, and sometimes more often.

The reason that software is updated used to be to fix problems or to introduce new features. But, honestly, the main reason for new versions of programs appearing now is to make more money for the software developers. Upgrading means that everyone who owns the software may buy a new version and generate revenue for the company. Yep, it's greed.

My advice: Order the update only if it has features or makes modifications you desperately need, or if the update is for security reasons. Otherwise, if the current version is doing the job, don't bother.

✔ Consider each upgrade offer on its individual merits: Will you ever use the new features? Do you need a word processor that can print upside-down headlines and bar charts that show your word count? Can you really get any mileage out of the intranet version when you're a sole user sitting at home?

✔ Here's something else to keep in mind: If you're still using Doodle Writer 4.2 and everybody else is using DoodleWriter 6.1, you may have difficulty exchanging documents. After a while, newer versions of programs become incompatible with their older models. If so, you need to upgrade.

✔ In an office setting, everybody should be using the same software version. (Everybody doesn't have to be using the *latest* version, just the *same* version.)

What about upgrading Windows?

Upgrading Windows is a *big deal.* Why? Because everything else in your computer relies on Windows. Therefore, it's a major change, and something to think long and hard about.

Often, the newer version of Windows has many more features than the older version. Do you need those features? If not, don't bother with the update.

After a time, you may notice newer software packages coming to roost on the newest version of Windows. The new stuff is better than your current stuff, so you need to upgrade if you want to take advantage of it.

Where does this leave you? *Don't bother updating Windows!* Just wait until you buy a new computer, and that PC will have the newest version of Windows, all preinstalled and set up nicely.

What about patching or updating Windows?

Occasionally, Microsoft comes out with patches, security updates, or other fixes to Windows. It makes these fixes available automatically over the Internet, or you may opt to manually select an update by using the Windows Update program.

At one time, I was against applying the Windows updates, mostly because the updates were risky and could cause your PC to stop working. Lately, however, Microsoft has gotten better about its updates. I now recommend applying all updates to Windows whenever they come out. You can configure Windows XP to do this automatically:

Control Panel

1. **Open the Control Panel.**

2. **Open the Automatic Updates icon.**

3. **Choose the Automatic option in the Automatic Updates dialog box.**

4. **Click OK and, optionally, close the Control Panel window.**

Note that if your PC is on a broadband modem connection, you can have the updates downloaded any time of the day, as long as the PC is turned on all the time. Otherwise, you want to have the updates happen whenever your PC is connected to the Internet.

You can also manually update by running the Windows Update program: Click the Start button and choose All Programs⇨Windows Update. This command connects you to the Internet, where you can choose which updates you want to apply to your PC.

Chapter 24

Making Your Own CDs

*W*hen the CD drive first became an option on the PC, one question was universal: "How can I write to the thing? I want to make my own CDs!" At the time, computer users were familiar with floppy disks — removable and writable media. But CDs, they said, could be written to only by huge, complex, and expensive machines. In fact, there were only three such machines on the entire planet. Writing to a CD? Ha! It was a pipe dream.

My, how things have changed!

Today, any teenager with a properly equipped computer can produce more CDs in a day than the local music store sells in a week. Computers can easily create CDs, for storing either data or music. It's easy. This chapter tells you how it's done.

Making Your Own Data CD

Yes, you can make a CD, which doesn't involve crystals, nuclear power, or an insane laboratory assistant named Craig. You need three only things:

✔ A CD-R disc specifically designed for storing computer data

✔ A CD drive capable of writing to a CD-R disc

✔ Software to make it all happen

What to put on the CD-R?

The burning burning question is "What kind of data should you put on a CD-R?" Obviously, you don't want to use a CD-R like a removable hard drive. That's because the disc can be used only once. When it's full, it's done! It cannot be erased. Therefore, I recommend using CD-R data discs for *archiving*.

For example, when I'm done writing a book, I archive all the text documents, figures, pictures, — even the contract — on a CD-R disc. Though the files may not equal the disc's full 600MB capacity, that's fine; it's an archive. With the files safely saved on the CD-R, I can delete them from my hard drive and make that space available for something else. And, if I ever need the files again, they're handy on the archive CD.

I also use CD-Rs to send files in the mail that are too big to send by e-mail. (How big? Anything larger than 10MB is too big for e-mail.)

The CD-R discs, you have to buy. The CD drive must come with your computer, though external CD-R drives are plentiful and cheap. The software also comes with Windows, though better software exists on the Internet or up on the shelf at the Software-O-Rama.

Got all that stuff? You're ready to burn!

- ✔ CD-R discs are cheap. Buy 'em by the hundreds.

- ✔ Some CD-R discs are better than others. Although a pal of mine says that any old CD-R will do, I stick with the brands I know and use those special high-speed disks. My data is important to me, so I don't mind paying extra.

- ✔ CD-R drives are generally also capable of using CD-RW discs. They're called CD-R/RW drives.

- ✔ For more information on creating CD-RW discs, see the section "A few words about CD-RW," later in this chapter.

Mounting the CD-R

Just as floppy disks must be formatted, roads must be paved, and babies must be properly swaddled in diapers, CD-R discs must be prepared for use. Windows handles this task automatically. It's known as *mounting* the disc. Here's the 411:

1. **Put a blank CD-R disc into the drive.**

   Windows XP is smart enough to recognize the disc and asks you what to do with it, as shown in Figure 24-1.

Figure 24-1:
A blank
CD-R is
detected.

2. **Select the option Open Writable CD Folder Using Windows Explorer.**

3. **Click OK.**

   Windows mounts the CD-R.

You can now use the CD-R just as you can use the hard disk.

✔ Your computer may automatically recognize the CD-R and mount it without interrupting you. Groovy.

✔ If the CD-R drive doesn't recognize the disc, the disc could be defective. Fetch another.

✔ If you're running other CD-R burning software, it takes over and does I-don't-know-what, but probably something similar to what Windows XP does.

✔ If you're using software other than Windows, ensure that you create a standard CD, one that can be read by any PC.

✔ Some CD-R discs can hold up to 700MB of data or 80 minutes of music. It usually says on the CD-R case, so look when you buy.

Copying files to the CD-R

After mounting the CD-R, you can work with it just like you work with the hard drive: Copy files to the CD-R drive's window. Create folders, even subfolders. Rename and manage files as you normally would.

Making sure that the CD-R drive is up to writing a CD-R disc

If you're having trouble mounting a CD-R, check to ensure that Windows is set up to properly use the CD-R drive for disc recording. Heed these steps:

1. **Open the My Computer icon on the desktop.**

2. **Right-click the CD-R drive icon in the My Computer window.**

3. **Choose Properties from the pop-up menu.**

4. **In the CD drive's Properties dialog box, click the Recording tab.**

If you see no Recording tab, either you don't have a CD-R drive or it may be defective. Return it to your dealer. Note that some DVD/CD-RW drives may not have the Recording tab but can still record.

5. **Put a check mark by the option Enable CD Recording on This Drive.**

6. **Click the OK button.**

7. **Close the My Computer window.**

The trick here is that nothing is written to the CD-R until you direct Windows to burn information to the disc. So, technically (and rather sneakily), you're merely messing with an *image* of what the CD-R will eventually look like; nothing is burned to the disc yet.

✔ Avoid saving files directly to the CD-R. Instead, save the file first to the hard drive, preferably in the proper folder. After that, you can save a copy of the file to the CD-R. Only after the CD-R has been successfully written should you consider deleting the original files on the hard drive, if at all.

✔ The fewer times you write to the CD-R disc, the more data the disc can hold. Writing to the disc a little bit at a time consumes extra space because of the overhead required to keep track of the file information.

✔ Note that Windows updates its File⇨Send To submenu to include the CD-R drive, which allows for the quick right-click copying of files and folders.

Burning the CD-R

As files are prepared for the CD-R disc, Windows pops up a message on the system tray, as shown in Figure 24-2. This is your reminder that files are waiting to be burned to the CD-R.

Figure 24-2:
Files are
awaiting the
flames.

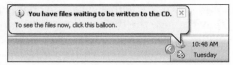

By clicking in the bubble (refer to Figure 24-2), you can see the CD-R drive's window. Or, you can open the CD-R drive's icon in the My Computer window.

 The CD-R drive's window displays a list of icons prepped for burning. Each icon is flagged with a straight-to-hell arrow, as shown in the margin.

To burn the files-in-waiting to the CD-R disc, choose File⇨Write These Files to CD. This action starts the CD Writing Wizard.

Work through the wizard and answer the questions as best you can; fear not — nothing is that difficult. In fact, most of your time is spent waiting for the files to burn, so get a cup of coffee or catch up on your e-mail.

When the files have all been burned, the disc is automatically ejected from the drive. It's now ready to use, and readable on any PC, just like any other CD.

✔ The speed at which the information is written to the CD-R is based on the drive's (hardware) speed rating. The first value in the rating is the speed at which data is written to disc.

✔ Note that one available option when the CD Writing Wizard is done allows you to create another CD with the same information on it. This feature is handy for making duplicates of your CD backups.

Labeling the CD-R (or not)

I highly recommend labeling all removable disks, even digital media cards. Even if you name things only A or B, that's fine because it helps you keep track of things.

Label your CD-R *after* it's been written to. That way, you don't waste time labeling what could potentially be a bad disc (one that you would throw away). I use a Sharpie to write on the disc. Write on the label side; the other side is the one containing your important data. You don't want to write on that.

Do not use a label on your CD-R. Only if the label specifically says that it's chemically safe for a CD-R should you use it. Otherwise, the chemicals in the standard type of sticky label may damage the disk and render the information that's written to it unreadable after only a few months.

Messing with files on a burnt CD-R

Some CD-burning software may finish the task after the disc is ejected. But, with Windows, you can continue to burn files to a CD-R until it's absolutely full. (In other words, no "final burn" occurs, as it does with some CD-writing software.)

For example, if you want to add more files to the CD-R, you can do so — if the disc has room. The files appear in the CD-R's window; existing files on the CD-R appear as normal, and the files waiting to be burned appear with the little arrow on them, as shown in Figure 24-3.

Note the Details listing in the lower-left corner of the CD-R disc's window. It tells you how much space is still available (Free Space) on the disc. In Figure 24-3, it shows 237MB — plenty of room!

You can also manipulate the files already on the CD. You can rename and even delete files. Note, however, that messing with those files consumes disc space.

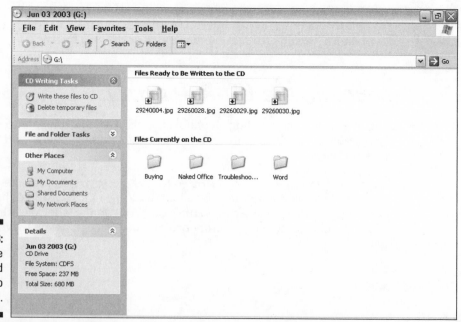

Figure 24-3: Files on the CD and waiting to be burned.

Unlike with a regular disk drive, information is never really erased from a CD-R. So, when you rename a file, Windows simply covers up the old name and creates a new one — which uses disc space. Similarly, when you delete a file from a CD-R, the space used by the file isn't recovered. Keep this in mind if you change anything already burned to the disc.

A few words about CD-RW

CD-RW discs work just like CD-R data discs. All the information in the previous sections applies to CD-RW discs just as it applies to CD-Rs. The main difference is the addition of a command used to reformat the CD-RW disc and start over.

To reformat the CD-RW, open its window (from the My Computer window), and then choose File➪Erase This CD-RW. This command starts the CD Writing Wizard, which you work through, and eventually it wipes the disc clean.

After reformatting the CD-RW disc, you can use it over again — which is the advantage of the CD-RW over the CD-R (which cannot be reformatted).

✔ Most CD-R drives double as CD-RW drives.

✔ CD-RW discs are different from CD-R discs. It says CD-RW on the label, and the disc is more expensive, which is most obvious when you try to taste this disc.

✔ CD-RW discs may not be readable in all CD drives. If you want to create a CD with the widest possible use, burn a CD-R rather than a CD-RW disc.

✔ Erasing, renaming, or moving a file after it has been burned to a CD-RW disc wastes disc space, just as doing so on a CD-R disc wastes space. If possible, try to do your file manipulations *before* you burn the files to the disc.

✔ It's often said that CD-RW discs are best used for backing up data because they can be reused over and over. However, on a disc-per-disc basis, it's cheaper to use CD-R discs instead.

✔ The speed at which the drive rewrites the CD-RW disc is the middle number in the drive speed rating-thing.

Disposing of a CD or CD-R

Sure, you can just toss a CD or CD-R into the trash. That's okay — in most places. Some communities classify a CD as hazardous, and it must be properly disposed of or sent off for recycling.

What about DVD-R/RW and the zillion other DVD formats?

Sadly, Windows doesn't support burning DVDs as it does burning CDs. The reason is most likely that there are about half a dozen recordable DVD standards, and Microsoft would rather sit out the battle to see who wins. Even so, most PCs that come with recordable DVD drives also come with special software that lets you make your own DVDs.

There are now two popular recordable DVD standards: DVD-R and DVD+R, known commonly as *minus* and *plus* standards. There are also similar DVD-RW and DVD+RW standards. Aside from minor technical differences, you really need to know only that DVD-R is more compatible with home movie DVD players, yet the DVD+R format is faster.

Future editions of this book will document how to create your own DVDs as this technology matures and is fully supported by Windows.

If you don't want anyone else to read the CD-R, you probably don't want to throw it away intact. The best solution is to destroy the CD-R by getting a paper shredder that can also handle CDs.

Some folks say that you can effectively erase a CD-R by putting it in a microwave oven for a few seconds. I don't know whether I trust or recommend that method. And, don't burn a CD-R; the fumes are toxic.

Burning a Music CD

Creating the music CD involves three steps:

1. Collect the music or sound files from their sources.

2. Manage the files inside the media software.

3. Write selected files to a music CD.

The first step is to use your media software to collect the music you want to burn to a CD. The music can be downloaded from the Internet, copied from an existing CD, or entered using the PC's sound input from any audio device. The music files are saved on disc and managed by your media software.

Next, you create *playlists,* or collections of the songs you have stored on disk. For example, you can collect a smattering of road tunes and create a playlist of those songs — like building your own album on your computer.

Finally, you simply copy one of your playlists to the CD-R disc. The media software then converts the music files and burns the CD-R.

This section details these steps in Windows Media Player. Note that your version of Media Player may have subtly different options than those I have outlined.

✔ I'm particularly fond of the MUSICMATCH Jukebox program as a great alternative to Windows Media Player. Look it up on the Web, at www. musicmatch.com.

✔ You use specific CD-R discs for recording music, which are often cheaper than the computer data CD-Rs. If you plan to create music only, consider buying some of these cheaper discs.

✔ It's assumed that you own whatever music it is that you're copying and that you're using the copies for only your personal use. Making a copy of a commercial CD or copyrighted music and distributing it without paying for it is theft.

Collecting tunes

Copying music from a CD into the computer is cinchy to do in Windows Media Player. Follow these steps:

1. **Insert a music CD into your CD-ROM drive.**

   This step automatically runs Windows Media Player. If not, from the Start panel, choose Programs➪Windows Media Player.

   In a few moments, information about the CD appears in the Media Player window. (The Internet may even be called up; this isn't necessary, so cancel the operation. Be warned, though, that it's a persistent calling, so consider giving in and connecting anyway.)

2. **Click the Copy from CD button.**

   It's on the left edge of the Media Player window, as shown in Figure 24-4.

3. **Click to select the tracks you want to copy from the CD.**

4. **Click the Copy Music button.**

   It's in the upper part of the Media Player window, just above the Composer column. (It appears as Stop Copy in Figure 24-4.)

Note that it takes a little time to copy over the tracks to the hard drive. That's because the CD-ROM can read from disc many more times faster than it plays the music — that's the last X (multiple) in a CD-ROM drive's speed rating.

Figure 24-4:
A file is
copied from
a CD to the
hard drive.

After the songs are copied, they appear in the Media Library. Click the Media Library button. Then, in the Media Library tree structure, you find the album and its copied tracks listed under Audio\Album. Click to select the album title, and you find the copied tracks on the right side of the window.

Creating a playlist

Before you can burn the music CD, you must create a playlist in Windows Media Player. The playlist is a collection of tunes, which doesn't necessarily have to be copied to a CD. For example, if you want, you can create a playlist of all your favorite afternoon songs or driving tunes or cleaning-the-house music. A *playlist* is merely a collection of songs that Media Player can play.

For creating a music CD, however, you probably want to assemble several dozen songs specific to the kind of CD you want to burn. For example, I can create my list of show tune highlights so that I can sing in the car and pretend that I'm on Broadway.

To create a playlist in Windows Media Player, follow these simple sample steps:

1. **Click the Media Library button on the left edge of the Media Player window.**

2. **Click the New Playlist button.**

3. **Type a descriptive name for the playlist.**

4. **Click OK.**

   The new playlist is placed in the My Playlists part of the Media Library tree, on the left side of the Media Player window.

   The next step is to add music tracks to the playlist. The music tracks can be found under the Audio branch of the Media Library tree. They're in the All Audio, Album, Artist and Genre branches.

5. **Click an audio source in the Media Library tree.**

   For example, I clicked one of my show tunes albums. The list of songs I copied from that CD appears on the right side of the Media Player window.

6. **Click to select a song, or Ctrl+click to select several songs.**

7. **Click the Add to Playlist button.**

8. **Choose your playlist from the drop-down menu.**

   If it doesn't appear, choose the Additional Playlist command; choose your playlist in the dialog box and click the OK button.

9. **Repeat Steps 6 through 8 to collect the songs you want in your playlist.**

10. **Click to highlight your playlist in the Media Library tree.**

    On the right side of the Media Player window, you find all the songs you copied into that playlist.

After the playlist is created, listen to the songs. Confirm that they're what you want.

 To remove a song from the playlist, click to highlight the song and then click the Delete Media button; choose Delete from Playlist from the Delete Media button's menu.

How an MP3 player fits into the picture

Beyond making your own CDs, it may be time to invest in a portable digital music player, also known as an *MP3 player.* (The term *iPod* is also used, though iPod refers specifically to the portable music player made by Apple Computer.)

The MP3 player may have come with its own software, or it may work directly with Windows Media Player. Either way, the idea is to connect the player to the computer and then use the music software to update the portable player. This works just like creating a musical CD, though the portable media player contains lots of storage for thousands and thousands of songs.

The songs play and are recorded to CD in the order they appear on the playlist. To rearrange the songs, use the up- or down-arrow buttons just above the list.

A playlist can contain many more songs than you eventually end up copying to CD; the CD need not contain all the songs on the playlist.

Burning a music CD

Burning a music CD is a snap after you have created a playlist in Media Player. Here are the steps to take to burn your music CD:

1. **Insert the CD-R into the drive.**

    If Windows attempts to open it or displays the "What the heck do I do now?" dialog box, just cancel out of the operation.

2. **Click the Copy to CD or Device button on the left edge of the Media Player window.**

3. **Ensure that you have your playlist selected on the left side of the window.**

    In Figure 24-5, it's the PCs for Dummies Sample Playlist, though my editor tells me that the *For* should be capitalized. Like, *whatever.*

Figure 24-5: A playlist is being prepared to be burned to CD.

4. Ensure that each title you want to copy has a check mark by its name.

If you don't want to copy a specific track, remove the check mark. Remember that you don't have to copy them all.

Keep an eye on the amount of time used by the songs you have selected to copy. Media Player lets you know if you have too many files to copy over. When that happens, you must unselect some songs to make room for others.

5. Ensure that the CD-R drive is chosen on the right side of the window.

It says `CD Drive (G:)` in Figure 24-5.

6. Click the Copy Music button.

It's in the upper-right corner of the Media Player window.

After clicking the Copy Music button, Windows dutifully copies the tracks you have selected to the CD-R disc. First, the tracks are converted into the proper CD format one at a time. Then, the files are copied over to the CD-R.

When the operation is complete, the disc is ejected and is ready to be played in any CD player. The disc's name is the same as the playlist you copied over.

✔ Some older CD players may not be able to read the CD-R music disc.

✔ The speed at which you can write to the CD-R drive is the *writing speed*. That would be the first number in the drive's speed rating. So, if you have a 40X–16X–48X drive, it creates a 40-minute music CD in only 1 minute.

✔ Unlike with data CD-Rs, you cannot add more music to a CD-R after it has been burned once.

✔ Not all sound files can be copied to an audio CD. MIDI files, for example, must be converted into WAV files to be recorded to a CD-ROM. Special software is required in order to make this conversion. Also, some WAV files may be recorded in a low-quality format that makes them incompatible with CD audio. Again, the files must be converted by using special software.

Chapter 25

Your Basic Internet Introduction

*I*t's information! It's communications! It's entertainment! It's shopping! It's research! It's the future! It's a colossal waste of time! Yes, it's software too!

It's the Internet, and it's practically indescribable. What began as a method for scientists and researchers to exchange information from remote locations has grown into a way for teenagers to type text messages at each other though they live next door. Truly, the Internet is one of the most remarkable things humans ever developed.

This chapter provides an introduction to the one computer concept that most likely doesn't need an introduction: the Internet. Even if you think that you already know everything, consider giving this chapter a skim. The Internet is ever changing, and there's always a chance that you may learn something new.

What Is the Internet?

The *Internet* is composed of hundreds of thousands of computers all over the world. The computers send information. They receive information. And, most important, they store information. That's the Internet.

Some common misconceptions about the Internet

The Internet is a piece of software or program you buy. Although you use software to access the Internet and you need software to send or retrieve information from the Internet, the Internet itself isn't a software program.

The Internet is a single computer. The Internet consists of all the computers connected to the Internet. Whenever your computer is "on" the Internet, it's part of the Internet.

Bill Gates, AOL, the government, or something or someone else owns the Internet. The Internet began as a military project run by the government. Large corporations and communications companies now supply most of the resources for the Internet. No lone person can own the Internet, just as no lone person can own the oceans.

The Internet can be turned off. Although your connection to the Internet may "go down" and parts of the Internet occasionally fail, because of its decentralized organization the Internet can never be turned off or cease to exist. After all, the military originally designed the Internet to survive a nuclear war. It's not going down.

Getting information from the Internet

The information on the Internet is next to useless unless you can access it. So, the whole idea behind getting on the Internet is to access all that information and take advantage of the Internet's communications abilities.

To use the Internet, you must connect your computer to some other computer already on the Internet. That's usually done through an ISP, or Internet Service Provider, which is covered later in this chapter. But, just connecting to the Internet doesn't allow you to access any information. For that, you need specific Internet software, such as a Web browser. You can also exchange information via e-mail, which people use more than they use the Web.

  ✔ Chapter 26 is about the World Wide Web and using a Web browser.
  ✔ Chapter 27 covers e-mail.

How to Access the Internet

Getting on the Internet is no ordeal. Yet, like many rites of initiation, it takes some time and organization. The good news is that it's tough only the first time. After that, all this stuff is a snap. The bad news is, of course, that it *is* tough the first time.

Five things you need in order to get on the Internet

You need five things to access the Internet, four of which you probably have and one of which you have to go out and get:

✔ **A computer**

✔ **A modem**

Rare is the PC without a modem. If yours is one of the rare ones, mull over your modem options, as covered in Chapter 13.

✔ **Internet software**

Windows comes with nearly all the software you need.

✔ **Money**

This item is perhaps the toughest thing to come by. Access to the Internet costs money: You subscribe to it, just like with cable TV. Expect to pay anywhere from $5 to more than $100 a month to get on the Internet, depending on the type of service and various options you need. The average cost is less than $20 a month.

✔ **An Internet Service Provider, or ISP**

This item is the thing you need to go out and get. Just as the cable company provides you with cable TV, an *ISP* is the outfit that provides you with Internet access. Obtaining an ISP is a big deal, so it's covered in the next subsection.

In some situations, you may not need any of these things. For example, if you work for a large company, it may already give you Internet access through the network at your office. Ditto for universities and some government installations. And, you can always find free Internet access at a community library near you.

✔ Though I hate using acronyms, *ISP* is becoming popular enough that I feel I must. Not only is it easier to type, but many people also now say "ISP" and don't even know that it stands for Internet Service Provider.

✔ Though no one owns the Internet, an ISP is necessary in order to provide access to it. Sure, they could give away access, but that makes for a bad business plan.

✔ You can find ISPs by looking in the Yellow Pages, under *Internet*. I recommend using a local ISP because the tech support for those national ISPs tends to be iffy at best.

✔ The S in ISP stands for *service*. You pay them a fee, and they provide you with Internet access *and* service. That means technical support: someone you can phone for help, classes, software — you name it. The more support, the better the ISP.

✔ Though the Internet isn't a program, you need special software in order to access the Internet and to send or retrieve information.

Configuring Windows for the Internet

Setting up your PC to access the Internet isn't all that hard, if you have these three things:

✔ A silver bowl

✔ A ceremonial knife — preferably, bejeweled

✔ An unblemished goat

No. Wait. You needed those things in the *old days*. Now, all you need is some information from your ISP, and the New Connection Wizard does the rest.

Odds are good that if you chose a decent ISP, someone there can provide you with a Getting Started booklet or CD that has all the information you need to set up Windows for the Internet. That's your first, best option. Otherwise, you need the following specific information from your ISP:

✔ For a dial-up modem, the phone number to call

✔ For a broadband modem, the modem's IP address, the DNS address, and possibly a gateway address

✔ Your ISP's domain name — the `blorf.com` or `yaddi.org` thing

✔ Your Internet login ID and password

✔ Your Internet e-mail name, address, and password (if it's different from your login ID and password)

✔ The name of your ISP's e-mail server, which involves the acronyms POP3 or SMTP.

The information listed here is necessary to run the New Connection Wizard in Windows. Heck, there may even be more information. Keep it for future use!

To run the New Connection Wizard, heed these steps:

1. **From the Start button's menu, choose All Programs⇨Accessories⇨ Communications⇨New Connection Wizard.**

2. **Read. Obey. Answer the wizard's questions by using the information provided by your ISP.**

3. **Click the Next button to continue working through the wizard.**

4. **Click the Finish button when you're done.**

 After the wizard completes its interrogation and you click the Finish button, your Internet connection information is saved as an icon in the Network Connections folder (as shown in the margin). It means that you're ready to go.

✔ Refer to Chapter 18 for more information about the Network Connections folder, networking, and the Internet.

✔ You need to run the New Connection Wizard only once.

✔ I lied: If you change or add ISPs or switch from a dial-up to broadband connection, you need to run the New Connection Wizard again.

✔ Never toss out the booklet or sheet of information your ISP gives you! You need those numbers.

✔ Your Internet login ID and password are different from the user ID and password you use to get into Windows. You need a different ID and password for each system you access.

✔ $111{,}111{,}111 \times 111{,}111{,}111 = 12{,}345{,}678{,}987{,}654{,}321$.

Connecting to the Internet

Connecting to the Internet is cinchy: Simply run any Internet program on your computer. Windows is smart enough to connect automatically. If you have a broadband connection, Windows merely starts using that connection. Otherwise, Windows directs the modem to dial into the ISP and make the connection manually.

Hello, Internet

Here's how you connect to the Internet most of the time:

1. **Start your Web browser.**

   The Web browser software that comes with Windows is *Internet Explorer.* Double-click the Internet Explorer icon on your desktop or choose All Programs⇨Internet Explorer from the Start button's menu.

   For a broadband or always-on connection, such as through a local-area network, ta-da! You're on the Internet. That's it. That's all you need to do. As they say at the end of a French movie, *Fin!*

   For dial-up modems, the madness continues:

2. **Fill in the connection dialog box (if it appears).**

   If you see a Connect dialog box, as shown in Figure 25-1, fill it in. Use the information provided by your ISP, though most of the information may already be there. Click the Dial button to connect.

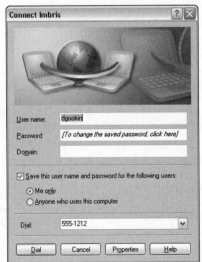

Figure 25-1: Dialing in to the Internet.

3. **Wait while the modem dials.**

   Doh-dee-doh.

4. **You're connected!**

   When a dial-up connection is established, a new, itty-bitty icon appears on the system tray, looking like the graphic shown in the margin. That's your Connected to Whatever teensy-weensy icon indicator telling you that you're online with the Internet and ready to run your Internet software.

✔ For several reasons, you may always have to manually enter your password. The first is that you're using a laptop, which doesn't save your Internet password, for security reasons. The second is that you didn't properly log in to Windows with a password-protected account. The third is that, for some reason, Windows forgets your password and forces you to reenter it (perhaps for security reasons).

✔ For other Internet Connection problems, woes, and worries, refer to my book *Troubleshooting Your PC For Dummies* (Wiley Publishing, Inc.), available only in bookstores with good-looking employees worldwide.

Not connecting to the Internet

You don't always have to connect to the Internet. For a broadband connection, you're online all the time anyway, so it isn't such a big deal. But, for dial-up modems, don't feel compelled to connect just because the connection seems to automatically dial itself — especially when the computer starts.

✔ To cancel the connection, click the Cancel button when you see it dialing.

✔ Why is your computer connecting to the Internet? Most likely, it's because some program or Windows itself is requesting information. Canceling that request isn't a problem, nor does it mess things up. Programs can wait until *you* want to connect to the Internet to conduct their business. Dammit! You're in charge!

Doing Something on the Internet (Using Internet Software)

After you have made the connection to your ISP, you're ready to run any or all of your Internet software. Fire up your Web browser, e-mail package, chat room, or any of a number of applications designed for fun and folly on the Internet.

✔ As long as you have an Internet connection, you can run any program that accesses information on the Internet.

✔ Yes, you can run more than one Internet program at a time. I typically have three or four of them going. (Because the Internet is slow, I can read one window while waiting for something to appear in another window.)

✔ You can also stay on the Internet while using an application program, like Word or Excel. Just don't forget that you're online.

✔ Close your Internet programs when you're done with them.

Adios, Internet!

To wave bye-bye to the Internet, simply close all Internet programs. That's it!

For a broadband connection, you're done. In fact, you don't even have to close your Internet programs because the connection is active all the time. For dial-up, you want to disconnect. After closing the last open Internet program's window, you see a Disconnect dialog box. Click the Disconnect or Disconnect Now button.

 If you don't see the Disconnect dialog box, double-click the wee Connection icon on the system tray. That displays the connection's Status dialog box; click the Disconnect button there to hang up.

✔ Dial-up connections must always disconnect from the Internet. Do not forget!

✔ Sometimes, the connection may drop automatically, especially if you haven't done anything on the Internet for a while.

✔ Your ISP may sport an idle-time disconnection value. After a given amount of time, the ISP may just hang up on you if it thinks that you're not alive.

✔ Keep track of how much time you have spent online by viewing the Status dialog box; double-click the connection icon on the system tray. This information is important when you eventually spend several more hours on the Internet than you intended. View the time. Exclaim "My goodness, that's a long time!" and then click Close.

Nasty programs!

The Internet may be a thriving community and full of information, but it's not exactly the safest place to be. Because just about anyone can get on the Internet, and because the Internet is an open system, lots of bad guys are prowling out there. They make nasty programs and can do nasty things to your computer if you're not careful.

Perhaps you have heard the words: spam, spyware, viruses, worms, or pop-ups. These are all nasty or annoying things that can make the Internet less fun to use. Fortunately, you have ways to prevent disaster and thwart the bad guys. Your ISP should be your biggest source of help in this area. You can also check out my book *Troubleshooting Your PC For Dummies* (Wiley) for more information on dealing with nasty things on the Internet.

If you're just starting out on the Internet, you should know about and use two basic Internet concepts: The first is the World Wide Web, and the second is e-mail.

The World Wide Web — or "the Web" — is directly responsible for making the Internet as popular as it is today. The Web introduced pretty graphics and formatted text to the Internet, which propelled it from its ugly all-text past. And, e-mail is the most compelling reason to use the Internet. Something about the instant nature of electronic communications makes some folks live for e-mail.

Chapters 26 and 27 cover the Web and e-mail. They're the two things you waste time, er, spend time doing on the Internet more than anything else.

Chapter 26

It's a World Wide Web We Weave

*T*he Internet existed for many years before everyone and his aunt joined the party. The main reason behind the surge in use was the World Wide Web. Before the Web, information was available on the Internet, but not really easy to get to. What the Web did was present the information on the Internet in a magazine-like format, with pictures, fancy text — and lots of advertising! Because the Web is on a computer, and not printed on paper, it has animations, games, and all sorts of fun and frivolity.

Honestly, the Web isn't that hard to use; just about anyone can figure things out, and you don't really need a book to help you. Even so, I'm compelled to write this chapter, which contains a quick review of basic Web operations and then concentrates on some Web issues you may not be aware of. Oh, and it has lots of tips.

Welcome to the Web

The chief piece of software used to access information on the Internet is a Web browser, or *browser,* for short. It's used to view information stored on Web sites throughout the Internet.

The most popular Web browser is Internet Explorer, or IE. It comes with Windows, and it's your key to viewing the World Wide Web. Other Web browsers are available, some that boast more features or are faster than IE. They all work pretty much the same.

Starting Internet Explorer

 Open the Internet Explorer icon on the desktop to start your Web browser. (Note that the icon is also found in numerous other places in Windows; it's ubiquitous.)

If you're not already connected to the Internet, after starting Internet Explorer, you are (refer to Chapter 25). Soon, the Internet Explorer main window fills with information from the World Wide Web, such as the *Web page* shown in Figure 26-1.

Toolbar   Address bar   Links bar   Busy thing

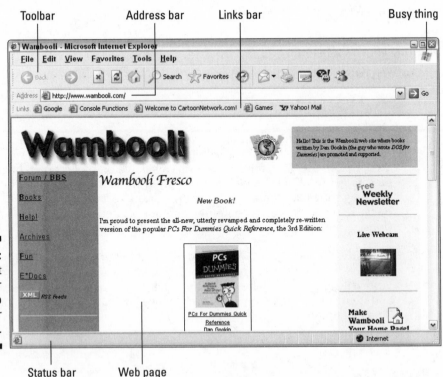

Figure 26-1: The Internet Explorer Web browser program.

Status bar   Web page

The first Web page you see in the Web browser's window is the *home page*. It's merely your starting point on the Web, and it can be changed. (See the section "There's no place like home page," later in this chapter.)

Touring the Internet Explorer window

You should notice a few things in the Web browser window:

Toolbar: You find, below the menu bar, a series of buttons. You use these buttons to visit various places on the Web and do basic things with your Web browser. If you don't see this bar, choose View➪Toolbars➪Standard Buttons from the menu.

Busy thing: The far right end of the button bar has what I call the *busy thing*. The busy thing becomes animated when your Web browser is busy doing something, which usually means that it's waiting for information to be sent from the far-flung parts of the Internet. That's your signal to sit, wait, and be patient; the Web is busy.

Address bar: This box holds the addresses of the pages you visit, and it's also an input box where you can type Web page addresses and other commands. If you don't see this box, choose View➪Toolbars➪Address bar from the menu.

Links bar: This handy toolbar lists popular places you like to visit on the Web. See the section "Using the Links folder and Links toolbar," later in this chapter, for the details on using this handy toolbar.

Web page: The Web browser displays a page of information on the Web — the Web page itself. In Figure 26-1, you see the Wambooli page, which is my own Web page (`http://www.wambooli.com`).

Status bar: This final chunk of information attached to the Web browser window often tells you important things or displays useful information. To view it, choose View➪Status Bar.

The Web browser shows you how simple it is to view information on the Internet. In its window, you see graphics and text — almost like reading a magazine — and more; keep reading.

- ✔ The busy thing is busy a lot. It's often said that the World Wide Web should be World Wide Wait.

- ✔ If you have trouble seeing the text on a Web page, consider changing the text size. Choose View➪Text Size from the menu and then choose a larger or smaller size from the submenu.

✔ Web pages can be wider and often longer than what you see displayed in your browser's window. Don't forget to use the scroll bars! Better still, maximize the browser window to get the full-screen effect.

✔ The thing you type in the Address box is officially known as a *URL* ("you are ell"). It's an acronym for Uniform Resource Locator. Essentially, it's a command you give the Web browser to go out and find information on the Internet.

Closing Internet Explorer

After you're done browsing the World Wide Web — meaning that it's 4 a.m. and you need to get up in 90 minutes to get ready for work — you should close Internet Explorer. This task is easy: Choose File⇨Close from the menu.

Closing Internet Explorer doesn't disconnect you from the Internet. If you're using a modem connection, you must manually disconnect if Windows doesn't automatically prompt you. Refer to Chapter 25 for more information on disconnecting from the Internet.

Visiting a Web page

The Web is divided into billions of locations called *Web sites.* These are sources of information built by companies, communities, individuals, time travelers, and others. The Web site itself is often divided into Web pages, like pages in a magazine. Using the Web is all about viewing those Web pages by using your computer's Web browser.

There's no place like home page

The Internet has two types of home pages. The first is the page you first see when you start your Web browser. You can quickly return to this page, the *home page,* by clicking the Home button on the Web browser's toolbar.

The beauty of a home page is that you can change it. Your home page can be any Web page on the Internet — or even a blank page, if you like.

To set a home page, follow these steps:

1. **Visit the page you want to call home.**

   For example, my Web page is at www.wambooli.com. Type that in the Address box to visit that page.

2. **Choose Tools⇨Internet Options.**

   The Internet Options dialog box appears; click the General tab, if necessary, so that it looks like Figure 26-2.

Figure 26-2:
The Internet
Options
dialog box.

3. **In the Home page area (in the top part of the dialog box), click the Use Current button.**

4. **Click OK.**

The new home page is now set. And, you can change it again at any time. After all, it's _your_ home page!

Note that you can also set the home page to be blank, if that's what you desire.

The other home page? That's a personal page you create, your electronic home on the Internet. Many ISPs offer you a place to create this home page. Refer to your ISP for more information. And, yes, your personal home page can also be the Web browser's home page.

Typing a new Web page address

The most common way to visit one of the estimated three billion pages of information on the World Wide Web is to type that Web page's address into your Web browser's Address bar. Suppose that you want to visit the popular Yahoo! Web portal. Its address is written like this:

```
http://www.yahoo.com/
```

Use the mouse to select any text already on the Address bar; press the Backspace key to delete that text.

Type **http**, a colon, two forward slashes, **www**, a period, **yahoo**, another period, and **com**. (Don't type a final period at the end of the address.)

Double-check your typing and then press the Enter key. Soon, the Yahoo! Web page appears in the browser's window.

If something goes wrong: The most obvious reason for something going wrong is that you mistyped the address. Double-check it! Everything must be *exact*. Upper- and lowercase mean different things. Use the forward slash (/), not the backslash (\). Go ahead and edit the address if you can, or just start over and type it again.

- ✔ If the Web page doesn't load, you may see some type of error message. The first thing you should do is try again! The Web can be busy, and often when it is, you get an error message.

- ✔ If you get a `404` error, you probably didn't type the Web page address properly. Try again: Just click the green arrow by the word *Go* on the far right end of the Address bar.

- ✔ Web page addresses are often listed without the `http://` part.

- ✔ Technically speaking, the `http://` part is required if the Web page address doesn't begin with `www` (and quite a few are like that).

- ✔ If the URL starts with `ftp://` or `gopher://`, you're required to type those commands.

Clicking a Web page link

The automatic way to visit a Web page is to click a Web page link. It appears as underlined text on a Web page, often colored blue (though that's not a hard-and-fast rule). The clear sign that you have found a link is that when you point at it, the mouse pointer changes to a pointing hand, as shown in the margin.

To use the link, click it once with the mouse. The Web browser immediately picks up and moves off to display that Web page — just as though you had typed the address manually.

✔ It's called the *Web* because nearly every page has a link to other pages. For example, a Web page about the end of the world may have links to other Web pages about Nostradamus or the guy who walks around with a sandwich board that says "Doom is near."

✔ Not all links are text. Quite a few links are graphical. The only way to know for certain is to point the mouse pointer at what you believe may be a link. If the pointer changes to a pointing hand, you know that it's a link you can click to see something else.

✔ Links can appear anywhere on a Web page.

✔ *Link* is short for *hyperlink* — another bit of trivia to occupy a few dozen neurons.

Navigating the Web

Using the Web is often like becoming engrossed in an encyclopedia or distracted by multiple articles in a newspaper. The folks who make Web browser software understand this distraction, so they have created a number of ways for you to not become lost or to retrace your steps as you surf the Web. Here are some handy tools you can use:

 To return to the Web page you were just ogling, use your browser's Back button. You can continue clicking the Back button to revisit each Web page you have gawked at, all the way back to the first page you saw 18 hours ago.

If you really need to dig deep, click the down arrow by the Back button. A list of the last several Web pages you have visited appears.

 If you need to return to where you were after going back, use the Forward button. Back. Forward. It's like playing the game Sorry! with a sadistic 8-year-old.

 If you accidentally click a link and change your mind, click the Stop button. The Internet then stops sending you information. (You may need to click the Back button to return to where you were.)

 The browser's Refresh button serves a useful purpose in the world of ever-changing information. Refresh merely tells the Internet to update the Web page you're viewing.

Here are the reasons for clicking the Refresh button:

Web page not found: Don't give up too easily! The Internet can lie; click the Refresh button and give that Web page another try.

Changing information: Some Web pages have updating information on them. Clicking the Refresh button always gets you the latest version of the Web page.

Missing pictures: Occasionally, a graphical image may not appear. In that case, a *blank* icon shows up, to tell you that the image is missing. Often, clicking the Refresh button works some magic that causes the image to reappear.

Accidentally clicking the Stop button: Oops! Click Refresh to unstop and reload the Web page.

Finding Things on the Web

The Web is like a library without a librarian. It doesn't have a card catalog, either. And, forget about finding something on the shelves: Web pages aren't organized in any fashion, nor is the information in them guaranteed to be complete or accurate. Because anyone can post anything on the Web, well, anyone does.

Engines for searching

You find something on the Web by using a *search engine*. It's a Web page that features a huge catalog of other Web pages. You can search through the catalog for whatever you want. Results are displayed, and you can click links to eventually get to the Web page you want. It's all very nifty.

My main search engine these days is Google, at `www.google.com`. I admire it for its simplicity and thoroughness. Simply type what you're looking for in Google's sole text box. Click the Google Search button. After a few moments, Google displays a new page full of findings — Web pages on the Internet that more or less match what it is you're looking for in one way or another.

When the search engine finds more than one page of information, you see a Next 20 Matches link (or something similar) at the bottom of the page. Click that link to see the next list of Web pages that were found.

Google isn't the only search engine, though I believe that it's probably the best. I have listed a variety of others in Table 26-1.

Table 26-1	A Smattering of Search Engines
Site	**Address**
Ask Jeeves	www.ask.com
Dogpile	www.dogpile.com
C|NET Search.com	www.search.com
KartOO	www.kartoo.com
Teoma	www.teoma.com
Vivísimo	www.vivisimo.com
WebCrawler	www.webcrawler.com

Tips for a successful Web search

The more information you give in the Search text box, the more accurate the Web page results. Avoid using small words (such as *the, of, and, but, with,* and *for*) and put the most important words first.

Suppose that you want to find a MIDI file of the theme from the old "Dragnet" TV show. Type this line:

```
Dragnet theme MIDI
```

If words *must* be found together, enclose them in double quotes, such as

```
"Gilligan's Island" theme MIDI
```

or

```
"Toro riding lawnmower" repair
```

This search finds only Web pages that list the words *Toro riding lawnmower* together in that order.

If the results — the matching or found Web pages — are too numerous, click the link (near the bottom of the page) that says Search within results. That way, you can further refine your search. For example, if you found several hundred pages on Walt Disney World but are specifically looking for a map of the Animal Kingdom, you can search for "Animal Kingdom map" within the results found for Walt Disney World.

We All Have Our Favorites

TIP

Often, you find some Web place you love and want to visit again. If so, drop a *bookmark* on that page. That way, you can visit it at any time by selecting the bookmark from a list.

To drop a bookmark, use the Ctrl+D command — D for drop.

This command places the bookmark on the Favorites menu in Internet Explorer. That way, you can revisit the Web page by plucking it from the Favorites menu. It's a walk in the park, minus the bunions.

- ✔ Never fear to add a Web page to your Favorites! It's better to add it now and delete it later than to regret not adding it in the first place.

- ✔ If you forget to drop a bookmark, use the drop-down list on the Address bar's Back button to locate a Web site you have visited recently. Or, you can use the History list; see the section "History 101," later in this chapter.

- ✔ I really wish that Microsoft would call *favorites* by their proper name: bookmarks. Every other Web browser uses bookmarks instead. That name is just so much more descriptive than *favorites*.

Organizing your Favorites

The Favorites menu can get messy quickly. The solution to that, or to any mess on the computer, is to *organize*. You can organize your Favorites menu by deleting unwanted bookmarks or by creating submenus and sub-submenus full of Web pages you have visited. It's all quite easy.

To organize the Favorites menu in Internet Explorer, choose Favorites⇨ Organize Favorites. The Organize Favorites dialog box appears, as shown in Figure 26-3.

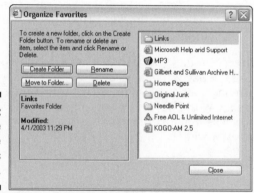

Figure 26-3:
The
Organize
Favorites
dialog box.

To move a selected bookmark into a folder, you can drag and drop the bookmark with the mouse or use the Move to Folder button.

To create a new folder, click the Create Folder button. The New folder appears, named New Folder, though you can type a new name for it at that time.

Rename a bookmark by selecting the bookmark and then clicking the Rename button. This is a good idea, especially for long bookmark names, which make the Favorites menu very wide. For example, I changed the quite long name of my 235-character local weather Web page to read only "Weather," which is all I need to know when choosing that site from the Favorites menu.

And, of course, to delete unwanted bookmarks, select them with the mouse and click the Delete button.

✔ I try to keep on the Favorites menu only as many bookmarks as will fit on the screen. If I open the Favorites menu and it starts to scroll off the screen, I know I need to go in and do some organizing.

✔ Create folders for specific categories of bookmarks: News, Weather, Sports, Music, Movies, Fun Stuff, Computer Reference, or whatever you're into.

✔ You can use submenus to further organize your topics.

✔ Feel free to delete any favorites that Microsoft preinstalled on the Favorites menu. Those bookmarks are from companies that paid money to have their products advertised there.

Using the Links folder and Links toolbar

One special folder that comes already set up inside the Internet Explorer Favorites menu is the Links folder. The items that appear in that folder also appear on the Links toolbar in Internet Explorer, which makes those links even handier to get at.

To make the Links toolbar appear, choose View➪Toolbar➪Links from the menu. The toolbar displays whatever links are saved in the Favorites\Links folder. That's where I put my most favorite Web pages: news, weather, Wambooli, and shopping, for example. They appear right on the Links toolbar, as shown in Figure 26-1.

Subfolders in the Links folder appear as menus on the Links toolbar.

History 101

Internet Explorer remembers every Web page you have visited today, yesterday, and sometimes for the past several weeks. Many people like this feature; it lets them review where they have been and revisit those places. Many more people despise this feature because it lets anyone else snoop on where they have been on the Internet.

Looking at the History list

 To see the History list, click the History button on the Internet Explorer toolbar. The History panel appears on the left side of the Internet Explorer window. The panel is divided into areas by date: Today, Last Week, 2 Weeks Ago, and 3 Weeks Ago, similar to what's shown in Figure 26-4.

Figure 26-4:
The Internet
Explorer
History
panel.

Beneath each date are folders representing the Web sites you have visited. Open a folder to view the list of individual pages.

Close the History list when you're done with it: Click the X (close) button in the History panel, or just click the History button on the toolbar.

➖ To revisit a page, simply choose it from the History list. For example, open the Last Week item, choose the Scandinavian Puns Web site, and choose an individual page from the site you visited last week.

➖ The keyboard shortcut for the History list is Ctrl+H.

Clearing the History list

Often, history doesn't reflect kindly on you. Fortunately, Internet Explorer offers several ways to delete, if not rewrite, your history:

✔ To remove a page or Web site from the list, right-click that item. Choose Delete from the pop-up shortcut menu.

✔ To clear all items from the History list, choose Tools⇨Internet Options. In the Internet Options dialog box, on the General tab, click the Clear History button. Click OK.

✔ To disable the History list, choose Tools⇨Internet Options to display the Internet Options dialog box. On the General tab, locate the History area. Reset the Days to Keep Pages in History option to zero, which disables the Internet Explorer History feature. Click OK.

Printing Web Pages

To print any Web page, choose File⇨Print from the menu. No tricks.

Some Web pages, unfortunately, don't print right. Some are too wide. Some are white text on a black background, which doesn't print well. My advice is to always use the Print Preview command to look at what's printing before you print it. If you still have trouble, consider one of these solutions:

✔ Consider saving the Web page to disk; choose File⇨Save As. Ensure that you choose from the Save As Type drop-down list the option labeled Web Page, Complete. Then you can open the Web page file in Microsoft Word or Excel, or any Web page editing program, and edit or print it from there.

✔ Use the File⇨Page Setup program to select landscape orientation for printing wider-than-normal Web pages.

✔ Use the Properties button in the Print dialog box to adjust the printer. These settings depend on the printer itself, but I have seen printers that can reduce the output to 75 or 50 percent, which ensures that the entire Web page prints on a single sheet of paper. Other options may let you print in shades of gray or black and white.

Chapter 27

Basic E-Mail

• •

In This Chapter

▶ Using Outlook Express

▶ Creating a new e-mail message

▶ Getting e-mail

▶ Replying to e-mail

▶ Understanding the Address Book

▶ Creating Address Book entries

▶ Using nicknames

▶ Making mail groups

• •

 ail call!

Nothing perks up your Internet day like getting fresh e-mail. *Ahhhh, people care enough about me to write! I'm loved!*

This chapter deals with e-mail, which can be an obsession for some folks. In fact, if you're like most people, you probably run both your Web browser and e-mail program at the same time. That way, you don't "miss anything" while you're on the Internet.

✔ This book assumes that you have Outlook Express (Version 6), the e-mail package that comes free with Windows.

✔ Outlook Express is *not* the same program as Outlook, which is another e-mail program distributed with Microsoft Office. Outlook Express is also not the only e-mail program available. A popular alternative, and a favorite of mine, is Eudora: www.eudora.com.

✔ If you haven't yet set up e-mail accounts on your computer, the first time you run Outlook Express it starts a wizard that walks you through the necessary steps.

Starting Outlook Express

Start Outlook Express by opening the Outlook Express icon on the desktop (as shown in the margin). You may also find the icon on the Quick Launch bar.

If you aren't already connected to the Internet, starting Outlook Express connects you. If not, refer to Chapter 25 for information on connecting to the Internet.

You cannot send or receive e-mail unless your computer is connected to the Internet.

The main screen

The first thing Outlook does is check for new mail. See the section "Reading e-mail," later in this chapter, if you *really* can't wait to get started. Outlook also sends any mail you have waiting.

Figure 27-1 details the Outlook Express screen. It consists of three parts:

Folders list

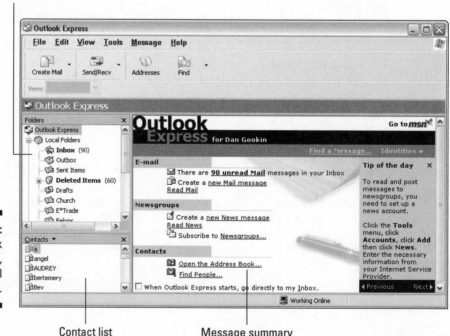

Figure 27-1:
Outlook
Express,
your e-mail
program.

Contact list   Message summary

Folders list: In the upper-left area of the window is the list of folders where sent, received, trashed, and filed mail goes.

Contact list: In the lower-left area is a list of *contacts,* people with whom you may normally communicate.

Message summary: On the right is a home page of sorts for messages, newsgroups, and stuff. You may or may not see this screen. Instead, you can configure Outlook Express to display your Inbox whenever you switch it on: Click to put a check in the box by the option When Starting, Go Directly to My Inbox Folder.

The inbox

The opening screen for Outlook Express is something you really don't want to see. No, you want to get that mail! Click the Inbox link to see any old or new messages you have received.

When you go to the Inbox (see Figure 27-2), the right side of the screen splits into two parts. The upper-right part shows the queue of e-mail in the Inbox. Bold text indicates unread mail; normal text indicates read mail (and the open/closed envelope icon confirms this information).

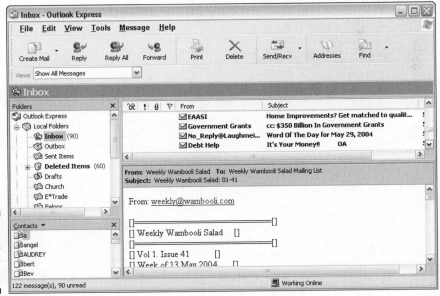

Figure 27-2: The Outlook Express Inbox view.

The lower-right part of the window shows a preview of the message's contents.

Between the left and right sides of the window is a separator bar. You can drag that bar with the mouse, to make either side larger. My advice is to drag the separator bar to the left, to make the Inbox and preview windows larger.

Closing Outlook Express

To close Outlook Express when you're done, close the program's window. Or, choose File⇨Exit from the menu.

If Outlook Express is the last Internet program you close, dial-up connections are prompted to disconnect from the Internet. If you're finished, disconnect!

Composing and Replying to E-Mail

The reason you use an e-mail program like Outlook Express is to both compose e-mail and — you hope — receive e-mail. ***Remember:*** To get e-mail, you must first send some.

This section assumes that you're using Outlook Express as your e-mail program. Other e-mail programs behave similarly.

Sending e-mail

To create a new message in Outlook Express, click the Create Mail button. The New Message window appears, as shown in Figure 27-3. Your job is to fill in the blanks — four of them:

To: To whom are you sending the message? Type the person's e-mail address in the To field. Important things to note:

- ✔ Don't put spaces in an e-mail address. If you think that it's a space, it's probably an underline or a period.

- ✔ You must enter the full e-mail address: zorgon@wambooli.com. Note the single exception: If you have e-mail nicknames set up, you can type the nickname rather than the full e-mail address in the To field. (See the section "The Valued Address Book" later in this chapter, for information on nicknames.)

- ✔ You can type more than one address in the To field. If so, separate each with a semicolon or comma, as in

```
president@whitehouse.gov, first.lady@whitehouse.gov
```

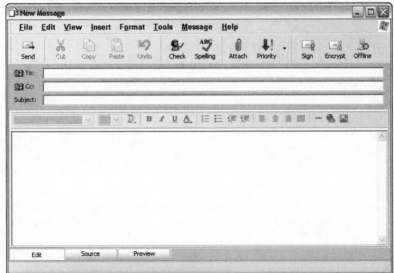

Figure 27-3:
The New
Message
window.

Cc: The *carbon copy* field is used to send a copy of the e-mail to another person, as sort of a For Your Information type of thing. People whose e-mail addresses are put in the Cc field receive the message, but they know that the message wasn't directly intended for them.

Subject: Type the message's subject. What is the message about? It helps if the subject is somehow related to the message (because the recipients see the subject in their Inboxes, just like you do).

The message: The last thing to fill in is the contents. Type the message!

When you're done composing your e-epistle, check your spelling by clicking the Spelling button. Your message is scanned, and potential misspelled words are flagged. Select the properly spelled word from the dialog box — the same drill you go through with your word processor's spell check feature.

Review your message! Spell checking doesn't check for grammatical errors or potentially offensive outrageous statements. Remember that you can't recall e-mail after it's sent!

Finally, you send the message. Click the Send button, and it's off to the Internet, delivered cheaper and more accurately than by any post office on earth.

If you don't want to send the message, close the New Message window. You're asked whether you want to save the message. Click Yes to save it in the Drafts folder. If you click No, the message is destroyed.

✔ You can start a new message by pressing Ctrl+N or choosing File⇨New⇨ Mail Message from the menu bar.

✔ If you type the wrong e-mail address, the message *bounces* back to you. It isn't a bad thing; just try again with the proper address.

✔ An e-mail message is sent instantly. I sent a message to a reader in Australia one evening and got a reply from him in fewer than 10 minutes.

✔ Please don't type in ALL CAPS. To most people, all caps reads like YOU'RE SHOUTING AT THEM!

✔ Spell checking in Outlook Express works only if you have Microsoft Word or the entire Microsoft Office package installed. Otherwise, you cannot spell-check in Outlook Express.

✔ Be careful what you write. E-mail messages are often casually written, and they can easily be misinterpreted. Remember to keep them light.

✔ Don't expect a quick reply from e-mail, especially from folks in the computer industry (which is ironic).

✔ To send a message you have shoved off to the Drafts folder, open the Drafts folder. Then double-click the message to open it. The original New Message window is then redisplayed. From there, you can edit the message and click the Send button to finally send it off.

✔ Also see Chapter 28, which covers e-mail file attachments.

Reading e-mail

To read a message, select it from the list in the Inbox. The message text appears in the bottom of the Outlook Express window, as shown earlier, in Figure 27-2. You can read any message on the list like this, in any order; selecting a new message displays its contents in the bottom part of the window.

Of course, you're not stuck viewing the message in the crowded jail of the Outlook Express multiple-window inferno. No, if you like, you can open a message window by double-clicking the message in the Inbox. A special message-reading window opens, similar to the one shown in Figure 27-4.

Because the message has its own window, you can resize or drag around the message anywhere on the screen. And, you can open more than one message-reading window at a time, which helps if you need to refer to more than one message at a time (those he-said-she-said things, for example).

The message-reading window also has two handy buttons: Previous and Next.

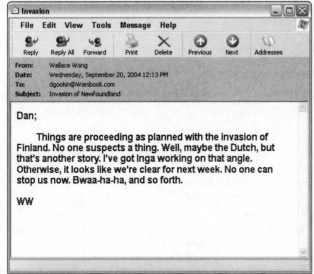

Figure 27-4:
An individual mail message in its own window.

Click the Previous button to read the previous message in the Inbox, the one before the current message.

Click the Next button to read the next message in your Inbox. If you're reading the last message in the Inbox, clicking the Next button makes an annoying sound.

As with a Web page, if you have trouble seeing the text in an e-mail message, choose View➪Text Size from the menu and choose a larger or smaller size from the submenu.

After reading e-mail

After reading a message, you can do one of many things to it.

To print an e-mail message, choose File➪Print from the menu. The Print dialog box appears; click OK to print. You can also print a message by clicking the Print button on the toolbar.

To send an answer or follow-up to an e-mail message, click the Reply button.

Note that Outlook Express does several things for you automatically:

- The sender's name is automatically placed in the To field. Your reply goes directly to the sender without your having to retype an address.

- The original subject is referenced (Re) on the Subject line.

- Finally, the original message is *quoted* for you. This feature is important because some people receive lots of e-mail and may not recall the train of the conversation.

Type your reply and then click the Send button to send it off.

Forwarding a message is the same as remailing it to someone else. To forward a message, click the Forward button. The forwarded message appears *quoted* in the body of the new message. Type any optional comments. Fill in the To field with the address of the person to whom you're forwarding the message. Finally, click the Send button to send it off.

To delete the message you're reading, click the Delete button. Poof! It's gone. (To be accurate, the message is merely moved into the Deleted Items folder on the left side of the Outlook Express window.)

- You don't have to do anything with a message after reading it; you can just keep it in your Inbox. There's no penalty for that.

- You can edit the quoted text when replying to or forwarding a message. The quoted text isn't "locked" or anything. I typically split up quoted text when I reply to e-mail — even delete chunks — so that I can address topics individually.

- Use the Reply All button when you reply to a message that was carbon-copied to a number of other people. By clicking Reply All, you create a reply that lists *everyone* the original message was sent to so that they can all read the reply.

- You can use the Forward button to resend bounced e-mail messages to the proper address. The forwarding keyboard command is Ctrl+F. Just type the proper address and maybe an explanation of how you goofed or something, and click the Send button to send it off again.

- Deleted mail sits in the Deleted Items folder until you clean out that folder. To clean it out, choose Edit⇨Empty Deleted Items Folder from the menu.

The Valued Address Book

Whenever you get e-mail from someone new, or whenever you learn a friend's new online address, you should note it in the Outlook Express Address Book. Not only does the Address Book let you keep the addresses in one spot, but you can also easily recall an address for sending mail later.

Adding a name to the Address Book

You can add an e-mail name to your Address Book in one of two ways: manually or automatically.

Manually adding names: To manually add a name to your Address Book, choose File⇨New⇨Contact from the menu. Outlook then creates a new Address Book entry (as shown in Figure 27-5), which you fill in.

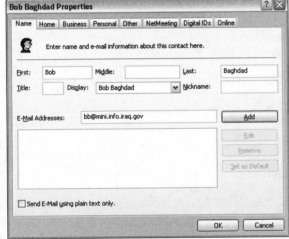

Figure 27-5:
Filling in a new Address Book entry.

The dialog box has many tabs and gizmos for you to work, but you need to fill in only four items on the Name tab: First, Last, Nickname, and E-Mail Addresses.

The Nickname item is optional, though it can be handy. For example, you can type **goober** rather than your brother's full e-mail address in the To field of a new message. Outlook Express recognizes the shortcut and replaces it with the proper, full e-mail address.

After filling in the four fields (or more, if you're entirely bored), click the Add button and then click OK.

Automatically adding names: To automatically add a name to the Address book, display an e-mail message from someone whose name you want to add. Choose Tools⇨Add to Address Book⇨Sender from the menu. Outlook instantly adds the name to the Address Book.

Addresses

Click the Addresses button on the toolbar to display the Address Book window. From there, you can edit or manage the entries in your Address Book.

Using the Address Book when sending a message

The Address Book really comes in handy when you're creating a new message. With the New Message window on the screen, click the To field's button, as shown in the margin. A special Address Book window appears, as shown in Figure 27-6.

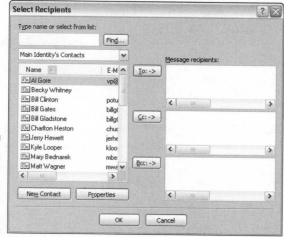

Figure 27-6: Select people here to send e-mail to.

To add someone to the To field, select that person's name and click the To button; likewise for the Cc or Bcc fields. To select more than one e-mail address at a time, press and hold the Ctrl key and then Ctrl+click to select the names. (Release the Ctrl key when you're done selecting.)

When you're done, click OK, and the message's To, Cc, and Bcc fields are already filled in for you.

Creating a group

Often, you want to send e-mail to more than one person — for example, all the folks on your Jokes, Sappy Stories, Family, or whatever lists. By creating a group, you can save yourself some time spent typing all those addresses over and over.

To create a group, follow these steps:

1. **Choose Tools⇨Address Book to open the Address Book.**

2. **Choose File⇨New Group.**

   A dialog box appears, where you can create the group.

3. **Type a name for the group.**

   Be clever and descriptive. The Jokes group can be named Jokes. The people you send messages to regarding your nude quilting group can be named Nude Quilters.

4. **Add members to the group.**

   Use the Select Members button to pick whom you want to be in the group. This action displays another dialog box, from which you can cull your list of e-mail contacts and add them to the group: Select the names and addresses from the left side of the window and use the Select button to add them to the group on the right side.

5. **Click OK when you're done adding members.**

6. **Click OK to close the group's Properties window.**

7. **Close the Address Book window.**

   You're ready to use the group.

To send a message to the group, type the group's name in the To, Cc, or Bcc field. The message is then sent to that group of people automatically.

You can also click the To button, as described in the preceding section, to choose a group from the list in your Address Book.

TIP

Putting Bcc to work

The sneaky Bcc field is used to *blind carbon-copy* a message, which involves sending a copy of a message to someone and having that person's name *not* appear in any copy of the e-mail. That way, you can clue people in to a message without having its true recipients know the names of everyone else who received the message.

To access the Bcc field, choose View⇨All Headers from the New Message window's menu. The people in the Bcc field receive a copy of the e-mail message just like everyone else; however, the people in the To or Cc fields don't see the Bcc field names listed.

Remember that you must always have a name in the To field; if you don't want to put anyone specific there, just use your own e-mail address.

By the way, putting the group in the Bcc field is a wonderful idea; see the nearby sidebar "Putting Bcc to work" for more information.

A great way to use Bcc is when you send a message to several people. For example, when sending out That Latest Joke, just put everyone's name in the Bcc field and put your own name in the To field. That way, everyone gets the joke (or not, as the case may be), and they don't see the huge stack-o-names at the start of the e-mail message.

Chapter 28

Files to Here, Files from There!

*T*he Internet was borne of the need to fling files far and wide between the early steam-powered computers of the past century. Thank goodness, it's much easier to do today. You can send a file to anyone by adding an attachment to your e-mail. You can fetch files either through e-mail messages or by grabbing them from Web pages. Or, you can venture into the mysterious waters of FTP. This chapter tells you the details.

Grabbing Stuff from a Web Page

The Internet is brimming with files and programs just waiting for you to seize a copy. Work some magic, and the file is piped into your PC just as though you had copied it from a CD-ROM (though not as fast). You can grab files, programs, fonts, graphics — just about anything and everything you want. And, it's as cinchy as clicking your mouse.

✔ Copying a file to your computer is known as *downloading*. When someone sends you a file over the Internet, you *download* it. (Think of the other computer as being on top of a hill; it may not be, but it helps to think of it that way.)

✔ Sending a file to another computer is known as *uploading*.

✔ Complaining to your best friend over a beer is known as *unloading*.

Saving an entire Web page to disk

To save an entire Web page to disk, choose File⇨Save As in Internet Explorer. A Save Web Page dialog box appears, similar to the Save As dialog box in any other application. Use the dialog box to save the Web page to disk.

✔ Saving a Web page saves an *HTML file* to disk. That file contains the formatting instructions for the Web page. (It's basically a text file, though not that readable.)

✔ You can view the Web page offline by using Internet Explorer; the saved Web page opens and is displayed just as though you were connected to the Internet.

✔ You can also view saved Web pages by using a Web page editor, such as FrontPage. Business applications, such as Microsoft Word and Excel, can also be used to view Web pages.

✔ I know many people who save Web pages for reading later, offline. In fact, saving a fun Web page for reading during a long airplane flight is a great way to spend your time.

Saving an image from a Web page

To save an image from a Web page to your PC's hard drive, right-click the image and choose Save Picture As from the pop-up menu. Use the Save As dialog box to find a happy home for the picture on your hard drive.

✔ Nearly all images on the Web are copyrighted. Although you're free to save a copy to your hard drive, you're not free to duplicate, sell, or distribute the image without the consent of the copyright holder.

✔ To set the image as your desktop wallpaper, choose Set As Background from the pop-up menu after right-clicking the image.

✔ If you point the mouse at a picture long enough, an image toolbar appears. The buttons are, from left to right, Save the Image to Disk, Print the Image, Send the Image As an e-Mail Attachment, and Open the My Pictures Folder.

Saving text from a Web page to disk

Most Web pages display plain text. You can copy that text and save it to disk just as you would copy text from one application and paste it into another. Here's how:

1. **Select the text you want to copy.**

   Drag the mouse over the text, which highlights it on the screen. The text is now selected.

2. **Choose Edit⇨Copy.**

3. **Start any word processor.**

   You can start Notepad, WordPad, or your word processor, such as Microsoft Word.

4. **Paste the text into your word processor.**

   Ctrl+V or Edit⇨Paste.

5. **Print. Save. Whatever.**

   Use the proper menu commands to save or print or edit the text you copied from the Web page.

Getting Software from the Internet

The Internet is a great repository of software, various programs for free or nearly free, which you can download to your computer for use, tryout, or just because. This section covers downloading software from the Internet.

   ✔ A *repository* is a location where things are stored.

   ✔ A *suppository* is medicine you eat, but not with your mouth.

Searching for programs

The first step to getting software from the Internet is to find it. Many software companies have a direct Internet presence, so by merely finding their Web pages, you can visit the download area and see which files they have up for grabs.

You can also use a search engine to locate files, or, specifically, you can use file-searching engines to find things. Two examples are the C|NET Shareware.com (`www.shareware.com`) and IT Pro Downloads (`http://itprodownloads.com`) sites. Use these sites just like search engines: You can search for files of a specific type, or you can browse by category to see what's available.

Creating a Downloads folder

Because downloads need a place to be saved on your computer, I recommend creating a special Downloads folder for them. That way, you can always keep your downloaded programs and files together and quickly locate a downloaded file if you ever need to reinstall it.

Follow these steps to create a special Downloads folder:

1. **Open the My Documents icon on the desktop.**
2. **Choose File⇨New⇨Folder.**
3. **Name the folder** My Downloads.

   Or, just name it **Downloads** if the entire My prefix-thing bugs you.

Whenever you download a file, use the Save As dialog box to browse to the My Downloads folder and save your downloaded file there.

✔ Keep a copy of the program's registration number in the Downloads folder, in case you eventually buy the software. Most registration numbers are e-mailed. When you receive that e-mail, choose the File⇨Save As command to save a copy of the message in the Downloads folder.

✔ It's okay to delete a file from the My Downloads folder after the file's program has been installed. I don't do it, however, because I like to keep everything in case I need to reinstall it again.

✔ Another folder, found in the Windows folder, is named Downloaded Program Files. This folder is used for updates to Internet Explorer, and its contents aren't for you to play with.

Downloading a file from the Internet

To download a file, simply click the proper link or wait for the download to start automatically. This instruction is apparent whether you're using a file search engine or downloading a program from a developer's Web site; clicking the link starts the downloading process.

After the download begins, you see a File Download dialog box, as shown in Figure 28-1. Click the Save button. Do not click the Open button! The Save button lets you save the file on your hard drive, which is where you want it. If you click Open, Internet Explorer attempts to run the program over the Internet, which is probably not what you want, not to mention slow and a high security risk. *Click Save instead!*

Clicking the Save button displays the Save As dialog box. Use it to browse to the Downloads folder (which you may have created in the preceding subsection).

Rename the file. In the Save As dialog box's File Name box, type a new, more descriptive name for the file. Be sure *not* to rename the EXE or ZIP filename extension (if it's visible).

For example, rename the file DSLST45.ZIP to DSL Speed Test 45.ZIP. That's a much more memorable name than the original name. There's nothing wrong with renaming a file you're saving on your computer.

Click the Save button, and the other computer on the Internet begins sending your computer the file.

While the file is downloading, feel free to go off and do something else on the Web; you don't have to sit and watch the file download — but you must stay connected to the Internet. If the connection drops, you have to start over and redo everything.

To find out what to do after the file is downloaded, see the next section.

How long does it take to download a file?

Honestly, the progress meter you see when a file is being downloaded is for entertainment value only; no one really knows how long it takes to download a file. If the Internet is busy, it may take longer than estimated — even for a fast modem. Consider the time that's displayed as only a rough estimate.

Installing and using downloaded software

Two things need to happen after you successfully download a file. These two things depend on the type of file you have downloaded.

If you just saved to disk a regular EXE or program file, you should run it: Double-click its icon in the Downloads folder, which runs the installation or Setup program and gets you going. Follow the instructions on the screen.

If the file is a zip file, you have more work to do. Zip files open as compressed folders in Windows XP, so your first step is to open the compressed folder and see what lies inside. Hopefully, you see a README document that you can open and view to see what to do next.

If you see no README document, your job is to extract all the files from the compressed folder archive, to copy them into their own folder on the hard drive. Right-click the Compressed Folder icon and choose Extract All from the pop-up menu. Then, use the Extraction Wizard to determine a folder in which the files are extracted.

For example, create a new folder in the C:\Program Files folder for a program or utility you just downloaded.

After extracting the files from the Compressed Folder archive, check to see whether it has a Setup or Install program you then have to run to complete installation.

- ✔ Downloading the file is free. If the file is shareware, however, you're expected to pay for it if you use it.
- ✔ Even though the file was downloaded, if you don't want it, you have to uninstall it as you would uninstall any program (refer to Chapter 23).

Look, Ma! It's an E-Mail Attachment!

E-mail attachments are fun — fun to send and fun to receive. They're a convenient and popular way to send files back and forth on the Internet.

This section covers sending and receiving e-mail file attachments by using the Outlook Express (OE) e-mail program that comes with Windows. The steps described are similar for other e-mail programs. (Refer to Chapter 27 for more basic information on e-mail.)

Grabbing an attachment with Outlook Express

 The secret of attachments in Outlook Express is the paper clip icon. When you see the paper clip icon next to the message subject in the Inbox, it indicates that the e-mail message has one or more files attached to it. Yee-haw!

When you read the message, you see an Attach Header line appear on the regular list of From, Date, To, and Subject. That header appears by the file or files attached to the message.

Attachments aren't anything until you open them. To open an attachment, double-click its icon by the Attach heading. A warning dialog box may appear; my advice is to always save the attachment to disk; choose that option and click OK. Then, use the Save Attachment As dialog box to save the file to a memorable place on your computer's hard drive.

An exception for attached files is graphics files. They appear as images below the message body itself. You don't have to do anything; the images just show up. (If not, the images that were sent aren't proper Internet graphics files, such as JPEG or PNG.)

With the attachment saved, you can reply to or delete the message as you normally would.

- ✔ I save my attachments in the My Documents folder. After looking at them or examining their contents, I then shuffle them off to the proper folder.

- ✔ To save multiple attachments at one time, choose File➪Save Attachments. You can then use the Save Attachments dialog box to save them all at once to a folder on the hard drive.

- ✔ Even if Outlook Express displays graphics files directly in your message, you may still want to choose File➪Save Attachments to save them to disk.

- ✔ Don't open attachments you weren't expecting, especially program files — even if they're from people you know. Just delete the message. Or, if you're using antivirus software (which I highly recommend), the antivirus program may alert you to the nasty program's presence even before you open the e-mail.

- ✔ For more information on fighting nasty programs on the Internet, refer to my book *Troubleshooting Your PC For Dummies* (Wiley Publishing, Inc.).

- ✔ At some point, you may receive a file that your PC cannot digest — a file of an unknown format. If so, the dreaded Open With dialog box appears. Quickly, ignore it! Choose Cancel. Then respond to the e-mail and tell the person that you can't open the file and need to have it re-sent in another format.

Things you don't need to know about FTP

FTP is one of those ubiquitous three letter acronyms (TLAs) that litter computer jargon like empty Pabst cans at a NASCAR race. It stands for File Transfer Protocol, and it's also a verb that generically means "to send files hither and thither on the Internet." For example, when you grab a file from the Web, as described in this chapter, your PC is really using FTP to get the file.

You can also use specific FTP programs if all you want is to get files. Just as there are Web servers on the Internet — computers that dish up Web pages — there are *FTP servers,* or computers that just list a host of files. You can use your Web browser to access an FTP server, or you can use specific FTP software, such as SmartFTP, from www.smartftp.com.

Theoretically, using FTP is just like working with files in Windows. The difference is that rather than copy files between one disk drive and another, you copy them from one computer to another over the Internet. Also, some FTP servers require a password for access, and that seems to bewilder some folks.

The only real reason to mess with FTP any more is when you plan to create your own Web page. In that case, you need an FTP program, or to use FTP as part of your Web page creation program, to get the Web page from your computer onto the Internet. That's a whole other book, so I think I'll stop writing about FTP right here.

Sending an attachment in Outlook Express

You attach a file in Outlook Express by — can you guess? — clicking the big paper clip Attach button in the New Message window. Yup, it's that easy.

Start by creating a new message or replying to a message. (Refer to Chapter 27 for the details.) When you're ready to attach a file, click the Attach button or choose Insert⇨File Attachment from the menu.

Use the Insert Attachment dialog box to find the file you want to attach. It works exactly like an Open or Browse dialog box. After finding and selecting the file, click the Attach button.

The file you attach appears on a new line in the New Message window, right below the Subject line.

To send the message and the file, click the Send button. And it's off, on its merry way. . . .

✔ Sending a message with a file attached takes longer than sending a regular, text-only message.

✔ You should ensure that the recipient of a message can read the type of file you're sending. For example, sending a Word file to a WordPerfect user may not meet with the results you want.

✔ Note that some folks cannot receive large files. Sometimes, the limit is 5MB, but I have seen it as low as 1MB. The alternative? Burn a CD-R and send the files through the regular mail. (Refer to Chapter 24 for information on burning CD-Rs.)

✔ Send JPEG or PNG pictures. Any other picture format is usually too large and makes the recipient wait a long time to receive the message.

✔ You can send more than one file at a time — just keep attaching files.

✔ Or, rather than send several small files, consider putting them all in a compressed folder and just sending the single compressed folder instead.

✔ Don't send file shortcuts; send only originals. If you send a shortcut, the people receiving the file don't get the original. Instead, they get the 296-byte shortcut, which doesn't help.

✔ Try not to move or delete any files you attach to e-mail messages until *after* you send the message. I know that it sounds dumb, but too often, as I wait for my e-mail to be sent out (while I'm not busy), I start cleaning files. Oops!

Part V
The Part of Tens

The 5th Wave   By Rich Tennant

"I got this through one of those mail order PC companies that let you design your own system."

In this part . . .

Making up lists is a fun, if perhaps useless, exercise. Remember the old chestnut "Ten books you would want to have on a desert island"? It's just a mental exercise. I mean, if you were really stranded on a desert island and someone else were proud of the fact that they had these 10 books with them, wouldn't you want to strangle that person? I know folks who have their lists of "10 desert island CDs" and "10 desert island friends." But, folks, it's not about the desert island — it's about creating lists, which is what you will find in this part of the book.

Chapter 29

Ten Common Beginner Mistakes

Sure, you can make a gazillion mistakes with a computer, whether it's deleting the wrong file or dropping the color laser printer on your toe. But I have narrowed the list to ten. These are the day-to-day operating mistakes that people tend to repeat until they're told not to, or they read about it here.

Not Properly Shutting Down Windows

When you're done with Windows, shut it down. Choose the Turn Off Computer command from the Start panel, click the Turn Off button, and wait until your PC turns itself off.

✔ Don't just flip the power switch when you're done.

✔ Refer to Chapter 4 for detailed PC shutdown instructions.

Buying Too Much Software

Your PC probably came out of the box with dozens of programs preinstalled. (No, you're not required to use them; refer to Chapter 23, the section about uninstalling software.) Even with all that software preinstalled, don't overwhelm yourself by getting *more* software right away.

Buying too much software isn't really the sin here. The sin is buying too much software and trying to learn it all at once. The buy-it-all-at-once habit probably comes from buying music, where it's okay to lug home a whole stack of CDs from the store. You can listen to several CDs over the course of a few days. They're enjoyable the first time, and they age well. Software, on the other hand, is gruesome the first day and can take months to come to grips with.

Have mercy on yourself at the checkout counter and buy software at a moderate rate. Buy one package and figure out how to use it. Then, move on and buy something else. You learn faster that way.

Buying Incompatible Hardware

Whoops! Did you forget to notice that the new keyboard you bought was for a Macintosh? Or, maybe you thought that you were getting a deal on that FireWire scanner, and, lo, your PC doesn't have a FireWire port. The biggest disappointment: You buy a new AGP expansion card, and all you have available are PCI slots.

Always check your hardware before you buy it! Especially if you're shopping online — if you're not sure that the hardware is compatible, phone the dealer and ask those folks specifically.

Not Buying Enough Supplies

Buy printer paper in those big boxes. You *will* run out. Buy extra paper and a variety of papers for different types of printing (drafts, color, high-quality, and photo, for example). Buy a spool of 100 CD-Rs. Get a few extra media cards. Keep extra printer ink cartridges on hand. You get the idea.

Not Saving Your Work

Whenever you're creating something blazingly original, choose the Save command and save your document to the hard disk. When you write something dumb that you're going to patch up later, choose the Save command too. The idea is to choose Save whenever you think about it — hopefully, every few minutes or sooner.

Save! Save! Save!

You never know when your computer will meander off to watch wrestling on TV while you're hoping to finish the last few paragraphs of that report. Save your work as often as possible. And, always save it whenever you get up from your computer — even if it's just to grab a Fig Newton from the kitchen.

Not Backing Up Files

Saving work on a computer is a many-tiered process. First, save the work to your hard drive as you create it. Then, at the end of the day, back up your work to an external disk drive, a removable disk, such as a CD-R, or a flash memory drive. Always keep a duplicate, safety copy of your work somewhere because you never know.

At the end of the week (or month), run a backup program. I know that this process is a pain, but it's much more automated and easier to do than in years past. I recommend checking out the Dantz Retrospect Backup software and using it to back up your important stuff to a CD-R. You'll be thankful!

`www.dantz.com`

Opening or Deleting Unknown Things

Computers have both hardware and software rules about opening or deleting unknown items. On the software side, I have a rule:

Delete only those files or folders you created yourself.

Windows is brimming with unusual and unknown files. Don't mess with 'em. Don't delete them. Don't move them. Don't rename them. And, especially, don't open them to see what they are. Sometimes opening an unknown icon can lead to trouble.

On the hardware side, don't open anything attached to your PC unless you absolutely know what you're doing. Some hardware is meant to open. New console cases have pop-off and fliptop lids for easy access. They make upgrading things a snap. If you open a console, remember to unplug it! It's okay to open your printer to undo a jam or install new ink or a toner cartridge. Even so, don't open the ink or toner cartridges.

Other hardware items have Do Not Open written all over them: the monitor, keyboard, and modem.

Trying to Save the World

Avoid that hero instinct! People new to PCs and fresh on e-mail somehow feel emboldened that they're personally responsible for the health, safety, and entertainment of everyone else they know on the Internet. Let me be honest: If you're just starting out, be aware that those of us already on the Internet have seen that joke. We have seen the funny pictures. We know the stories. And, everyone has already sent us that e-mail saying that if you send it to seven people you know, somehow Bill Gates will write you a check for $4,000.

Please don't be part of the problem. Telling others about viruses and *real* threats is one thing, but spreading Internet hoaxes is something else. Before you send out a blanket e-mail to everyone you know, confirm that you're sending the truth. Visit a few Web sites, such as www.truthorfiction.com, www.ciac.org/ciac/, and www.vmyths.com. If the message you're spreading is true, please include a few Web page links to verify it.

Thanks for being part of the solution, and not part of the problem!

Replying to Spam E-Mail

Don't reply to any spam e-mail unless you want more spam. A popular trick is for spammers to put some text that says "Reply to this message if you do not want to receive any further messages." Don't! Replying to spam signals the spammers that they have a "live one," and you then get even more spam. Never, ever, reply to spam!

Opening a Program Attached to an E-Mail Message

You can receive photos via e-mail. You can receive sound files. You can receive any types of documents. You can even receive zip file archives or compressed folders. These files are all okay to receive. But, if you receive a program (EXE or COM) file or a Visual Basic Script (VBS) file, do not open it!

The only way to get a virus on a PC is to *run* an infected program file. You can receive the file okay. But, if you open it, you're dead. My rule is "Don't open any EXE file you're sent through e-mail."

✔ Zip files (compressed folders) are okay to receive. You can open them and see what's in them. If they contain programs you're unsure of, just delete the whole deal. You're safe.

✔ If you have to send a program file through e-mail, write or phone the recipient in advance to let the person know that it's coming.

✔ When in doubt, run antivirus software and scan the file before you open it.

✔ Some types of viruses can come in Microsoft Word documents. Antivirus software may catch these viruses, but in any case, confirm that the sender meant to send you the file before you open it.

Chapter 30

Ten Things Worth Buying for Your PC

I'm not trying to sell you anything, and I'm pretty sure that you're not ready to burst out and spend, spend, spend on something — like another computer (unless it's someone else's money). Still, there are some toys — or, shall I say, *companions* — worthy of your PC's company. Here's the list of items I recommend. Some are not that expensive, and I don't sell any of them on my own Web site!

Mouse Pad and Wrist Pad

If you have a mechanical (not optical) mouse, you need a mouse pad upon which to roll it. Get one; the varieties are endless — plus, the mouse pad ensures that you have at least one tiny place on your desktop that's free of clutter for rolling the mouse around.

A *wrist pad* fits right below your keyboard and enables you to comfortably rest your wrists while you type. This product may help alleviate some repetitive-motion injuries that are common to keyboard users. Wrist pads come in many exciting colors, some of which may match your drapery.

Antiglare Screen

Tawdry as it may sound, an *antiglare screen* is nothing more than a nylon stocking stretched over the front of your monitor. Okay, they're *professional* nylons in fancy holders that adhere themselves to your screen. The result is no garish glare from the lights in the room or outside. An antiglare screen is such a good idea that some monitors come with them built-in.

Glare is the number-one cause of eyestrain while you're using a computer. Lights usually reflect in the glass, either from above or from a window. An antiglare screen cuts down on the reflections and makes the stuff on your monitor easier to see.

Some antiglare screens also incorporate antiradiation shielding. I'm serious: They provide protection from the harmful electromagnetic rays spewing out of your monitor even as you read this page! Is this necessary? No.

Keyboard Cover

If you're klutzy with a coffee cup or have small children or spouses with peanut-butter-smudged fingers using your keyboard, a keyboard cover is a great idea. You may have even seen one used in a department store: It covers the keyboard snugly, but still enables you to type. It's a great idea because, without a keyboard cover, all that disgusting gunk falls between the keys. Yech!

In the same vein, you can also buy a generic dust cover for your computer. This item preserves your computer's appearance, but has no other true value. Use a computer cover only when your computer is turned off (and I don't recommend turning it off). If you put the cover on your PC while the PC is turned on, you create a minigreenhouse, and the computer gets way too hot and could melt. Nasty. This type of heat build-up doesn't happen to the keyboard, so the keyboard cover on all the time is okay — cool, in fact.

More Memory

Any PC works better with more memory installed. The upper limit on some computers is something like 4GB of RAM, which seems ridiculous now, but who knows about two years from now? Still, upgrading your system to 512MB or 1GB of RAM is a good idea. Almost immediately, you notice the improvement in Windows and various graphics applications and games. Make someone else do the upgrading for you; you just buy the memory.

Larger, Faster Hard Drive

Hard drives fill up quickly. The first time, it's because you have kept lots of junk on your hard drive: games, things people give you, old files, and old programs you don't use any more. You can delete those or copy them to CD-Rs for long-term storage. Then, after a time, your hard drive fills up again. The second time, it has stuff you really use. Argh! What can you delete?

The answer is to buy a larger hard drive. If you can, install a second hard drive and start filling it up. Otherwise, replace your first hard drive with a larger, faster model. Buying a faster model is a great way to improve the performance of any older PC without throwing it out entirely.

Ergonomic Keyboard

The traditional computer keyboard is based on the old typewriter keyboard (the IBM Selectric, by the way). Why? It doesn't have to be. No mechanics inside the keyboard require the keys to be laid out in a staggered or cascading style. Repetitive typing on this type of keyboard can lead to various ugly motion disorders (VUMDs).

To help you type more comfortably, you can get an ergonomic keyboard, such as the Microsoft Natural Keyboard. This type of keyboard arranges the keys in a manner that's comfortable for your hands, keeping everything lined up and not tweaked out, like on a regular computer keyboard.

Get a UPS

The *uninterruptible power supply (UPS)* is a boon to computing anywhere in the world where the power is less than reliable. Plug your console into the UPS. Plug your monitor into the UPS. If the UPS has extra battery-backed-up sockets, plug your modem into it too.

- ✔ Chapter 4 has information on using a UPS as well as using a power strip.
- ✔ Using a UPS doesn't affect the performance of your PC. The computer couldn't care less whether it's plugged into the wall or a UPS.

USB Expansion Card

USB is the *thing* to have for expanding your PC. If your computer lacks a USB port, you can buy a USB expansion card.

My advice: Get a 4-port USB PCI card. (Sorry about all the acronyms and jargon.) Four ports are plenty. I prefer the Belkin line of products. Refer to Chapter 7 for more USB information.

Scanner or Digital Camera

Scanners and digital cameras are really the same thing, just in different boxes. A *scanner* is a flat-bed-like device used for scanning flat things. A *digital camera* is a portable scanner with a focused lens, which lets it "scan" things out in the non-flat real world. Both gizmos do the same thing: Transfer some image from the cold harshness of reality into the fun digital world of the computer.

If you already have a manual camera, getting a scanner is a great way to start your computer graphics journey. You can easily scan in existing photos and, after they're digitized, store them in the computer or e-mail them off to friends. (Refer to Chapter 28.)

Digital cameras are also great investments, though they're more expensive than scanners. The future of photography is digital, so buying one now or later is probably on your list of things to do before you die.

Portable Digital Music Player

In case you haven't heard or read it somewhere, the CD player is dead. In fact, music pundits are saying that music CDs will soon be a thing of the past. The next and final resting place for all your music will be your computer. The portable extension of that music will be a digital music player, also known as an *MP3 player*.

The most popular digital music player is the Apple iPod. Though the iPod is an Apple product, it's fully compatible with your PC, including the popular iTunes music program. Other digital music players exist as well. Ensure that the one you get has enough storage for all your music, is compatible with your PC, and has a handy way of talking with the computer as well as recharging its battery.

Chapter 31

Ten Tips from a PC Guru

I don't consider myself a computer expert or genius or guru, though many have called me all those names. I'm just a guy who understands how computers work. Or, better than that, I understand how computer people think. They may not be able to express an idea, but I can see what they mean and translate it into English for you. Given that, here are some tips and suggestions so that you and your PC can go off on your merry way.

Remember That You Control the Computer

You bought the computer. You clean up after its messes. You feed it CDs when it asks for them. You control the computer — simple as that. Don't let that computer try to boss you around with its bizarre conversations and funny idiosyncrasies. It's really pretty dopey; the computer is an idiot.

If somebody shoved a flattened can of motor oil in your mouth, would you try to taste it? Of course not. But stick a flattened can of motor oil into a CD drive, and the computer tries to read information from it, thinking that it's a CD. See? It's dumb.

You control that mindless computer just like you control an infant. You must treat it the same way, with respect and caring attention. Don't feel that the computer is bossing you around any more than you feel that a baby is bossing you around during 3 a.m. feedings. They're both helpless creatures, subject to your every whim. Be gentle. But be in charge.

Realize That Most Computer Nerds Love to Help Beginners

It's sad, but almost all computer nerds spend most of their waking hours in front of a computer. They know that it's kind of an oddball thing to do, but they can't help it.

Their guilty consciences are what usually make them happy to help beginners. By passing on knowledge, they can legitimize the hours they while away on their computer stools. Plus, it gives them a chance to brush up on a social skill that's slowly slipping away: the art of *talking* to a person.

- ✔ Always be grateful when you're given help.
- ✔ A great place to get help online is my Wambooli Forums, where real, live nerds really do help beginners. See for yourself, at

  `http://forums.wambooli.com/`

- ✔ Beware of Bogus Nerds. These people don't love computers, but went to some sort of school to learn a few by-rote tricks. They may not be helpful or know anything about computers, other than what they're told. You can detect Bogus Nerds because they lack the enthusiasm of True Nerds, the ones who help you.

Use Antivirus Software

It's a sad statement, but to really enjoy your computer, you have to invest in some antivirus software. You really need the protection such a program offers — even if you're careful. Every PC that's running Windows and connected to the Internet is at risk. There are no exceptions.

I recommend Norton AntiVirus. It's the leader of the pack and very efficient. The McAfee virus protection program is also a good choice. But I don't recommend Web-based antivirus scanners. Get a real program. Pay money for it. If your data is important, it's worth the cost.

- ✔ Yes, pay the money and buy the annual subscription to keep your antivirus software up to date.

- ✔ Some antivirus programs come with other Internet security software as well, including spyware protection and perhaps a firewall. Yes, those things are worth the cost.

- ✔ There's no need to run two antivirus (or spyware or firewall) programs at once. One program is enough to do the job.

- ✔ For more information on nasty things that can happen to your PC and how to prevent them, refer to one of my favorite books — because I wrote it — *Troubleshooting Your PC For Dummies* (Wiley Publishing, Inc.).

Understand That Upgrading Software Isn't an Absolute Necessity

Just as the models on the cover of *Vogue* change their clothes each season (or maybe I should say "change their *fashions*" each season), software companies issue perpetual upgrades. Should you automatically buy the upgrade?

Of course not! If you're comfortable with your old software, you have no reason to buy the new version. None!

The software upgrade probably has a few new features in it (although you still haven't had a chance to check out all the features in the current version). And, the upgrade probably has some new bugs in it too, making it crash in new and different ways. Feel free to look at the box, just as you stare at the ladies on the cover of *Vogue*. But don't feel obliged to buy something you don't need.

Don't Ever Reinstall Windows

A myth floating around tech-support sites says that the solution to all your ills is to reinstall Windows. Some suspect tech-support people even claim that it's common for most Windows users to reinstall at least once a year. That's rubbish.

You *never* need to reinstall Windows. All problems are fixable. It's just that the so-called tech-support people are lazy and resort to a drastic solution as opposed to trying to discover what the true problem is. If you press them, they *will* tell you what's wrong and how to fix it.

In all my years of using a computer, I have never reinstalled Windows or had to reformat my hard drive. It's not even a good idea just to refresh the bits on the hard drive or whatever other nonsense they dish up. There just isn't a need to reinstall Windows ever. Period.

Refer to my book *Troubleshooting Your PC For Dummies* (Wiley) for all the various solutions you can try instead of reformatting your hard dive or reinstalling Windows.

Perfectly Adjust Your Monitor

I don't have much explaining to do here. Keeping the monitor turned up too brightly is bad for your eyes, and it wears out your monitor more quickly.

To adjust a CRT monitor to pink perfection, turn the brightness (the button with the little sun) all the way up and adjust the contrast (the button with the half moon) until the display looks pleasing. Then, turn the brightness down until you like what you see. That's it!

Unplug Your PC When You Upgrade Hardware

Newer PCs don't have a flippable on-off switch, like the older models do. When you open the case to upgrade or add an expansion card, your belly (if it's like my belly) may punch the power-on button, and, lo, you're working in a hazardous electrical environment. To prevent that, unplug the console before you open it for upgrading.

You don't need to unplug the console or even turn off the PC when you add a USB or FireWire device. (You do need to unplug it if you add a USB expansion card, however.)

Subscribe to a Computer Magazine

Oh, why not? Browse the stacks at your local coffeehouse-slash-music-store-slash-bookstore. Try to find a computer magazine that matches your tastes.

✔ One magazine that seems to be worthy for computer beginners is *SmartComputing*. Look for it in a magazine stand near you.

✔ What sells me on a magazine are the columns and the *newsy* stuff they put up front.

✔ Some magazines are all ads. That can be great if you like ads, or it can be boring.

✔ Avoid the nerdier magazines, but I probably didn't need to tell you that.

Shun the Hype

The computer industry is rife with hype. Even if you subscribe to a family-oriented computer magazine, you still read about the latest this or the next-biggest-trend that. Ignore it!

My gauge for hype is whether the thing that's hyped is shipping as a standard part of a PC. I check the ads. If they're shipping the item, I write about it. Otherwise, it's a myth and may not happen. Avoid being lured by the hype.

✔ When hype becomes reality, you read about it in this book.

✔ Former hype I have successfully ignored: Pen Windows, push technology, Web channels, Shockwave, Microsoft Bob, Windows CE, and tablet PCs.

✔ Hype that eventually became reality: USB, CD-R, shopping on the Web (or *e-commerce*), DVD drives, digital cameras, and home networking.

Don't Take It So Seriously

Hey, simmer down. Computers aren't part of life. They're nothing more than mineral deposits and petroleum products. Close your eyes and take a few deep breaths. Listen to the ocean spray against the deck on the patio; listen to the gurgle of the marble Jacuzzi tub in the master bedroom.

Pretend that you're driving a convertible through a grove of sequoias on a sunny day with the wind whipping through your hair and curling over your ears. Pretend that you're lying on the deck under the sun as the Pacific Princess chugs south toward the islands with friendly, wide-eyed monkeys that eat coconut chunks from the palm of your hand.

You're up in a hot air balloon, swirling the first sip of champagne and feeling the bubbles explode atop your tongue. Ahead, to the far left, the castle's spire rises through the clouds, and you can smell Chef Meisterbrau's awaiting banquet.

Then, slowly open your eyes. It's just a dumb computer. Really. Don't take it too seriously.

Index

• E •

• N •

BUSINESS, CAREERS & PERSONAL FINANCE

0-7645-5307-0

0-7645-5331-3 *†

Also available:
- Accounting For Dummies †
0-7645-5314-3
- Business Plans Kit For Dummies †
0-7645-5365-8
- Cover Letters For Dummies
0-7645-5224-4
- Frugal Living For Dummies
0-7645-5403-4
- Leadership For Dummies
0-7645-5176-0
- Managing For Dummies
0-7645-1771-6

- Marketing For Dummies
0-7645-5600-2
- Personal Finance For Dummies *
0-7645-2590-5
- Project Management For Dummies
0-7645-5283-X
- Resumes For Dummies †
0-7645-5471-9
- Selling For Dummies
0-7645-5363-1
- Small Business Kit For Dummies *†
0-7645-5093-4

HOME & BUSINESS COMPUTER BASICS

0-7645-4074-2

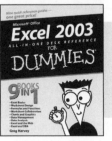

0-7645-3758-X

Also available:
- ACT! 6 For Dummies
0-7645-2645-6
- iLife '04 All-in-One Desk Reference
For Dummies
0-7645-7347-0
- iPAQ For Dummies
0-7645-6769-1
- Mac OS X Panther Timesaving
Techniques For Dummies
0-7645-5812-9
- Macs For Dummies
0-7645-5656-8

- Microsoft Money 2004 For Dummies
0-7645-4195-1
- Office 2003 All-in-One Desk Reference
For Dummies
0-7645-3883-7
- Outlook 2003 For Dummies
0-7645-3759-8
- PCs For Dummies
0-7645-4074-2
- TiVo For Dummies
0-7645-6923-6
- Upgrading and Fixing PCs For Dummies
0-7645-1665-5
- Windows XP Timesaving Techniques
For Dummies
0-7645-3748-2

FOOD, HOME, GARDEN, HOBBIES, MUSIC & PETS

0-7645-5295-3

0-7645-5232-5

Also available:
- Bass Guitar For Dummies
0-7645-2487-9
- Diabetes Cookbook For Dummies
0-7645-5230-9
- Gardening For Dummies *
0-7645-5130-2
- Guitar For Dummies
0-7645-5106-X
- Holiday Decorating For Dummies
0-7645-2570-0
- Home Improvement All-in-One
For Dummies
0-7645-5680-0

- Knitting For Dummies
0-7645-5395-X
- Piano For Dummies
0-7645-5105-1
- Puppies For Dummies
0-7645-5255-4
- Scrapbooking For Dummies
0-7645-7208-3
- Senior Dogs For Dummies
0-7645-5818-8
- Singing For Dummies
0-7645-2475-5
- 30-Minute Meals For Dummies
0-7645-2589-1

INTERNET & DIGITAL MEDIA

0-7645-1664-7

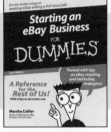

0-7645-6924-4

Also available:
- 2005 Online Shopping Directory
For Dummies
0-7645-7495-7
- CD & DVD Recording For Dummies
0-7645-5956-7
- eBay For Dummies
0-7645-5654-1
- Fighting Spam For Dummies
0-7645-5965-6
- Genealogy Online For Dummies
0-7645-5964-8
- Google For Dummies
0-7645-4420-9

- Home Recording For Musicians
For Dummies
0-7645-1634-5
- The Internet For Dummies
0-7645-4173-0
- iPod & iTunes For Dummies
0-7645-7772-7
- Preventing Identity Theft For Dummies
0-7645-7336-5
- Pro Tools All-in-One Desk Reference
For Dummies
0-7645-5714-9
- Roxio Easy Media Creator For Dummies
0-7645-7131-1

SPORTS, FITNESS, PARENTING, RELIGION & SPIRITUALITY

0-7645-5146-9

Parenting

0-7645-5418-2

Also available:

- Adoption For Dummies
  0-7645-5488-3
- Basketball For Dummies
  0-7645-5248-1
- The Bible For Dummies
  0-7645-5296-1
- Buddhism For Dummies
  0-7645-5359-3
- Catholicism For Dummies
  0-7645-5391-7
- Hockey For Dummies
  0-7645-5228-7

- Judaism For Dummies
  0-7645-5299-6
- Martial Arts For Dummies
  0-7645-5358-5
- Pilates For Dummies
  0-7645-5397-6
- Religion For Dummies
  0-7645-5264-3
- Teaching Kids to Read For Dummies
  0-7645-4043-2
- Weight Training For Dummies
  0-7645-5168-X
- Yoga For Dummies
  0-7645-5117-5

TRAVEL

0-7645-5438-7

0-7645-5453-0

Also available:

- Alaska For Dummies
  0-7645-1761-9
- Arizona For Dummies
  0-7645-6938-4
- Cancún and the Yucatán For Dummies
  0-7645-2437-2
- Cruise Vacations For Dummies
  0-7645-6941-4
- Europe For Dummies
  0-7645-5456-5
- Ireland For Dummies
  0-7645-5455-7

- Las Vegas For Dummies
  0-7645-5448-4
- London For Dummies
  0-7645-4277-X
- New York City For Dummies
  0-7645-6945-7
- Paris For Dummies
  0-7645-5494-8
- RV Vacations For Dummies
  0-7645-5443-3
- Walt Disney World & Orlando For Dummi
  0-7645-6943-0

GRAPHICS, DESIGN & WEB DEVELOPMENT

0-7645-4345-8

0-7645-5589-8

Also available:

- Adobe Acrobat 6 PDF For Dummies
  0-7645-3760-1
- Building a Web Site For Dummies
  0-7645-7144-3
- Dreamweaver MX 2004 For Dummies
  0-7645-4342-3
- FrontPage 2003 For Dummies
  0-7645-3882-9
- HTML 4 For Dummies
  0-7645-1995-6
- Illustrator CS For Dummies
  0-7645-4084-X

- Macromedia Flash MX 2004 For Dumm
  0-7645-4358-X
- Photoshop 7 All-in-One Desk Reference For Dummies
  0-7645-1667-1
- Photoshop CS Timesaving Technique For Dummies
  0-7645-6782-9
- PHP 5 For Dummies
  0-7645-4166-8
- PowerPoint 2003 For Dummies
  0-7645-3908-6
- QuarkXPress 6 For Dummies
  0-7645-2593-X

NETWORKING, SECURITY, PROGRAMMING & DATABASES

0-7645-6852-3

0-7645-5784-X

Also available:

- A+ Certification For Dummies
  0-7645-4187-0
- Access 2003 All-in-One Desk Reference For Dummies
  0-7645-3988-4
- Beginning Programming For Dummies
  0-7645-4997-9
- C For Dummies
  0-7645-7068-4
- Firewalls For Dummies
  0-7645-4048-3
- Home Networking For Dummies
  0-7645-42796

- Network Security For Dummies
  0-7645-1679-5
- Networking For Dummies
  0-7645-1677-9
- TCP/IP For Dummies
  0-7645-1760-0
- VBA For Dummies
  0-7645-3989-2
- Wireless All In-One Desk Reference For Dummies
  0-7645-7496-5
- Wireless Home Networking For Dummi
  0-7645-3910-8

ALTH & SELF-HELP

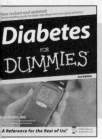

0-7645-6820-5 *†

0-7645-2566-2

Also available:

- Alzheimer's For Dummies
  0-7645-3899-3
- Asthma For Dummies
  0-7645-4233-8
- Controlling Cholesterol For Dummies
  0-7645-5440-9
- Depression For Dummies
  0-7645-3900-0
- Dieting For Dummies
  0-7645-4149-8
- Fertility For Dummies
  0-7645-2549-2

- Fibromyalgia For Dummies
  0-7645-5441-7
- Improving Your Memory For Dummies
  0-7645-5435-2
- Pregnancy For Dummies †
  0-7645-4483-7
- Quitting Smoking For Dummies
  0-7645-2629-4
- Relationships For Dummies
  0-7645-5384-4
- Thyroid For Dummies
  0-7645-5385-2

UCATION, HISTORY, REFERENCE & TEST PREPARATION

0-7645-5194-9

0-7645-4186-2

Also available:

- Algebra For Dummies
  0-7645-5325-9
- British History For Dummies
  0-7645-7021-8
- Calculus For Dummies
  0-7645-2498-4
- English Grammar For Dummies
  0-7645-5322-4
- Forensics For Dummies
  0-7645-5580-4
- The GMAT For Dummies
  0-7645-5251-1
- Inglés Para Dummies
  0-7645-5427-1

- Italian For Dummies
  0-7645-5196-5
- Latin For Dummies
  0-7645-5431-X
- Lewis & Clark For Dummies
  0-7645-2545-X
- Research Papers For Dummies
  0-7645-5426-3
- The SAT I For Dummies
  0-7645-7193-1
- Science Fair Projects For Dummies
  0-7645-5460-3
- U.S. History For Dummies
  0-7645-5249-X

Get smart @ dummies.com®

- **Find a full list of Dummies titles**
- **Look into loads of FREE on-site articles**
- **Sign up for FREE eTips e-mailed to you weekly**
- **See what other products carry the Dummies name**
- **Shop directly from the Dummies bookstore**
- **Enter to win new prizes every month!**

parate Canadian edition also available
parate U.K. edition also available

lable wherever books are sold. For more information or to order direct: U.S. customers visit www.dummies.com or call 1-877-762-2974.
customers visit www.wileyeurope.com or call 0800 243407. Canadian customers visit www.wiley.ca or call 1-800-567-4797.

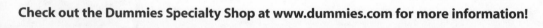